Down on the Shore

D0851888

The patchworks
of our lives
wear thin . . . in time;
those quilted squares and stars
those fading steps of stairs
unravel handsewn stitches
and years.
Unknown
perhaps forgotten—
as often we forget the brave
but learn by rote
their feats in history—
are hands that labored long
designing every piece
to make it fit . . .
reworked the tight-drawn seams
that came unsewn
in fabrics worn too pale
to hold the weight
of new-spun threads.
Yet moments woven
within each patterned piece
endure
as if skilled hands
that racked the quilt
and let it be
had not
long decades past
settled to dust.
Memory beckons
alien and native blessed
to scan our Shore:

its low and grassy grounds . . .
gray sands of trampled paths . . .
damp black plow-plaited earth
in fresh-turned fields . . .
main streets that parallel
quiet of country roads . . .
vast rippling seas of green,
cornfields defining farms . . .
white buildings, shuttered bright,
dwarfed by giant barnyard reds . . .
dark waters, ever-yielding . . . deep,
shore-fringed with cypress trees . . .
and Shore-small towns—
each one
still boldly marked
in white on black,
hard clinging to the myth
that black always has been . . .
must ever be
here for . . .
held after . . .
white.
Back . . . moving slowly back
the finger points
to one small trace
in time—
one little town
deep-etched, held fast . . .
indelibly inscribed
and woven
in the patchworks
of our lives . . .

—AVH 1990

Down on the Shore

THE FAMILY
AND PLACE
THAT FORGED
A POET'S VOICE

Adele V. Holden

Tidewater Publishers
Centreville, Maryland

Copyright ©2000, 2003 by Adele V. Holden

All rights reserved. No part of this book may be reproduced in any manner whatsoever without written permission except in the case of brief quotations embodied in critical articles and reviews. For information, address Tidewater Publishers, Centreville, Maryland 21617.

Library of Congress Cataloging-in-Publication Data

Holden, Adele V., 1919-
   Down on the Shore : the family and place that forged a poet's voice / Adele V. Holden.—1st Tidewater Publishers ed.
      p. cm.
   ISBN 0-87033-547-2
   1. Holden, Adele V., 1919—Homes and haunts—Eastern Shore (Md. and Va.) 2. Poets, American—20th century—Family relationships. 3. Eastern Shore (Md. and Va.)—Social life and customs. 4. Holden, Adele V., 1919—Childhood and youth. 5. English teachers—United States—Biography. 6. Poets, American—20th century—Biography. I. Title.
   PS3515.O326 Z465 2003
   811'.54—dc21   2003012635

Front cover photo: Adele Holden, her sister Elizabeth Marie, and father Snow Holden in the mid-1920s; *back cover photo:* postcard from Pocomoke City, Maryland, sent to Adele Holden by her grandmother.
Opposite: Laura Jane and Snow Henry Holden

Manufactured in the United States of America
First Tidewater Publishers edition, 2003

In memory of my dear parents,
Snow Henry and Laura Jane Holden;
my treasured sister and brother,
Dorothy Emily and Leon Henry;
my beloved grandmother, "Mom";
and
other family and dear friends

And when we had accomplished those days, we departed and went our way; and they all brought us on our way, with wives and children, till we were out of the city: and we kneeled down on the Shore, and prayed.

—Acts 21:5

Contents

Acknowledgments

I would like to thank every person who has contributed to *Down on the Shore*. However, that is impossible; the ones who were most important have passed. But they knew my gratitude because I expressed it in various ways while they could appreciate it.

Still, there are many persons whose encouragement, suggestions, research assistance, manuscript readings, and editorial acumen have helped me to plough through an unpublishable creation to the reality of this memoir. My gratitude embraces each of them.

For their invaluable assistance during the initial writing of this memoir, I thank Richard Hart, Josephine Jacobsen, and Robert Brugger.

For their immeasurable support and encouragement from my first writing efforts to the beginning of this memoir, I honor the memory of my dear sister, Dorothy Holden Stokes, and my favorite professors and mentors, Jean Fisher Turpin and Elliott Coleman.

For allowing me to use the "books" of the old *Worcester Democrat* in my research on the Eastern Shore during the Depression, I thank William H. Kerbin, Editor.

For their critiques of my manuscript (critiques that led to my making important changes in the manuscript), I thank Barbara Phillips of Bridge Works Publishing and Frances G. Conn, Baltimore author.

For his belief in the worth of this memoir and for his patience in piloting me through the extensive changes vital to *Down on the Shore*, I thank Gregg A. Wilhelm.

For typing and proofreading a revision-in-progress, I thank Carolyn Boyd and Carolyn Hull Anderson, respectively.

For prodding me to keep at it when I was weary of all the problems involved in this production, I thank my faithful adoptive sister, Ruth Margret Land.

Down on the Shore

Author's Note

Down on the Shore vividly portrays my life and my family's experiences living on Maryland's segregated Eastern Shore during the Depression, complete with happy times, holidays, births, graduations, and deaths, plus instances of racial injustice that we and other black families suffered. Conversations and events took place at which I was not present, but which were shared with me by my parents, friends, and relatives. The third person form is used to identify such dialogues and incidents; for example, references to my parents as "Momma" and "Poppa" become "Jane" and "Snow" and so on.

The poems that introduce and conclude this memoir, as well as the verse excerpts leading off each chapter, are from my own original body of work—some published, some not—written over the course of many, many years. My indebtedness to poets who encouraged me and people who inspired me never can be fully repaid.

Prologue

"Greetings from Pocomoke City, Maryland." I never shall forget the placid riverside scene on the postcard that bore those words. On the back, the cramped, laborious writing by my grandmother reaffirmed her love. The card was postmarked November 13, 1953.

Forty years later, I still wondered what could have happened to that treasured card, even after I gave up expecting to find it in some unlikely place. But I never stopped hoping that it might one day miraculously turn up. It was my only keepsake from my beloved grandmother Adell Dickerson—"Mom," as all her children and grandchildren called her. She shared her name with me, her first granddaughter.

Perhaps it was, as I've been told, Fate. I don't know. But I do know what happened a few years ago. I was all set to spend an afternoon browsing through the mall when conscience, or something, seemed to force me toward a long-postponed, dreaded job in the den. When I was almost through vacuuming dust from one shelf of books, I paused and removed a book from the adjoining shelf. And there, between pages of *Remembrance of Things Past,* was my grandmother's card!

It was propitious that Mom's card should be found a few days before my planned trip to the Eastern Shore to surprise my Uncle Ray, who had suffered a broken hip and major surgeries and was recuperating in a nursing home in Princess Anne, Maryland. Now, I could share with him my newfound treasure—his mother's card.

◆

Upon requesting my uncle's room number, I was told he would be any place except in his room, as he usually was all over the place in that wheelchair of his. Ray spied me from halfway down a long corridor and turned on the speed, wheeling vigorously toward me as I rushed to meet him.

"Can't hardly b'lieve my eyes—it's you!" he cried. "All the way from Baltimore. Umph, umph, umph."

At first, he seemed determined to convince me that he was ready and able to go home to Pocomoke City, a few miles south of Princess Anne. Although he did appear to be younger than most people the same age, he was well past ninety. He argued that it made not one bit of sense for him to stay in a nursing home—"not when I got my own home to go to." But the old home on Pocomoke's Bank Street, where generations of family were born, was vacant. No one lived there now to welcome Ray on his return. I really think he knew what he could not admit, even to himself. And his sadness hurt my heart.

But remembering and talking about all the fun the family shared in Pocomoke—at the Holden homes on Bank Street and then Fourth Street, down Mom's, at Mount Zion Church— cheered Ray up a little; so I asked for news from home. He said there was none worth telling, although he mentioned how big chain stores were going up way out where there was once nothing but fields and woods, and a whole lot of new houses popping up past Mom's "for *them,* not for us."

I had been waiting for the right moment to ask Ray to tell me all about the way life used to be down on the Shore when he was young—something our elders never seemed to tire of relating. But his response really jarred me. He did not open his mouth— just bolted straight up in his wheelchair, shoved the cap far back on his balding head, and exhaled the longest sigh he could muster. Allowing ample time for the performance to sink in, he sat there measuring me with stern, unwavering eyes. Then, cocking his small head to one side, he squinted up at me and shouted, "Great day in the morning, Ginny! You mean you asking *me* to tell you about how it was 'round here? *You?* Can't b'lieve my own ears!"

He knew that I knew what life was like for poor blacks on the Shore. Indeed I did, but I pretended to need some help remembering. Hoping to get him started, I told him about my work on a book that should provide insight into life on the Shore as our people have lived it and have known it to be. Upon hearing that his contribution would become a part of that book, Ray doffed his cap, grinned, and exclaimed, "Great day in the morning!"

When I gave him Mom's postcard, he stared at the message for several minutes before turning it over and commenting on its looking like new after such a long time. We tried to determine where in Pocomoke the card's scene might be found. Ray eyed each item, from winding clay road to the river, but could not be certain. He speculated that it just might be out Dividing Creek way, but declared the Pocomoke River couldn't look that blue "not even under the bluest sky the good Lord ever made." Of course, we realized it was only a postcard scene, and Ray conceded, "Guess they free to make it anyway they want—still don't make it no Pocomoke River. That old river's more like brown than blue anyway."

"Ginny," Ray said, "you asking me to tell you about Pocomoke. Sure, it's a whole lot I can tell. But, first and last, ever' thing I know wouldn't even be a drop in the bucket. Old folks use t'say if ever' last Negro 'round here up and told all they know about all the meanness white folks done to us, not even the short half'd be told—not nowheres near half. Not going to be told neither—not to that old river rise up and speak!"

When I asked what they meant, he could tell no more than what Mom used to say. In her words, "Lots of crimes done 'round here to us by white people—and some we done to each other, too—been a long time buried in that old river. And if God ever let that river speak, many a body moored in watery graves going rise up. Then all them that put 'em in there and still be living's going be wishing they was dead. But onliest way all the truth ever going to be told is for that river to rise up and speak."

I heard Ray moan; then he began to sing softly and sorrowfully:

Old Jordan's river is chilly and cold—
One more river to cross.
It chills the body but not the soul—
One more river to cross.

"Make you think 'bout singing in the old Mount Zion Church, don't it?" he lamented. "Ye-e-es, Lord."

Minutes later, he resumed talking about Pocomoke. "No need looking to no old folks' sayings to know what's what around here, Ginny. We both been born and bred right here, and it's where I been most all my life. Far's I can see, 'tain't been no whole lotta changing. Onliest thing worth talking about was school integration—what they was bound and determined wouldn't *never* happen in Pocomoke. But Uncle Sam had final say on that. Still makes my blood boil ever' time I think about all the trouble piled up on your pop just so's you all could get your schooling same's whites got. It's a sin and shame, ain't it?"

Still trying to account for the unaccountable, my uncle recalled his old boss's impression of Eastern Shoremen. Chief, a northerner, was convinced that Eastern Shoremen were "hell-bent on cutting themselves off from the rest of the world, as if nature hadn't done a good enough job already." Furthermore, he believed that the area's geographical location probably was what made the people so everlastingly backward. He maintained that they were unneighborly, distrustful people, whose ancestors reportedly made several attempts to secede and who desired to separate themselves not only from Delaware but also from the rest of Maryland. Chief made a point of letting the locals know he knew more of their history than they did, but that perhaps they were too ashamed to learn it.

Ray's recollection of Chief's observations reminded me of a geography lesson back in elementary school. We were supposed to be learning all about the Eastern Shore and its people. Our teacher Miss Waters introduced two terms: "physical barriers" and "invisible barriers." She explained their differences and their respective effects on inhabitants of a given area. To illustrate, she outlined the little state of Maryland on the blackboard map of the United States. Then she double-lined a tiny blob that appeared to be barely hanging onto the mainland—our Eastern Shore. Even then, I wondered how on earth such, a small piece of land—buffeted by Bay and ocean waters—could still be there.

Back at the map, Miss Waters, pointer at work, guided us to see the makings of physical barriers; by seeing, we could relate to them. But we were not able to grasp the concept of invisible barriers, not even when she used the speech of Eastern Shoremen as an example. She described our speech as distinctive—"set apart"—even from that of other Marylanders. We did not understand. Unmindful of drawls and dialects, we saw nothing wrong with our speech. Our teacher's "proper talking" was pleasingly strange, but ours was all right, too.

Not until I was a college freshman did I fully appreciate Miss Waters's efforts. During the first meeting of our oversized speech class, the professor asked that we call out—distinctly and in consecutive order—an assigned number for attendance check. After number thirty-nine, I uttered a nervous, high-pitched "Farty!" which echoed through the high-ceilinged room. While number forty-one waited for the laughter to subside, I sat confused and embarrassed with no place to hide.

"Tell 'em this here's just about far down as you can go and not be right smack in Virginia," Ray said in response to how I should tell people where Pocomoke's located. "Guess we got around about three thousand or so folks. Now, the one who could tell all anybody'd need to know was Mom. Remember how she always talked about her Indian relations? She said 'twas Indians that named the river Pocomoke on account of its murky water, dyed dark that way from rotted swamp roots draining in there. Another thing she told us was, in Indian talk, 'pocomoke' meant land of plenty. Guess 'twas, too, plenty hunting and fishing and trapping and planting and all."

Back in the late 1800s, Pocomoke was a bustling river town. Big freighters and schooners came and went from up and down the East Coast and even from faraway countries. All that loading and unloading provided plenty of work. Pocomoke was the "metropolis" of Worcester County, and people from outlying areas—including Virginia—came to town to shop. On Saturdays, the downtown business district was one busy place. But just about everything was beholden to the river—trapping, fishing, sawmills, shipbuilding. All that changed when trains came through, making it impossible for river traffic to keep up with the rails.

Ray and I spent the remainder of the afternoon trading memories of the town we know so well—memories of Bedlam, "the colored section" on the other side of town; of paved streets and sidewalks that became either dusty or muddy roads immediately past the last white home and just in front of the first "colored"; of the "as-it-was, same's-it-is" depressed lot of our people there; of the scarcity of decent housing and jobs, matching the scarcity of hope for a better life; of the perils of working in the "Can House," the local tomato-canning factory; of the painful sight of what once was the attractive Fourth Street home my parents provided for us; of sleepy children riding in back of dilapidated trucks to farms to pick strawberries, tomatoes, beans, potatoes, and other seasonal crops; of unforgettable Christmas joys that neither poverty nor segregation could dim; of my parents' struggles to further their children's education in that time and place; of the horrors branded into our minds and hearts by lynchings in nearby towns.

Adell Dickerson, "Mom,"
late 1800s

We talked until no time was left for sharing. As I prepared to leave, Ray spoke of the fatal heart attacks of both my beloved father, in 1968, and sister, Dorothy Emily, in 1984. Then, noting that even mention of those awful losses was upsetting me, he said, "I miss 'em, too, Ginny; so I know just about how you feeling, close as you was to both of 'em."

Before letting me go, he said, "Now, Ginny, you be sure and hold onto that postcard. Long's you got it, Mom'll be right there with you!"

Whenever I gaze upon that treasured card, I sense Mom's comforting presence and am transported back down on the Shore to the days of my youth.

1 · *The Shore We Knew*

When life was April hued
and Momma sang pure soul
soft rocking a hymn
or sudsing her washboard
with the blues . . .
when days were summer long
and Poppa—garage grease over all—
walked strong and proud . . .

Bank Street in the 1920s was a typical dirt road found in "colored sections" of Pocomoke City, Maryland. About three blocks long, the narrow road had a crooked path, trampled through weeds on one side and a ditchbank on the other. Frame houses, separated by strips of yards or cornfields, lined both sides of Bank Street. Most of its small boxy houses contained four rooms, two up and two down. Several were partitioned to shelter two families. Three buildings, larger houses with porches and grassy yards, stood out from the rest, in appearance and because they were owned by the occupants. Almost all the other houses were owned by whites. But in their midst there was a lone gray house—the rented home of Snow and Jane Holden, who had moved there from her parents' home after the birth of their first child, Henry.

My mother had a meaningful role in getting that house painted gray. One day, she said, she heard Ed Taylor was planning to paint all his Bank Street houses red. She hurried downtown to ask—if necessary, beg—him not to paint "their house" red, in spite of the fact that she knew he had gotten wind of the renters' dissatisfaction with the idea.

Ed was annoyed. "The nerve of some niggers nowadays," he told his handyman. "Looks like they'd be tickled to death just getting them houses painted any color at all. Ought to paint 'em jet black and be done with it!" Hardly glancing at Momma after she had blurted out her request, Ed let her stand by the counter, where he aimlessly arranged and rearranged piles of denim shirts. Finally he sneered, "What's matter, Jane, don't you all like red? I swear, I thought all colored folks like red."

She swallowed hard: She knew she would get nowhere with Ed if he even suspected what she felt like telling him. When she spoke, her voice was plaintive, but calm. "Please, Mr. Ed," she begged, "don't paint our house red. I never did like no red house, not even when I was a child. If you'd be so kind as to give us something other'n red, I'd be ever so much obliged to you and thank you, too."

After a few more minutes, without once looking in her direction, Ed mumbled, "Might be enough paint left over from the house on Maple Street to do your'n. Have to see." He gave a sarcastic grunt before adding, "That is, if gray don't offend you, too."

"Mr. Ed!" Momma exclaimed, "I just don't know how to thank you. Maybe one day Snow and me can do something for you. Come time, just say the word, and it's good as done."

In spite of himself, Ed grinned, "How about saving me a pan of them hot rolls next Saturday?"

"'Deed I will, Mr. Ed. Some cinnamon buns, too," she promised. "And thank you. Thank you ever so much."

So one little gray house stood in the midst of those painted red from eaves to steps. Immediately after that encounter, Momma said she began to wish she had left the matter for my father to handle when he paid the rent, but she knew his temper and was fearful of what might happen if Ed got nasty. More than likely there would have been trouble. Then Ed would paint the house red just for spite. Might even make them move. The nearer she got to the house, the more upset she became. By the time she got home, she knew she was going to be sick.

Throughout the years during which her three children were born—and most times thereafter—Momma described herself as "not so well." But she was much stronger than the frail image she nurtured. Lean and agile, she appeared to be taller than her mere five feet. Her skin—a smooth milk chocolate—molded the thin lines of her nose and mouth. Bold cheekbones sloped to hollows in her long face. Deep creases, etched from nostrils to the corners of her mouth, lent a tinge of sullenness to match her brooding eyes, which seldom lingered on any one object. Nervous, sensitive, sympathetic, moody—all those traits, plus a desperate need to worry about everything, characterized my mother. Yet, in spite of herself, her laughter, lusty and contagious, brightened many gloomy days. Then her singing, matching her mood of the moment as she did her housework or bent over a steamy washtub in the yard, moved neighbors and passersby to exclaim, "Just listen to that Jane Holden, wouldja? She sure singing up somethin' today. Can't nobody grab ahold a song and turn it loose like that gal! No siree!"

When Snow Holden was only three or four, his older cousin Edie described him as the "prettiest little boy I ever seen in my life." At that time Edie had gone with her mother Clara to visit her cousin Mary, my father's mother, who was critically ill. Being naturally talkative, the older child had complained, "Oh Mom, that little boy, he won't talk to me." Hearing Edie, Mary raised herself up in bed to explain, "He's shy like that, Edie. But he's friendly. He don't see girls like nothin' being Ah'm laid up here and can't take him nowheres. And his pop don't have time 'cause he be working." She paused, gasped for breath, and fell back onto the pillows. Afterward, she called her child and held out a bony, calloused hand, "Snow, come speak to your cousin Edie. Tell her where Pop gone to."

Obediently, the little boy spoke, "Hey, cousin Edie. Pop gone to church. He be back after while." That done, he turned his attention to the futile task of putting a wheel back onto a tiny wooden wagon. The wheel stayed in place just long enough for the wagon to roll halfway across a low bench beside the bed before it fell to the floor again. Patiently, as if each effort were his first, the child picked up the wheel and began to work on it again.

After that visit, Mary died. Edie shared the grief of the small timid cousin with dimpled cheeks, enormous black eyes, and lustrous hair that fell in soft curls past his shoulders. But when she saw him again, Edie cried to her mother, "Oh, Mom, why'd they go and cut off his pretty curls?"

"Because he's a boy, that's why!" came the sharp reply. Perhaps Clara said no more because it saddened her to talk about Mary, whose tears had dampened those curls—curls she had grown too weak to comb—as she placed them in a box for safekeeping shortly before she died, leaving her only child to be brought up by his father alone.

Decades later, Edie said her cousin—a muscular young man of medium height and build—was as "handsome a man as you're likely to set eyes on." Close-cropped, jet-black curls crowned his head. Eyes, still big and dark below thick, evenly curved eyebrows, were no longer shy and fearful. Either they appeared to search for elusive answers, or they twinkled mischievously, as if they harbored a coveted secret. Sun rays and time had darkened his skin to olive. A sculptured fineness marked his cheekbones and nose. A slight slant to the lower lip evoked oddly differing impressions of sensuousness, haughtiness, even bitterness. However, those who had known him as a boy saw, in the fixed set of his mouth, some reflection of the struggles he had endured following the death of his mother. When he smiled, though, his countenance exuded a warmth that shattered barriers—until the smile faded. Popular with the boys and brazenly sought after by women, he would not be swayed from one truth: his family was his life. And he resolved to make possible a better life for his children than what he had known. With our mother beside him, he vowed to reach that goal.

Happy in a world of our own, we children—the impetus behind our parents' dreams—numbered just three then: six-year-old Henry; myself, three years younger; and Marie, the baby. Henry was a curious, inventive boy who bore a marked resemblance to his father and whose feelings about first grade alternated between moderate praise and subtle resistance. I was small for my age, a shy and pensive child, who liked to touch the blue and white morning glories that hung over the fence or to sit statue-still watching butterflies and hummingbirds flutter above flowering bushes with delicate and exquisite colors. And the baby Marie—whether playing on the floor, bouncing on someone's lap, or toddling about—proclaimed happiness as long as things went her way. Unappeased, she was apt to throw a tantrum—screaming and flailing her chubby arms, kicking, and soaking a freshly changed diaper. Looking cherubic and cuddly, the baby had her mother's rich brown skin. Big black eyes looked up trustingly to anyone who promised to rescue her from crib or playpen. And so we three, as different as we were similar in many ways, were a source of constant wonderment to our parents.

Two doors up the street from us lived Momma's Uncle Will, her father's brother, in a comfortable six-room house with a wrap-around porch that extended from the front around to a dining room side door. Uncle Will's property, the width of three average Bank Street plots, extended as far as the stone road, Sixth Street. Just beyond the stone road was a field—part of the "colored school" yard. Most areas that were not overgrown with tall weeds were covered with bits of coal and cinders and broken glass. On the far side of the school yard lived my grandmother, Adell Dickerson.

Mom's home, too, was a six-room frame dwelling. Front and side porches added to the appearance of the house, around which well-tended flower beds bloomed. The grassy lawn was fenced in by hedges; every sprig had been planted and coaxed to mature glossy green foliage by Mom alone. To the far side of the house, an occasional tuft of weeds sprouted from hard gray dirt, which became on rainy days a muddy mess to track indoors. Across the yard from the kitchen door, the iron pump—its mouth draped in a rust-stained rag—stood encased in a wooden pump box. In the yard behind the kitchen, rich black earth was hoed into neat rows, sprouting tender greens. Every seed had been sown, every shoot set out, and every row tended by my widowed grandmother. She was a handsome, middle-aged woman of medium height, stout but solidly built, her bearing strikingly regal. Long black plaits, high cheekbones and narrow nose, flawless nut-brown skin, deep-set piercing eyes, and a thin, firm mouth attested to her "first American" ancestry.

Mom's home was her pride. On those grounds, in the old part of the house, she was born. In that same part of the house

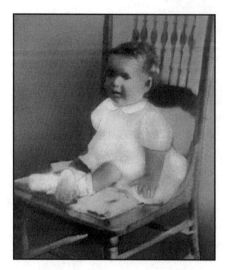

Adele Virginia Holden, "Ginny"

she had watched her mother waste away and die of consumption. There, too, her mother's ancestors had lived and died. And there she had given birth to seven children, of whom five survived. Seldom did she speak of the deaths of her two children or of the tragic railroad accident that took her husband's life when her first grandchild was a baby. At times, she reminisced about their early ups and downs in the same manner that she recalled their efforts to overcome them. Then, my mother pointed out, there were but four rooms in the house. The dining room used to be the parlor, where a crackling fire once blazed in the fireplace. But that had been bricked up long ago and hidden behind plaster and flowered wallpaper. Many years passed, and their family grew large before Momma's parents finally saved up enough to add on two rooms and to move their old kitchen back, apart from the house. Mom's pride in her home was no different from that of other black homeowners in Pocomoke, whose houses had been "in the family" for generations. Each owner kept his house in good repair, and each one boasted about the size and quality of his crops in gardens where usually the rows that outdid all others were the ones planted nearest outhouses.

✦

Sunday was a day of rest for the Holden household. When dinner was over in the little gray house on Bank Street, our family relaxed on the floor before the windows in the front bedroom. All the furniture—wrought iron double bed, a tan bureau, a white crib, and a dark, ancient rocking chair, even the matting on the floor—was secondhand. The roof of the A-frame house slanted so low that it appeared to be pressing the two windows against the floor. Only the baby and I could stand beside the windows and view the scene directly below, so our parents sat on the floor or lay propped on elbows. From the windows we could see far beyond the dense bushes behind houses across the street and recognize friends strolling on Linden Avenue or playing quietly in the field. Soon Momma spotted a familiar figure.

"Here come Ben," she said.

"Drunk or sober?" Poppa asked.

"Like usual, for Sunday," she groaned.

"Drunk again. Poor old Ben," Poppa mumbled, watching Ben stagger by. Ben Smith had been Poppa's friend ever since they began working together in "Chief" Whitney's garage. That was five or six years after Ben suddenly showed up in town, hungry, dirty, and friendless, according to my father. The story got around town that Ben came from somewhere in South Carolina. Folks said he was orphaned at the age of eight when his parents died in a car wreck. Relatives took him in, but nobody really had wanted the homely child. For several years, Ben was shuttled from one relative to another, whose treatment of the boy ranged from indifference to outright abuse. After having taken a brutal beating for something his cousin had done and blamed on him, the fourteen-year-old boy walked away from his uncle's house while the family slept.

He hopped a freight train and crouched terrified inside a box car until hunger forced him to jump off in Pocomoke. Dirty and afraid, without a penny in his pocket, the overgrown boy went from back door to back door begging for work in exchange for food and a place to stay. He had a very hard time before anyone took him in. People let him do heavy jobs that they didn't want to pay to get done, gave him something to eat, and sent him on his way. The townspeople were naturally suspicious of strangers, especially one who showed up looking as bad as Ben. Even blacks said he looked like somebody just one step ahead of the law.

A white man, old "Doc" Barnes, finally saw in Ben what others would not see. He gave Ben a cot in the attic, meals, and a little spending money. In return, Ben took excellent care of Doc's office as well as the big old house, doing all the odd jobs and heavy cleaning. Ben continued to work for Doc even after he started helping out in Chief's garage. And when Doc had a stroke, it was Ben who took care of him, diapering him and everything until the old man died. Long before he died, Doc had told his best friend—in Ben's presence—that the only one he could depend on to look after him was Ben. Doc said his children never took care of their mother during her last sickness, and they were treating him the same way. But he swore by Ben—said even though Ben was a black man, he was more like a son to him than his own. He declared that, as God was his witness, he'd "made provisions" for Ben so that he would never want for anything the rest of his life.

Ben never left Doc through the three years the old man lingered. After Doc's condition worsened, his children decided to put him in "the home" to die, but Ben begged them to leave their father with him. When they said they couldn't be worried with trying to get someone to come in and relieve him, Ben said he would make out by himself. And he did! He told Chief he'd come back to the garage, if he'd have him, after things got better for Doc. Doc took a long time dying; and when he finally passed, the children—after bickering over who got what—told Ben that their father had left no will. The only thing they offered him was the old man's clothes.

A short time after Doc's death, Ben met Al Collins, whose family recently had moved to town, and the two men became friends. At Al's suggestion, Ben stopped by Collins's house one Sunday and met his new friend's family. He said it made him feel good to be welcomed into the little house by Al's big noisy family. He liked them all, but he couldn't keep his eyes off the thin dark girl, whose sparkling black eyes and dazzling smile made him forget all the others. Her name was Rachel. Throughout their brief courtship, Ben declared that "Rachel's the bestest thing that's ever happen to me." Their love deepened after marriage, and when Rachel gave him a son, Ben was so overwhelmed with joy he could not speak. Instead, the big homely man sank to his knees beside their bed, buried his face into the sheet, and cried aloud. Then Rachel, spent from hours in labor, caressed her husband's convulsing shoulders as tenderly as she had touched her infant for the first time.

My father said that Ben already was working in the garage doing odd jobs when Chief hired him as a kind of apprentice automobile mechanic. A native New Yorker, Chief told his employees he didn't think much of the ways of Eastern Shoremen. But his business depended on the white people, so he had to cater to them. Nevertheless, he did not try to hide his belief that nobody could tell what kind of person a man is by his color, or, as he often put it, "A man ought to be treated like a man, no matter what color he is."

Chief never went around preaching his philosophy; he knew better than that if he wanted to stay in town. But his actions spoke volumes. For the first time in their lives, my father and Ben knew what it was to be treated the same as any other man, and by a white man. More than that, the three men working together— smeared with the same black grease and dirt, year after year—became close friends. Chief was like an older brother to his two employees, who prior to working together had no more than exchanged words in passing on the street.

Even to the black community, Ben was an outsider, one whom they knew nothing about except what he himself had told. They were suspicious about what he might have done back in South Carolina, or wherever he had come from. But one day Ben got in a scrape with a hometown boy and Poppa stood up for him against his buddies, convincing them that Ben was right. My father gained a friend for life. After that, the fellows stopped referring to Ben as "the hobo." They no longer made fun at his gorilla-like build; now they could see past the frowning, overhung brow and recognize in him a good man, who would share his last dime with a stranger.

Normally kind and gentle, Ben had been known to become violent when drunk. And as surely as Saturday was payday, Ben was certain to be drunk on Saturday night. But on Monday morning, haggard and morose, he would be waiting, as usual, for Chief to open up the garage. It had been that way with Ben for almost a year now. Before that, he was a different man.

"Wonder," Poppa said as he peered through the window, "if that poor boy'll ever get hisself together."

"Why don't you talk to him, Snow," Momma pleaded. "Most likely he'll listen to you, least more'n to anybody else. It's a sin and shame him doing like this ever' weekend the Lord sends. Ain't no way to fault him, though, not after what he's been through. And only the Lord knows what poor Rachel's going through, her baby dead and Ben more drunk than sober."

"No, Lord," Poppa agreed. "If we were in their place, don't know what I'd do."

She took the sleeping baby from him and slumped into the rocking chair. The squeak-squeak of the old chair was the only sound in the room. Henry and I stared at the man, who delighted in giving us pennies, as he reeled by. When Momma spoke again, her voice quivered, "Snow, we been blessed. I know we ain't got much, but Ben he's suffering so much; it really hurts me the way he's suffering. I pray for him. Just wish I knew what else to do."

"He won't talk none about Lil Ben," Poppa said. "If just now and then he'd let up and talk, might help him. Just keeps it all piled up inside. That's bad. Not but one time he really talked to me about it, and then he was cold sober. 'Twas 'round about quittin' time, and I was putting away my tools and stuff. I look up and Ben's standing by the door. He's just standing there watching me and looking kinda funny, like he's got something on his mind. Well, we brush up the shop, then we sat down to have a smoke 'fore going home. We sat there talking about nothing in particular when all a sudden Ben says, 'Snow, if I had enough money to take care of Rachel and Lil Ben like I oughter, my baby'd be livin' today, 'stead of buried out to Hall's Hill!'

"I says, 'Why you talk that way, Ben? You know that ain't so. Ever'body knows you was crazy about Lil Ben.'

" 'Yea,' he says, 'sure, I were crazy about him all right, but that didn't give him enough what he need. Why you think Rachel took Lil Ben to go along with her sister and them to stay in them shanties and pick berries? You think I wants my wife and baby to make out like hogs in them nasty, broke-down shanties? No Suh!

'Twarn't nothing for her to do 'cept go so's she can save lil somethin' to pay on them things she want for the front room. Lawd, she sure set her mind on that brown settee she seen in Fisher's window. Lawdy, Lawdy.'

" 'Most times,' " Poppa continued reporting what Ben said, " 'I'd mosey on down there to spend Saddy night and Sunday with 'em so's 'twouldn't be so lonesome. Last time I'm down, I says, 'Baby, com' on back with me now. Picking's pretty nigh over with anyways.' But she said she best stay the few days left and make most she can. Now, just how much you thinks she going make and they not payin' but two or three cent a box and them berries scarce as hen teeth? You got spend most what you make in the man's store for grub and all. No need tellin' you, Snow; you knows how they gotcha comin' and goin'. No way to save nothin' nohow. No Suh! But Rachel she won't listen. No Lawd! If she just come back with me like I ask her to. Umph, umph, umph,' he groaned, shaking his head from side to side.

"I didn't know what to say, Hon; so I just sat there feeling sorry," Poppa lamented. "After a while he starts talking some more. Seem like he's all wound up. 'Snow,' he says, 'that lightnin' bolt took the bestest thing ever I had in the world—my baby, my little baby boy!'

"I says, 'Ben, I know. It's a bitter pill to swallow.'

" 'Don't make no sense, Snow,' he cries, 'no sense in this world! I just keeps on a'seein' him, all burnt, with the mark of the bolt on his poor little head. I sees it ever' day and night the Lawd send. Can't get it outen my head. Nearbout drivin' me crazy. Onliest way I can shut it up's get full up with corn likker!'

"When he stop talking I says, 'Ben, I know it's terrible hard. Don't think I'd do good as you if I was in your shoes. But you just can't keep on drinking that way. 'Twill kill you, sure's you born.'

" 'Don't make no diffrence, Snow,' he says. 'I just soon be dead, and that's the Lawd's truth.'

"After that, he just sat there, looking pitiful, tears in his eyes. Shook me up, I tell you. 'Twas all I could do to keep from breaking down myself. Wish to God I'd know what to do to help that poor boy. Never wanted to help nobody so bad in my whole life."

19

Drying her tears, Momma reached out to stroke Poppa's shoulder. She told him to just keep on being Ben's friend, and that it would take a long time for Ben to get over his loss, but they'd do whatever they could to help him and keep on praying for him.

The silence made everything seem different. Their sadness made me feel sad, too. Turning away from the window, I saw the Sunday paper on the floor and waited for my father to make Sunday happy again.

"Poppa! Poppa!" I shouted.

Startled, he seemed to realize that in their concern for Ben, they had almost forgotten about us. Patting the floor beside him, he beckoned me to sit and asked, "What you want with Poppa, Honey?"

"You not read funny paper!" I pouted.

"That's right! Poppa supposed to read Mushmouth, ain't he?" he said, squeezing me playfully. Jumping up, I grabbed a diaper from the crib and wrapped it around me into a long apron. Instantly, I became Mrs. Stebbins, Mushmouth's mother. Pointing a finger at an imaginary little boy, I cautioned, "Be sure to look up an down 'fore ya cross the street!"

"Well, I declare," exclaimed Poppa, "if that ain't old Mushmouth's momma all over again!"

Soon a good Sunday feeling edged back into the room. Henry, unwilling to let me have all the attention, left the window and tugged at Poppa's arm asking, "Poppa, who this?" Grinning broadly, he bowed from the waist, gestured for someone to precede, and said, "After you, my dear Gaston!"

Scratching his head in mock amazement, Poppa played along, "You just got to be nobody but Alphonso! That's mighty good, Son."

And so Henry and I became our favorites: Mutt 'n' Jeff, Barney Google and Spark Plug, Kayo and Moon Mullins, Tillie and Mac, Felix the Cat, Agnes and Krazy Kat, and the pair we impersonated best of all, Maggie and hen-pecked Jiggs. Tired of acting, we flopped on the floor beside Poppa, eager to hear him make the funnies talk. And the earlier gloom cast by Ben's tragedy no longer threatened to spoil our best day of the week.

"That's all, children; Poppa done read all the funnies. Now you all want to look at the pictures," he told us.

By the time we had "read" all the funnies, we were ready for our Sunday nap. It was then, while we slept, that my parents added whatever they could from Poppa's wages to their "savings box." After dumping its contents onto the floor where they sat, Poppa would smooth out every bill and pat each coin as he arranged them in little piles of green and silver. Ever so slowly, as if the pace might swell the total, he handled each piece, then added the week's small savings. Momma watched him record the sum on a wrinkled sheet before announcing the new total. Together, they lamented the meager sum, but that did not lessen their eager planning. And so, together they embroidered a dream: they vowed to save enough, in spite of discouraging odds, to buy a house of their own.

"Don't make no difference, Snow, if we got to sit on boxes for chairs, long's we can save up enough to buy a house," Momma declared, as Poppa fumed about the few pieces of secondhand furniture they owned.

"You just keep on feeling that way, Girl, and we going get our house," he promised. "If I got to work my fingers to the bone, we going get it or my name's not Snow."

Later in the afternoon, peaceful quiet settled over the little gray house. While we slept, my parents savored precious moments all for themselves. But soon stirring sounds marked the end of quiet time. Marie lay making happy noises until she tired of solitude. From our room I watched her throw things from her crib, squealing as each item hit the floor. When the last thing not fastened down was tossed out, Momma knew "their time" was over. Marie, fat legs poking through the sides of her crib, squealed when Momma picked her up and began to talk to her.

"Why you wanta wake ever'body up, Dumplin', just 'cause you done had a nice long nap? You laughing at Momma 'cause she wants to lay down a lil bit longer? Bet that's just what 'tis. That's all right, Sugar Pig, you been right good. Com'ere to Momma."

After bathing Marie and patting powder in all the creases, she pinned on a snow-white diaper, eased her into rubber pants, and buttoned her into a ruffled pink pinafore. With the brushing of the baby's sparse soft hair, Momma had her all ready. She then noticed that we were awake.

"You two get a good nap?" she asked, before shaking Poppa to get up and dress.

Soon, we children were ready for our family's Sunday stroll. Henry, uncomfortable in his new Buster Brown suit, sat on the steps, enviously watching Bobby and Jamie play in the dirt next door. They called back and forth to each other. Twice Henry left the steps, casting furtive glances toward the house to be sure no one inside saw, and stood near his friends and their mud houses. He was careful not to get too close to the fence, for he knew the penalty for playing in dirt while wearing his new suit.

In the kitchen all was well. The baby chattered in her playpen, and Momma sighed aloud, "Now, maybe I can go get my things on." After warning me not to rock fast in the big rocking chair, she left me to watch Marie.

Henry returned to the steps where he had been told to sit. Suddenly there was a heavy crashing noise. Anguished cries, screams, racing footsteps on the stairs shattered the quiet. Frightened and alone, Henry crept into the kitchen. Momma, her hands trembling, was rinsing a blood-soaked cloth and dabbing the bleeding wound ever so gently while Poppa tried to hold me still and calm me. But my cries grew louder, alarming the baby, who began to whimper; unheeded, she let go full blast. Nevertheless, not until the heavy bleeding subsided did they have time for either tantrum or fright.

As she changed the water in the basin, Momma turned to Henry, "You be a big boy, Henry, and play with Baby so she'll stop crying."

In spite of his own fright, Henry tried as hard as he knew how to quiet Marie. Nothing worked. She just screamed louder and kicked harder. When every effort seemed futile, he stopped trying. Poppa, still trying to calm me, sensed Henry's frustration. "Give her them beads to play with, Son. Nothing wrong with her. She get tired hollering, she'll stop." Then, for the first time since everything happened, he spoke to Momma, his voice stern and angry. "What's this child doing getting her mouth all cut up like this anyway?"

"She fell outen that rocking chair. I keep telling Ginny, over and over, to not rock so hard. But her head's just hard as stone, turn that chair clean over. Told her to sit there to I got my things on," she mumbled.

"Oughten never leave her in no rocking chair anyway. Can't expect no lil child to know how fast to rock. Don't know what you must been thinking," he mumbled.

"Then whyn't you stay in here and watch 'em? That's what I'd like to know," she snapped, hurt that he could blame it all on her. "Didn't I have to get my things on, too? Here you all ready and just fooling around upstairs and me with all three children to get ready—not so much as time to catch my breath."

"You right, Sweetheart," he relented, "don't know what must come over me. Guess it just upset me to see Ginny's mouth cut so bad, that's all. Nobody's to blame. You go get dressed. Ever'thing'll be all right down here."

Momma cleaned up the last signs of the accident. She did not look at my father, did not say a word; but softly, almost inaudibly, she hummed "Must Jesus Bear the Cross Alone" as she moved toward the stairs. Then she turned back to the playpen, where Marie's shrill protests had dwindled to an occasional whimper. Henry still sat beside the pen. Seeing the fright that lingered in his eyes, Momma cradled his head and held him close. "Poor little boy," she murmured, "nobody took time to pay him no mind." She stooped to press her cheek to his. "Did all that fuss scare Momma's lil man? Thought she forgot all aboutcha, didn't you? No she didn't neither. Momma don't never forget her boy! Go sit back on the steps, and 'fore you can say 'Jack be nimble,' we going be ready to go down Mom's."

After giving Henry a playful pat on the backside, she picked up the whimpering baby, scolding as she carried her upstairs, "Now, why you want to carry on, alarming the place like that, Baby? Ain't one thing wrong with you. Now you hush that noise, right now!"

Some time later, after the rocking chair had been soundly thrashed, we finally were on our way down Mom's. As we walked along, my mother complained of an uneasy feeling, like trouble was waiting to pounce right down on us, she said.

"It's Ginny's fall," she told Poppa. "That's what 'tis."

Many years later, recalling that afternoon and the fall that left a permanent reminder of the accident on my lip, Momma divulged the root of her worries about the mishaps, one after another, that seemed to befall me. And she often said she wondered whether Poppa's thoughts also dwelled on "Harrison's prophecy."

According to Momma, one bright spring morning when I was only a few months old, Harrison Gray, who was said to possess strangely prophetic powers, spied her sitting in the side yard holding me and watching Henry play.

"Hey-o, Jane!" he said. "How you hittin' 'em this nice mornin'?"

"Hi, Harrison! Pretty good, I guess. How's yourself?"

"I'm fair, I reckon," he mumbled. "Ain't never going be no better'n that. Let's see that lil ol' ugly baby of your'n."

Momma said Harrison looked at me for a long minute before speaking. "That's sure one pretty lil baby you got there, Jane. Look just like a doll baby. Mighty puny though. It's a shame, though, a certain shame."

"What's a shame, Harrison? What you talking about, Boy?"

"Shame you not never going see her grow up, Jane, that's what," Harrison replied and gulped before continuing. "This child ain't going live that long. Now don't ask me how I knows, Jane. That I can't tell you. But sure's God be my witness, it's clear to me as daylight."

"Harrison! How can you say something like that about my baby?" she cried. But Harrison turned a troubled gaze in her direction and, without another word, shuffled from the yard.

On his way to work that morning, my father said he had felt good, mainly because Momma was in a cheerful mood—no sign of the lingering depression which had been bothering her. But the moment he stepped into the kitchen for lunch, he knew that his relief was short-lived.

"What's matter, Hon?" he asked.

"I tell you, Snow, and you just going say it's silly."

"Now how you know what I'm going say 'til you tell me?" he teased.

Ignoring his question, she moaned, "All morning long, keep hearing what Harrison said."

"Harrison! What's he doing here causing trouble?"

"He just stop by on his way from Beulah's, Snow. Never much as set foot in the door."

"Humph!" he grunted. "Next time he stops by on his way from Beulah's, or anywhere else, you tell him to keep right on walking, 'less you want me tell him. Now, what he say to get you all upset?"

"It's about the baby," she whimpered.

"About Ginny? What in name of common sense he got to say about her? What's matter," he joked, "he say she's ugly? You know that fool never could half see noway."

"No, he said she's pretty. But Snow, Harrison he said . . . he said she's not going live long enough to grow up! I know Ginny's frail and all but . . ."

"And that's what's gotcha all worked up?" Poppa cut in. "You mean you taking what that drunk says to heart, Jane? Well, I hope to die! How you figure Harrison'd know what's going happen to Ginny any better'n you and me? Humph! Now, I *know* he better stay away from here!"

"But, Snow," she cried, "you know well's me how Harrison's always saying things, and they always turning out just like he says. He's got me so worried and feeling like something awful's going happen to her. Just about made me sick."

"Jane, Honey," he began, trying to allay her fears, "now you know Harrison just well's me. You think he'd be in the shape he's in if he knows so much more'n ever'body else? Ain't nobody went to school with us that's half bad off as Harrison Gray, drunk more'n he's sober. And you mean you going let somebody like that put ideas in your head? Great day in the morning! Sure thought you got more religion than that. You the one always saying how the Lord's the onliest one can say which way we going. Best put Ginny in His hands and forget what that drunk's saying."

"You right, Snow. But, try as I will or may, I just can't help feeling it's something to what he says. Wasn't no smell of whiskey on him today. And you know yourself ever' time you turn around it's something else matter with Ginny. Wasn't nothing like this with Henry. Scares me, Snow. It's just making me feel weak all over."

After lunch, as Poppa sat beside the cradle watching his sleeping baby, Momma said she noticed that he had been sitting silently for an unusually long time, and she knew that soon she would have to remind him it was time to go back to work, something she never had to do. When she turned to speak, she caught a glimpse of his face. Although he smiled the moment he felt her eyes on him, the smile was too late. In that instant she had seen a reflection of her fears in his eyes.

2 · School Days

Then "school's out" time
stretched farther—
from berry-picking's May
to romping free in daisy fields . . .
living for children's day
or, barefoot, splashing rain fairies
through months as long as years
to September

Folks could hear the singing from a block away down Bank Street: "Goin' lay down my sword an' shield; Down by the riverside!" Sitting alone on the front steps, I waited to watch the children from the "big" school march by on their way to the Odd Fellows' Hall for noon devotions. "An' sto-uh-dee war no more, ain' goin' study war no more . . ." The older children came first, strutting in time with the rhythm of the song. From yards and doorways, housewives and old folks listened, proud that the young ones were getting the education they had missed. After getting her teacher's permission, a girl ran into our yard and asked Momma to let me go with them.

"Annie, Honey, she's not fit to go nowheres today," Momma replied, wiping her hands on a dishrag as she came to the door. "Maybe another day, but ask me ahead of time."

After my first school visit with Annie, all I talked about was school, wanting nothing as much as to go back again and again. Even playtime was play-school time, with a class consisting of two dolls and a rubber mouse. Occasionally Marie would sit long enough to play school, but because the pupil soon became disruptive, the sessions were short. Now and then Henry agreed to be in the class; however, he usually asked to be excused at the start of the lesson and didn't return. Nothing lessened the fascination that school held for me. Everything in my world included school. One day, as I played school with imaginary pupils, Poppa asked, "What you think, Hon, our lil girl's going be a schoolteacher?"

"Who on earth can know what somebody that little's going be, Snow? If truth be told, I'll be satisfied long's she just grows up healthy," Momma remarked solemnly.

"Course, we both want her to be healthy! But you know you just's anxious as me for these children to make something outen theirselves," he replied.

Refusing to join in his mood, she said, "No need you talking that way, Snow. *You* know what just crossed my mind. Wash up. It's just about ready."

She flipped over the thick slice of fresh ham browning in the heavily crusted black skillet and stirred potatoes and onions frying in a smaller pan. Then she swung the biscuits she was taking from the oven out of Poppa's reach, fussing, "No need spoiling your supper that way. Land sakes, gimme time to put it on the table! Made some applesauce, full of cinnamon and nutmeg way you like it, to go with them biscuits. You children go wash your hands and get to your places."

Heads bowed above the oilcloth-covered table as Poppa asked the blessing: "Dear Lord, make us truly thankful . . ."

✦

Being in first grade down at the Hall was even better than playing school. At the close of each day, I ran home to tell Momma what had happened at school: "Miss Williams gave Harold ten licks on his hand for hittin' Betty. Mandy got standed in the corner. Miss Williams says 'Don't say we *is.*' "

One day Sara Williams walked home with me. Momma jerked around from the clothesline to see the pleasant-faced, stout young woman standing beside me near the kitchen steps. Although she had grown accustomed to seeing Miss Williams since she started taking me to school, she certainly didn't expect to see her standing there in our yard. She didn't want strangers, especially teachers, visiting—not until she and Poppa were able to get some furniture for the front room. But there my teacher was, smiling, looking all nice and cool, while Momma, after having stood over the hot stove canning peaches all morning plus having done the Berrys' heavy, dirty washing, was wet through with sweat. As she walked toward us in her damp, limp, old gingham dress, she said all kinds of thoughts raced through her mind: "What on earth'd she come here for today . . . s'pose she's coming in . . . kitchen's a mess . . . don't know when I looked such a sight. "

"Good afternoon, Miss Williams. You have to excuse how I look. Been trying to can some peaches and washing too and trying to pacify the baby. She would pick today to be real fussy," she rambled on. "Ginny, whyn't you tell me Miss Williams coming home with you?"

"Ginny didn't know until after school that I was coming this way. She said she would show me where the Longs live, Mrs. Holden. There's not one thing wrong with you. I just stopped to speak and to tell you what a nice little girl you have," said Miss Williams.

"It's nice of you to say so," Momma beamed.

"Ginny's one of the brightest pupils I've had, and she never gives one bit of trouble."

"I'm mighty glad to hear she's doing good in school, Miss Williams. Just hope she'll keep it up. That's one child's sure crazy about school."

Miss Williams told Momma she wanted me to be in the Christmas play and asked her to lend a hand with preparations. Momma promised to help and asked Miss Williams whether she had time to come in. Later she told Poppa how relieved she was because my teacher didn't have time to visit that day.

After the good-byes, Miss Williams crossed the yard and turned toward Marsie Long's. Momma recalls that, from the first, she sensed a feeling of closeness with my teacher, almost as if the two of them were old friends, "not all stuck up and full of airs like a lotta teachers."

✦

On the Shore, it seemed as if another winter could barely wait to come—winter with its gray hard-frozen ground, razor-sharp winds, swirling sleet and hail, and heavy snows that lingered in ruts and corners and waited for the next blizzard. Meanwhile, the flaming glory of fall-colored leaves painted the countryside. The bluest of blue skies floated magnificent clouds through Indian summer. Then the last brilliant blooms of autumn faded and fell upon straw-colored grass. And the sun-warmed breezes turned into whistling winds.

The primary grades were preparing to celebrate Thanksgiving. We drew big lopsided pumpkins, colored them orange, and trimmed them with fat green leaves on stumpy brown stems. We took home cutout turkeys, Pilgrims, Indians, and corn shocks to color. Then we pasted our creations on windows, blackboards, and bulletin boards. On the day before school recessed for the holiday, Miss Williams read us the story of the first Thanksgiving and some Thanksgiving poems. Then we sat around a table of long, rough boards covered with brown paper. There were bowls of popcorn balls, big beautiful apples, ginger snaps, tangy-sweet apple cider, and yellow-tipped orange kernels of candy corn. When the party was over, we rushed home for the long holiday weekend. We would not feast on turkey. Thanksgiving Day dinners would be whatever our poor parents managed to provide. But we were happy and thankful.

Rehearsals for the Christmas program had begun long before Thanksgiving, and primary pupils were excited. We not only would be taking part in a special program, but also would be presenting our play along with the older schoolchildren at night in Mount Zion Methodist Church. While Miss Williams made crepe-paper costumes for wise men, shepherds, Mary and Joseph, and other characters, we children were doing special jobs. Some of us fluted red and green crepe-paper streamers; others cut strips of brown paper for the manger. Second-graders molded farm animals of papier-mâché and several cut out designs of stars, Christmas trees, bells, balls, gingerbread men, candles, wreaths, and candy canes. Hardly anyone misbehaved; we were too busy. Besides, no one wanted to be excluded from participating in that very special event.

There was no doubt about it: preparations for the Christmas play had a marked effect on our behavior, but Miss Williams pointed out another factor—one the parents tended to ignore—which had had a dramatic influence on behavior in the Hall. It concerned Wilbert Wilson's experience on a day in early November. Wilbert was a tiny boy, much smaller than most second-graders, and his inquisitive nature often led him into unpredictable situations. But never before had he gotten into anything to equal what happened that day. Probably no one, other than Wilbert himself, knew exactly what had precipitated the incident, which left the boy so upset that the doctor ordered his mother to keep him home from school for a long time. When Wilbert did come back to school, he seemed strange, almost like a different boy.

Everyone, including Miss Williams, remained puzzled about what actually had happened to Wilbert. That day, she recalled, was unusually warm—almost hot—for November. She had played several ring games with us when someone asked if we could play hide-and-go-seek. While Charles counted, children scurried out of sight to hide behind trees and bushes, under steps, and on all sides of the building.

"Read-e-e-e?" yelled Charles.

"Yeah! Yeah! Yeah!" we called back.

And the game was on. Seekers searched for hiders, who breathlessly shielded their secret spots as if they were playing the game for the very first time. As usual, recess ended too soon. With the summons of the heavy wooden-handled bell, undiscovered hiders reluctantly crept from their spots to line up at the steps—first-graders to the left, second-graders to the right. A monitor stepped out of line and peered down to the end. No Wilbert. So Joe reported his absence to Miss Williams, who determined that no one had seen Wilbert since we started playing hide-and-go-seek.

Then we heard the noise. It was like the wail of a trapped animal. All other noises ceased. We heard it again. Miss Williams ran down the steps in the direction of the noise. We followed her to the rear of the building. It was there we found Wilbert. And what we saw was a sight none of us would be likely to forget. Smeared and streaked with excrement, Wilbert was crawling from behind the toilet, where the rear bottom board had fallen back from piles of waste.

"Wilbert! What on earth?" shrieked Miss Williams. Turning to her astonished pupils, who backed away as one, she shouted, "Go inside, all of you!" She told one pupil to take charge and sent another for Wilbert's mother.

Once inside, we crowded at the windows to witness the scene unfold outside.

"Wilbert, sit on that box 'til I get something to clean some of this off you. Can't imagine what on earth . . ." Miss Williams threw up her hands, let them fall to her sides, and hurried around front. Inside, we laughed and talked, but a hush fell over the room when she closed the door. Scolding the noisemakers, she promised severe punishment for any disorderly pupils whose names Ella Mae took while she was outside.

Disheveled and out of breath, Hannah Wilson wiped her glistening face on her apron as she rushed across the school yard where Miss Williams was approaching Wilbert with a bucket, a broom, and some rags. When she was close enough to get a good look at Wilbert, she stared. Her mouth opened, but her voice failed. When she could speak, she roared, "You Wilbert! What the devil you doing all nastied up like that? If you ain't the worse mess I ever seen."

"Wah-ah-ahh . . . ," Wilbert cried, mouth open wide and eyes shut tight.

"Shut your mouth, Boy, lessen you wants some in there, too!" Mrs. Wilson told him. Then, with the initial shock behind her, she said, "Miss Williams, 'taint no while for you gettin' all messed up with him. Just gimme that piece of sheet to put 'round him. Onliest thing to do is plop him in my biggest washtub. Look like he's going need to soak to this time next week. Even got some in his hair!"

Mrs. Wilson put the sheet over Wilbert's shoulders. Then she asked in a quiet, bitter tone, "Miss Williams, just tell me one thing. What in the world's Wilbert doing *back* of the toilet anyhow?"

"Mrs. Wilson, I wish I knew. Last thing before recess was over, we played hide-and-go-seek. When recess ended and the children lined up as usual, we missed Wilbert. Then I heard him crying and found him crawling from behind the outhouse. He won't stop crying long enough to tell me what happened. I think the doctor should see him. He's shivering as if he might be having a chill," Miss Williams added.

"First thing's to get him in that washtub and scrub the stink off'n him. Ain't no doctor want fool with him, not like this. Come on here, Boy!" she snapped giving Wilbert an impatient shove.

No one knew whether it was the overall experience or what, but Wilbert was very sick after the incident. Weeks passed before the doctor allowed him to return to school. And before his return, Miss Williams gave strict warning: anyone who brought up the "outhouse incident" would be punished. So everyone was afraid to say anything to Wilbert about it. Whatever the actual circumstances, Wilbert refused to give one word of explanation. If anyone mentioned the incident in his presence, he would not speak for days. The emotional scars that experience left changed him, not for a few weeks or months, but for life.

It took the busyness of preparations for our Christmas program to restore an air of normalcy in the Hall. After weeks of preparations, we could hardly wait until Sunday. In the Sunday school room at Mount Zion, lights glowed through red and green streamers and sparkled on silvery ropes. A large star twinkled in the painted dark sky above the manger, all constructed by older boys in manual training class to transform the stage into a Christmas-card scene. All classes were assembled for a full rehearsal. First- and second-graders rehearsed before the upper grades. We begged to wear our costumes, but Miss Williams explained that crepe-paper costumes could be torn easily and there was no time for making replacements. So we satisfied ourselves by pretending to be dressed for our roles.

Even without costumes, we became excited upon hearing the first soft hum of "The First Noel," our cue. I was Mary; Richard was Joseph; Andrew was the donkey. It took a lot of practice before Andrew learned how to move on all fours, slowly without jerking so that I could sit sidesaddle on his back without tumbling off. But Andrew, a second-grade pupil, was as gentle as he was big for his age; the journey progressed without mishap, as "wise men" peeking from behind the curtain awaited their cues. At the close of the play, the entire student body sang "Silent Night" so beautifully that after the last note there was silence for several minutes. Next, we dramatized (with gift-bearing fairies dancing around the Christmas tree) a lively Christmas song:

> White fairies come down
> On the snowflakes, pretty snowflakes.
> Every one wears a crown.
> For fairies remember
> To celebrate December
> And they fasten lovely presents
> On the green Christmas tree.

With rehearsal over, the older children gathered younger ones and headed for home. But after I got home, everything changed drastically for me. Momma said she knew something was wrong the moment Annie let me into the kitchen, but she tried to ignore the feeling. Leaning over the hot stove, she placed one heavy flatiron down and picked up another. After testing the iron by the sizzling of a wet finger touched quickly against its bottom, she asked, "Well Annie, how'd rehearsal go?"

"Real good, Miss Jane. Lil children's play's best though. You ought seen Ginny. She done real good," Annie said.

"That's good. She sure practice hard enough. Ginny, com'ere; you don't act like you feeling good," she said, placing the back of her hand against my forehead.

"Um hum-m," she murmured, nodding her head. "Got a fever, just like I thought. Go getcha things off. I'm going give you some medicine and let you lay down in here. Annie, thankya for bringing her home. Not likely she'll be going to school tomorrow. "

When I didn't make a fuss about having to lie down, Momma felt concerned; when I didn't say anything about having to miss school the next day, she began to worry. I still was half out of my dress when she came upstairs. So she pretended to fuss, as she felt my hot forehead and asked, "Where you feel bad, Ginny?"

"Nowheres," I whimpered.

"Expect we better get the doctor to see you," she said on the way downstairs.

That really scared me, so I tried to sound all right, "But I ain't sick, Momma. Don't get the doctor, p-please."

"Now stop that fretting and lay down here so I can cover you up. Suppose we just wait to your father comes home and see how you feeling then," she said, smoothing the quilt over me. "Momma made some nice hot soup. I believe that's just what'll make this child feel better!"

"I ain't hungry."

"You ain't hungry, you must be sick for sure," she sighed. Cracking the door against the still, cold air, she called Henry repeatedly without response. Several minutes later a panting Henry bolted into the kitchen.

"Where you been, Boy? Thought I told you to not go outen the yard," Momma fussed.

"That's where I was, playing with Bobo and Herman. Ask 'em, Momma."

"Don't need ask nobody. How you going be right out front and not hear, loud's I been yelling? You go away from here one more time and you know what'cha goin' get. Now fasten that jacket and go get that kindling in here."

"When I full up the box, can I go back out and play?" he asked.

"You ask me one more thing, Boy, and I'm going tell your father on you! It's time you in the house anyway. Guess you want him to come home and find that woodbox empty again, Mister. Don't expect no help outen me next time. You getting too big for me to be after you all the time. Bet right now you ain't done the first homework. Just keep it up, Henry, and you going be in plenty trouble when Snow gets home," she cautioned.

"Done some in school," he muttered.

"How much? Lemme see."

Henry fumbled in his canvas bookbag. After a long search, he pulled out a wrinkled sheet of paper showing several raggedy columns of figures. Only two or three had been worked. Momma examined the sheet and shook her head.

"That all you done, Henry?" she asked. "That's some sorry looking work. I know you better get that wood in here and sit down to that table, no maybe-so about it!"

Henry had been working for a while when we heard the signal: Poppa always cleared his throat noisily as he turned into the yard. He came in, rubbing his hands together and crossed the kitchen to stand by the stove, not without complimenting Henry on his studiousness.

"Hi Hon! How's the ol' lady?" he teased. Her response was more of a sigh than a greeting.

He had swung a squealing Marie high over his head before noticing me on the lounge in the corner. Putting Marie down with a pat on the bottom, he came over to the lounge, where I lay, sad eyes beckoning.

"What's matter with my girl?" he asked, pushing back the blanket so he could sit down without smudging it with grease.

"She come home sick, Snow," Momma explained. "Got right smart fever. Could be cold. It's hard to tell. Ain't ate a thing since she got home. Wouldn't even try'n eat some soup."

"You going eat some soup for Poppa, Honey?" he asked caressing my face. I didn't answer.

"Think we ought get the doctor to her, Snow?" Momma asked in such an anxious voice that I started crying.

They talked it over and decided to wait until morning. After supper, they tried again to coax me to eat some soup. I swallowed two or three spoonfuls then began to gag. No more.

Poppa wasn't sure what woke him later that night; the only sound to be heard was the ticking of the clock. But he turned over and Momma wasn't there. He came into our room and whispered., "What's matter, Hon, she worse?"

"I'm not sure. She's half 'sleep, but the fever ain't down. Told me she hurt. I ask her where she hurt, and she start whimpering. I don't like way she looks, lips all parched," Momma lamented. "What time's it getting to be?"

"Nearbout five o'clock. Soon be morning. Aim to go after Dr. Hull 'fore he leaves home for his office. Com'on back to bed. She's 'sleep now," he whispered. But I wasn't sleeping.

"I'm going lay down here with them. You go ahead. 'Fore you know, it's going be time to go to work," she reminded him.

Momma said it seemed as if morning never would come as she lay listening to my restlessness, hearing night sounds, trying to shut out the faraway echoes of roosters outcrowing each other. Still no border of light outlined the window shade. Everything was darkness and waiting, and I was no better. Suddenly, she said she knew something was wrong. She bolted from the bed. The lamp was out. Daylight flooded the room, and Poppa was standing in the doorway all ready for work.

"What's matter, Snow? She worse or something? I must've dropped off to sleep!" she blurted.

"Just didn't want to leave without telling you. I'm going after Dr. Hull. Started not to wake you up—way you been up off'n on all night," he told her.

The moment they got me settled on the lounge in the kitchen, Poppa left to get the doctor; then Momma called Henry downstairs to get dressed by the stove. Soon coffee was perking in the blue-white speckled enamel pot. Slab bacon sizzled in the skillet. A bowl of buckwheat batter was ready to be dropped in sizzling circles on the heavy old black, grease-crusted griddle.

Although we both waited anxiously for the doctor's arrival the sharp rap at the door gave us a start.

"Morning! Smells like breakfast is all ready," observed the big formidable looking white man, who ducked automatically as he entered the low kitchen doorway.

"Morning Doctor," Momma said. "You welcome to such as we got. Thought sure Snow'd be with you."

"He was," Dr. Hull replied. "Went up to the garage to tell Chief he'd be late. Now what seems to be the trouble with this youngun?"

"'Deed I wish I could tell you. It's got me worried nearbout sick myself. She come home sick from school yesterday, kinda feverish, and she don't seem one bit better. Look how her lips all cracked."

"She complained of any pain?" Dr. Hull asked brusquely as he felt my pulse.

"Yessir. Says she hurts real bad. I ask her to show me where, and she says her knees and elbows—head, too. She won't eat much of nothing. Just turn and twist nearbout all night long, Doctor," Momma moaned. "I'm so worried I don't know what to do."

"Now, you listen to me, Jane," Dr. Hull cut in sternly. "Whatever's wrong won't be helped by you letting yourself get all worked up when you need to be taking care of your family. Told you the way you act can help make a sick child better or make it worse! Let this child see you acting all nervous and worried and she'll be twice as long getting better. That what you want?"

Without waiting for a reply, he continued, "Now, for God's sake, get that woebegone look off your face before she notices, and let me examine her. Go on with whatever you got to do. If I need you, I'll holler."

"Ginny," he called in an incredibly gentle voice, "your momma tells me you don't feel good. That right?"

I nodded, fixing a frightened gaze on him.

"Well now," Dr. Hull said, "we'll have to get you feeling better. I'm not going to hurt you. Just want to find out what's making you feel bad. First, let's see how that throat's doing. Open your mouth. Wider. Hmm. Let's take your temperature. Now Ginny, I want you to put your hand on every place that hurts."

"Um hum-m," Dr. Hull nodded. "Do the pains hurt like somebody's hitting on your knee hard, or does it feel like I'm squeezing it 'til it hurts bad?"

"Like they squeezin' on it, real hard," I whimpered.

"Well Ginny, we'll see if we can't get rid of that mean old pain. Might take a little time, but . . ."

"Doctor, what is it? Is it serious?" Momma interrupted, ignoring his earlier warning to not fret.

But before Dr. Hull could reply, Poppa rushed in, asking, "Well, Doctor, what's wrong with my girl?"

"She's going be all right, Snow," Dr. Hull said quickly.

"What's wrong with her Doctor?" Poppa repeated.

"Well she . . .," Dr. Hull began. "Suppose we let Ginny rest while we talk in the other room."

"Sure, Doctor. Best put your coat on—no fire in there," he advised.

But the door they thought they'd closed behind them was ajar. So I lay listening as they talked, and Poppa repeated his question again in a strained voice. Then I heard Dr. Hull say, "I'm afraid she's got all the symptoms of rheumatic fever, Snow. Can't say for sure just yet."

"Doctor!" Momma cried, "you mean my child's got the old-time fever? You mean she's that sick?"

"Looks that way," he said. "But Jane, I don't want you to get all worked up. If you want Ginny to get well, you've got to stay calm and listen to everything I tell you so you'll know how to take care of her."

"But, Doctor, what's happen to her all a sudden?" she asked. "'Fore she left for school, she didn't act sick."

"You know Ginny was a very sick child," Dr. Hull said, "when she had that bad throat. Well, it happens sometimes after that kind of illness, with the throat infection and all, the patient comes down with painful joints and fever, like Ginny. I'll give you a prescription for pain and to bring her fever down. But the main thing is keep her in bed."

"How long she got to stay in bed?" Momma asked.

"Well, that depends," he said slowly, "on how soon the symptoms disappear. Could be a few weeks. Could be longer. You just keep her in bed 'til I tell you she can get up. Try to get her to eat some oatmeal. Later on, some soup and maybe custard, until she feels more like eating. Give her one of these pills after meals and at bedtime. Keep her in bed. That's very important. This kind of sickness can cause more serious problems if the patient is not treated properly. But we won't go into that now," Dr. Hull added.

"Now, Hon, Doctor says she's going be all right. No need getting all upset. You do and soon's you go back in the kitchen, Ginny's going take notice," Poppa warned.

"That's right, Snow. You take care of Jane, and I'll take care of Ginny," Dr. Hull added as they returned to the kitchen.

I smiled, waiting for him to continue, when he said he thought I was looking better already. But his next words killed the smile.

"Tell me," he began cheerfully, "how would you like a nice long vacation from school?"

"We already going have vacation for Christmas," I informed him.

"That's right, so you will," he recalled. "Then what would you say if you could have a longer vacation than the other children? How about from now until way after Christmas holidays are over?"

I squirmed and began to stammer, "B-b-but I gotta be-be in the Chris-Christmas p-play. Can't I be in the p-play 'fore I got stay h-home?"

My tear-filled eyes sought first my father, then my mother. The moment I saw my mother's face, I knew there would be no Christmas play for me. I pulled the blanket up around my chin and cried. Later I watched as Momma, sniffling and sighing, wrote a note to Miss Williams while Poppa and Henry ate break-fast. Finally, I went to sleep and slept so long that Momma said she became uneasy and was about to shake me when I opened my eyes. When I asked whether I could be in the play if I felt better soon, she sighed before answering:

"Ginny, honey, you go outdoors 'fore Dr. Hull says so, then you going get sicker'n you are. And then you'd have to stay home in bed a great long time. You don't want that to happen, now do you?"

The holidays approached and the play went on without the original Mary—me. I fretted and whimpered more about having missed being in the special program than about my pains. Neither other children's colorful accounts of the program nor Christmas day—which my parents brought into our bedroom since I was still bedridden—helped cheer me up. When my teacher began vis-iting and going over our classwork, all I could think about was getting out of bed and going back to school.

It seemed as if the weeks in bed would last forever. But finally the day came when I was lifted into the rocking chair. I remember clutching the chair arms and moving my head carefully because it felt as if it might topple off. Looking about me, I felt strange, al-most as if I were seeing the old room with its familiar objects for the first time. After a few days of sitting in the chair, I was allowed to try standing. But I cried out that something was sticking into the bottoms of my feet. On the third day of trying, I stood without cringing, even took a few steps. For some time the short steps were unsteady, but the prospect of becoming well enough to return to school was the best tonic. Finally, I was allowed to try attending half-days. That first day, when Momma walked home from taking me to school, she said she was so filled with gratitude and relief that she walked right past our house.

School was fun and I loved Miss Williams dearly, but the second-grade school year was rapidly drawing to a close, and soon we would be leaving the Hall to go to third grade. It was confusing to be glad and sad at the same time. Glad because I was going to be in the "big school" next door to my grandmother's house. Sad because I would be leaving Miss Williams. On the last day of school, Miss Williams gave her pupils a party. Everyone was happy. We savored pink lemonade, cookies, popcorn balls, and candy, and we played ring games. I didn't want Edward Bailey to "pick me" to be his partner because he looked so funny with his front teeth missing. But when it was his turn to select, he skipped straight to me, as the children sang:

> How do you do my pardner?
> How do you do to-da-ay?
> Won't you dance in a circle?
> I will show you the way.
> Tra la la la la . . . tra la la la la . . .

Edward stood before me singing and grinning and holding out his hands, inviting me to skip dance around the circle of schoolmates with him. And I had to do it, even if Edward did look funnier than any other boys without front teeth, because the teeth he did have were marked with brown ridges and rotten.

After the games were over, we received report cards. Each child got a good-bye hug. Those leaving for the third grade got a special talking to by Miss Williams, who told us she would miss each of us and she was counting on each one to show his new

41

teacher that he deserved to be promoted. Each child, in turn, promised to make her proud of him. Then we all burst from the building, happy and free for a long, wonderful summer.

◆

Summer on the Shore for children and grown-ups alike, even the very poor, was a special time. So many sunny days, far more days than a small child could count. And time enough for everything, for chores rushed through to lazy hours of playtime, for romping on the church lawn after Children's Day rehearsals and for soaring almost to the sky in swings roped to sturdy limbs of towering churchyard trees. Time for so many simple pleasures during those wonderful days of summer on the Shore.

On one day every summer, colored Sunday schools from a number of Shore towns had their picnic day on the Ocean City beach, which at all other times was considered to be the exclusive province of whites. Even then, blacks were relegated to one distant section of the beach. Nothing, however, curbed the enthusiasm of bus- and carloads of picnickers on that special day. Bathing suits, packed away for a year, were shaken out, and sometimes moth holes were too numerous for mending. On the night before the picnic, women fried chicken, made beaten biscuits and potato salad, deviled eggs, and baked rolls, sweet potato pies, and their richest cakes. Some made freezers of ice cream early in the morning, to be packed with ice and salt and wrapped in several burlap bags.

Long before we were near the beach, Poppa always called our attention to the slate blue "water line" marking the horizon. He would turn to Momma, asking, "Smell it, Hon? Smell that water?" We children could hardly wait to jump from the borrowed garage car and feel the hot sand shift beneath our feet. For the first few minutes after tumbling from the car, we just stood in awe watching monstrous waves slap the shore, sending spray everywhere. Then, after Momma cautioned us repeatedly to stay together and to return every few minutes so she would know we were all right, we ventured forth.

When it was time to go into the water, we had to change in the car—blacks were not allowed to use facilities provided for bathers.

But after the first toes inched into chilly water, the splashing, kicking, and screaming surpassed any witnessed at a mass baptism. Exhausted, we would rest up, then go in again until we had had enough. All of us dried off in the cars while our mothers tried to free us of sand so we would not be too uncomfortable. But they knew the effort was useless.

By the time everyone had dressed, the feast was spread. And my father assured Momma every picnic day that nothing ever tasted as good as her crispy fried chicken, along with potato salad and tomatoes from our garden, cinnamon buns, chocolate layer cake, and everything. Friends and neighbors exchanged picnic goodies. Some complained about being confined to that remote part of the beach, but their children's carefree laughter drowned out the voices of discontent.

3 · *"Call Me Miss Blaine!"*

While these and still worse shames
are kept intact . . .
held fast by hands of whites opposing change
the blackest curse, plus poverty and fear,
lies in our same acceptance of this lot:
emancipated-chained men of the Shore,
steeped in "what was—is now—and will forever be."

Too soon the goldenrod began to flower along fields and ditch banks. We knew that noontime no longer would find us at play, watching minnows and tadpoles splash through sunlight on pebbles in crystal streams. It was a bittersweet time; we yearned to keep summer's lazy days, yet most of us eagerly awaited the first day of school. Meanwhile, mothers searched the stores for affordable school necessities to add to secondhand clothes they bought from women they worked for. Fall plaids, corduroy pants, sturdy shoes, and school supplies had to be bought for three now in our house. Momma was apprehensive about how Marie would take to school. Although Marie would play school with me, she wasn't overly enthusiastic about the playtime, no matter how much the fun of school was touted for her benefit. But one thing was certain: the school bell would ring for all three of us.

The first day of school was a big event in the black community. Some children proudly showed off new clothes even though they were stiff and uncomfortable, especially the shoes. After all, except to church on Sunday, few of us wore shoes regularly in summer. Before going inside and during recess, we greeted and romped with old classmates, many of whom we had not seen since May. We stared curiously at the few new faces. Some students visited with old teachers and wondered how the new ones would be.

The procedure for opening day was generally the same in all rooms. Teachers started devotions with the singing of an opening hymn followed by reading of scripture, the pledge of allegiance, and a closing song. Then we listened to teachers talk about the importance of a good education, especially for blacks. After the lecture, the teachers proceeded to get organized for work. Seats were assigned, monitors were selected, a devotions committee was organized. Textbooks were piled on front-seat benches of old-fashioned desks which were connected in long rows like the cars of a train. Under each desk was an enclosure, a shelf with fancy wrought iron sides, where we stored our books. Most of the seats were built to accommodate two; the newer single desk units had not been passed down to "colored schools." The furniture—hand-me-downs from white schools—was broken, marked up, and mismatched.

The sole new item black pupils in Pocomoke were likely to get was a label (to be pasted inside the textbook) that identified each book as property of the county board of education along with the pupil currently responsible for it. The new label was pasted over one containing names of children who had previously used the book. From most of those frayed-edge books—their scribbled-on pages syrup-smeared, torn, and dirty—pages, even entire sections, were missing. However, once in a while a delivery of new books reached our school. Oh, the thrill of receiving a brand-new book! To inhale its delightful newness, to smooth the hands over its unblemished back, to open it for the very first time, carefully as directed by the teacher, without damaging it, to slide a hand across clean fresh pages, to gaze upon glossy illustrations and pictures in color, to paste in the first label and write one's name into the unmarked space, and, at the day's end, to take home that precious possession and pester one's mother about finding a cover for it.

It was exciting to be going along with Henry to the "big school." Since it was next door to our grandmother's, the old school building was familiar to me from the outside. Inside, it seemed cavernous and strange with its entrance hall leading to steep stairs that divided the square building into halves, with two rooms up and two down. After the one big room in the Hall, we third-graders had to get accustomed to hearing voices from other rooms and the thunder of students' footsteps overhead, as well as tramping up and down the stairs. It was strange to hear four different hymns being sung in classrooms during morning devotions.

In the first-floor room on the right, things soon settled into a familiar routine. After two hectic weeks, our teacher, Miss Lela Blaine from New York State, said she began to feel that things might work out, in spite of everything. Although it surely was different from home, she declared that no teacher could ask for nicer children, so very polite and eager to learn. The parents were nice, too—a bit shy though, almost as if they were afraid, she confided, after having noticed their timidity whenever she mentioned inequities, both in school and out. Once when she pointed out the difference between specific provisions for their children and for the white children, one of the more vocal mothers said, "Yes'm. We all knows that ain't how's s'pose to be, but that's how 'tis 'round here, Miss Blaine. Honey, you don't know much about these parts. Stay here long enough—you'll see."

"Ain't it the truth!" another parent joined in. But the longer they talked, the more Lela Blaine tried to convince them that things did not necessarily have to remain exactly as they had been for some time, even when that time was for as long as they could remember.

Apparently it was equally frustrating for Miss Blaine to try to discuss the situation with coworkers. It was rumored that whenever she brought up the matter, they seemed anxious to change the subject. One day when she persisted in talking about their responsibility as teachers to the black community, Carrie Winder, who had taught in Pocomoke for several years, reportedly spoke up: "Listen, Lela, what you're saying we already know. You think we don't want things different from the way they are? Think we don't know what ought to be done about it? Oh, we know all right! We've even tried to do something about some of the very things you're talking about. And do you want to know what happened? Before we even got time to work out some definite plans for action with parents, one of them told everything we'd discussed to her 'madam,' the wife of a town official. Before we knew what was happening, Old Man Bluff came over here and laid out the whole faculty.

" 'You nigra teachers are going to teach these children and act as you're told,' he said, 'or you can look for another job! And, by golly, I'll see to it you won't get hired in any school in this state!' So you see," Mrs. Winder concluded, "we do know, Lela. You'll learn."

Still Miss Blaine refused to agree. But whatever she might have hoped to do, an unforgettable incident changed things, for her, at least. I'll never forget that day. Before I was inside the kitchen, Momma said she knew something was wrong: when I spoke, I didn't look at her and she could tell I'd run all the way home.

"Ginny, how many times I got to tell you to stop all that running? You want to be sick in bed again, I guess," she scolded.

Tears trickled down my face, but if she saw, she gave no sign—just told me to change my clothes and come get something to eat.

"I'm not hungry, Momma," I mumbled, as I took off my shoes and padded toward the stairs.

In a few minutes I crept back into the kitchen, feeling strange and sick. No pain, not the way it hurt when I was sick in bed. But, as sick as I was then, the hurt I experienced that day seemed worse.

Putting the pan of beans she was snapping on the table, Momma felt my forehead. "Don't seem to have no fever. S'pose you tell me what's matter. You didn't get in some trouble in school, did you?"

"No'm."

"Well, you better tell me what's matter, less'n you want me to ask Miss Blaine."

"'Twas that old white man!" I blurted.

"What old white man, Ginny?"

"Old man he come to our room and fuss with Miss Blaine bad."

"Fussed about what? How come he was in your room?"

"He come with Mr. Bland, you know, the supervisor. He the one watched us read that day when Miss Blaine said we did good. Well, he come with that white man today. We seen 'em outdoors when we was having spelling. Miss Blaine says we was s'pose to go on and work just like before if they come in our room. We already finish spelling and was reading a story 'bout Hercules when they come in our room," I explained.

I described to Momma how the two men listened to us read some, and how Mr. Bland told Miss Blaine that her class was reading better than children in the fourth grade. The other man—Mr. Bluff, the school superintendent—remained silent and looked mean. We couldn't quite hear, but he asked Miss Blaine something and she said something back to him, and suddenly his face got all red. In a loud voice, Mr. Bluff asked for her name, and although she told him he just went on and kept asking. He yelled and scared us. Then Mr. Bland and Mr. Bluff left the room and stood talking in the school yard for a long time. That old white man was still fussing when he got into his car. Miss Blaine looked like she was going to cry; she told us to sing "My Country Tis 'o Thee" until school let out. When the bell rang, we were all still wondering why Mr. Bluff shouted at Miss Blaine.

I asked Momma if she knew why.

"I don't know why he hollered at your teacher, Child," Momma said, "but you stop worrying 'cause Miss Blaine's going be alright. Sure would like to know what's matter though."

That night, after we were in bed, my mother said she discussed what I'd told her with my father.

"Wonder," he said, "what that's all about."

"Don't know no more'n what Ginny says, and you know well's me how children can get the cart 'fore the horse. Whatever 'twas, sure got her upset. I imagine Miss Williams knows what it's about. They both room with Miss Grace," Momma said, "but teachers'll keep it to theirself. Bet Miss Williams wouldn't breathe a word of it if I did see her. I just hope it won't be nothing more to it."

"Humph," he grunted, "I wouldn't bet on it. They say that ornery, dried-up cracker's a regular Simon Legree. Treats all our teachers like dirt. Could be it's somebody here with enough spunk to stand up to that old devil. If that's it, I say thank the Lord!"

"Hope nothing's going happen to Miss Blaine. Ever'body says she's a real good teacher, and Ginny's took to her nearbout much as she done to Miss Williams," Momma added.

"Since we don't know no more'n you say," Poppa concluded, "no need worrying. If's anything to it, we'll hear about it soon enough. You can count on that!"

By the end of the week, we had heard nothing more about Mr. Bluff's visit. Of course, neighbors talked about the incident, but they knew no more than my account had divulged. On Friday, the children in our class were happy, as usual, to be free until Monday. But on Monday, a substitute was in Miss Blaine's place!

Almost two weeks after Miss Blaine was fired, a totally unexpected incident thrust the matter into focus around town. According to Grace Wells, as she was getting Miss Blaine's old room ready for a new roomer, she came across a notebook and some papers. Mrs. Wells said she sat down and thumbed through the papers. Whatever it was, she noticed it had been rewritten several times. Some copies were all marked up, with words written between the lines. Curiosity led her to begin reading the unmarked copy. As she later told it, the first few lines didn't make sense to her, but she continued to read slowly, thinking what each line could mean. And before she realized it, she had read every word. Then she read it all over again, nodding and clucking as understanding began to come to her.

"Found these in Miss Blaine's dresser," she explained when Miss Williams came home. "Couldn't make head or tails outen some of it, but Ah can make out enough to know she's saying the truth about how 'tis around here. Reckon Ah ought send it to her?"

"Let me look at it, Mrs. Wells. Maybe then I'll know what you should do," Miss Williams answered.

"Yes'm," Mrs. Wells agreed.

Supper had been over for some time when Miss Williams brought the papers downstairs. Mrs. Wells, seated in her usual place on the settee, laid down her knitting and invited Miss Williams to sit and talk. But Sara Williams was on her way out.

"Mrs. Wells," she said, "if it's all right with you, I'll take this to the parsonage and discuss it with Reverend Waller. I think he'll know what's best. More than likely we'll call Lela. Frankly, I think the people of this town ought to know what she has written. Can't say how much good it'll do, but something needs to shake them up. Maybe this will."

"Amen!" said Mrs. Wells. "Do what you think's best, Miss Williams. Most our people around here's scared of their own shadow. Old folks ain't going stand up to nobody. But they's one or two younguns ain't going sit still much longer, no indeedy! "

Although only a third-grader at the time, I have a lasting recollection of Miss Blaine: of the injustice done, of a child's first awareness of racial bigotry. My elders recounted to me what transpired in the firing's aftermath, which included a special Wednesday meeting at Mount Zion. More than half the seats in the Sunday school room were filled. Many who were there had walked miles from out in the country, on a weeknight, too. Word spread that the meeting involved an urgent matter of concern to every colored person in and around town. On the platform with Reverend Waller were two other local ministers. Reverend Waller stood, the light gleaming off his bald head, and raised his hands. A hush settled over the room when he turned to Miss Williams and said, "Sister Williams, I think we could do with a little music. Will you be so kind as to play our 'Negro National Anthem'?"

Miss Williams seated herself at the piano, ran through the spirited chorus, hit a resounding chord, and said, "Sing!" They stood, singing, "Lift ev-ry voice and sing till earth and heaven ring, ring with the har-mo-o-ny of li-i-i-ber-ty," with soul-stirring emotion. When the song ended, a chorus of amens echoed throughout the room. After a word of prayer, Reverend Waller stood, his solemn gaze searching the audience, pausing first at one face, then another. He appeared to be searching for someone.

"Brothers and Sisters," he said, "it's good to be here. It's good to see all of you here this evening. I know some of you walked a few miles to be here, and that same long, dark road is waiting for you to walk back home. God bless you.

"We called this meeting because we are concerned and worried about the welfare of our people in this town. Especially are we upset about what's happening to our children. Sometimes, Brothers and Sisters, God puts stumbling blocks into our paths to test us, to make us wake up to what's going on around us. Whether or not you realize it, we are often like those who 'see and see not.' We go on existing day after day in what someone described as our 'blind contentedness.'

"Now I don't know about you, but I find precious little around here for you and me to be contented with! Two or three years ago I would have thought a long time before saying this—might never said it at all because I was new here and didn't quite belong. But things are different now, Praise God! My family and I have lived here with you long enough for us to belong together. Lord knows we've prayed together, suffered together, cried together, rejoiced together, been denied together, as we've shared things—good and bad—that have come our way. So this is our home, too. And a man can talk honestly about what he calls his own. Amen?"

"A-a-a-men!" they shouted.

"Late last summer," Reverend Waller continued, "we met the school's new teachers. I thanked God for sending us such bright, well-trained young people. One teacher in particular impressed me as being especially promising. That teacher, we learned, had stood at the top of her graduating class, both in high school and college. She started right off working in church, played the organ for us a few Sundays ago! And this I didn't know until recently: she is also a talented writer. Most important of all is the fact that she cared about our children, and she wasn't afraid to speak out against the deplorable conditions under which they are struggling to get an education!"

"Amen!" an old man voiced agreement.

"I don't need to name the teacher for you. I don't need to tell most of you that she is no longer with us. If you're wondering what happened and why Miss Blaine was fired, we're giving you the chance to find out through that brave young lady's own words. Brothers and Sisters, I beg you to listen well to what she

51

left behind on a few sheets in a bureau drawer. Let her teach her finest lesson, in her absence, to you! Let her make you see with unveiled eyes those two poor old buildings that have served as schools for Negroes here for far too long, the deplorable so-called 'facilities,' the meager provisions, the awful conditions delegated to Negroes, whose hard-earned tax money helps provide a much different world for white folks and their children."

"Amen! Amen!" chorused the audience.

"Miss Blaine was fired—called a troublemaker—because she dared simply to request that the superintendent call her 'Miss Blaine,' no more or less than he calls his white teachers," said Reverend Waller. "And our children have been robbed—yes, whether you realize it or not. We—all of us—have been robbed! Believe me, we need the very best leaders if we are ever to overcome these barriers facing us every day of our lives in this Shore town we call home!"

"Amen!"

"Nothing wrong with saying 'Amen,' Brothers and Sisters," he said, "but we got to do a whole lot more'n that. I believe God helps those that help themselves. Are we willing to go on doing nothing more than taking whatever happens to be shoved our way, and, maybe, complaining about it among ourselves? Is that the best we can do to help ourselves, even down here on the Shore? Are we going on being satisfied for us and, worse yet, for our children to make out with no more than their parents and grandparents had? Heaven help us. We must get together and stand together.

"Yes, Miss Blaine was fired because the kind of treatment she resented is still expected and accepted here. Believe me, firing's not going to end our struggle. Many brave men will die before justice and equality are a part of life for our people! Who among you are willing to be counted in the fight that's bound to come? And a long, hard fight *is* coming, Children—even to the Shore." Reverend Waller paused, mopping his face with a damp handkerchief.

"Well, Children," he continued, shaking his head, "it's all up to us. Before Miss Williams reads to us, let me tell you that we called

Miss Blaine to ask if she would object to us reading and typing some copies of this poem. 'Reverend Waller,' she said, 'I'm glad you want to use it. I only hope and pray it can do some good.' To that, I say whether or not it can and will do much good is up to us!"

With a gesture in Miss Williams's direction, he sat down saying, "Read it slow and clear, Miss Williams. Just take your time."

Sara Williams arranged the sheets on the table before her and began to read clearly and slowly:

> Of county Negroes who do stay in school
> For long enough, in these depressing days,
> To learn to figure, read and spell and write,
> Each is assured the memory of one man:
> The wizened czar assigned to superintend
> All teachers in the schools within his realm.
> To Negroes, he seems like a scrawny bird . . .
> Dark feathered, shod in tight-laced high-top shoes.
> Small gray-haired head bobbing a buzzard's beak
> Between his mean and sunken beads of eyes.
> Sharp Adam's apple jiggling in craned neck . . .
> Tight lips grimaced to grin or sneer, not smile.
> For his use, "nigras" have but lone first names.
> Though lately now and then 'tis said, he deigns,
> In lieu of title due, to use one word:
> Mincing on "Teacher" Jones, but never "Miss."
> That far, not one inch further, will he bend
> On shores sans thought of "equal for all men"
> Where habit and black fear add flaw to flaw
> And words of men like him erase the law.
>
> Crumbs brushed from poor white's tables are our fare
> But discontent is barely breathed aloud.
> All this the children see. The children watched
> That day their teacher from "up North"
> Clashed in first meeting with the little man:
> "What is your name?" he asked in master's tone.
> "Miss Blaine," said she . . . serene, equally clear.

"What-is-your-name?" he hammered every word.
With eyes fixed straight into his hate, she said,
"What's my name, Mr. Bluff? It is Miss Blaine."
He wasted words on who and what he was
And then he asked again, "What *is* your name?"
Unmoved and splendid in her calm she said,
"I call you Mr. Bluff; call me Miss Blaine."
He ranted, raved, issued a final threat
Then, seething in his rage, stormed from the room.
Her class lost more than one who taught them well
In reading, writing, arithmetic, and song.
Yet some did glimpse the bolt of dignity
That flashed like lightning through dark silent woods
A blinding light that flared but dimmed before
Most downcast eyes would see . . . then shone no more.

While these and still worse shames are kept intact . . .
Held fast by hands of whites opposing change,
The blackest curse, plus poverty and fear,
Lies in *our* same *acceptance* of this lot:
Emancipated-chained men of the Shore,
Steeped in "What was—is now—and will forever be."
We, long the burdened plowers of this land,
Stay sunken in our mean, "left-over" world
When we could change direction of our lives.
It's clear: the more we slave to make whites rich
The less of this Shore's bounty is our own
And none but us for us, will turn the tide.
O Brothers! Brothers, for our children's sake
Think on these truths and dare yourselves to wake!

The silence was ominous. Miss Williams looked to Reverend
Waller, but his gaze was fixed above the audience. Gathering the
papers, she left the platform. And each footstep echoed through
the silence as if the room were empty.

Shaking his head slowly from side to side, Reverend Waller
rose and said, "This is no time for a lot of talking. Talk too much

anyway. Go home, Children. Go home and 'think,' as Miss Blaine put it, 'on these truths.' May the good Lord bless that young woman. She's been fired. But, mark my words: firing's not going to stop her! She'll make it. Remember her in your prayers. Could be she's already done more for us than we know."

Slowly the congregation filed out into the darkness. Some spoke of how somebody really ought to do something, of how good it was to hear somebody talking about doing something, of the things "colored people" have to put up with, of the fact that a change was long overdue. So they talked. Then they went their separate ways. But three men stayed behind with Reverend Waller and the other ministers to make plans to do more than talk. One of those men was my father.

4 · *Our First Home*

Thine is the small dwelling
within the heart of every man . . .
the home for which we labor
to call our own . . .

Snow Holden's response to the call to action following Miss Blaine's firing reflected his determination to fight for basic rights, especially the right to pursue an education—a vital factor in his struggle to provide a better quality of life for his family. Both Snow and Jane were ever mindful of the trials and deprivations that shadowed the lives of their ancestors. Also, they knew that little, if anything, had been done to change the circumscribed lot of blacks—not in Pocomoke. Even those who seemed less fearful said they were afraid to instigate changes because "them white folks might make everything worse than ever." But those two young parents made up their minds to do whatever God enabled them to do—even challenge Shore "laws of the land"—in order to secure due rights for their children. Even so, they could not imagine what they would have to suffer in that time and place in order to get a token of what rightfully belonged to their people. Within their vivid recollections dwells a measure of the history of a people and the area in which they lived.

The unhurried mood of Saturday night permeated their little house on Bank Street. No rushing. No dreading tomorrow. Only the pause and respite marking the end of a week's labors. Sweet-smelling all over from baths, the children kissed their father good night and reluctantly preceded their mother upstairs. After hearing their prayers and tucking them in, Jane prepared herself for the rest of the evening. Meanwhile, alone in the kitchen, Snow emptied pots of hot water into Jane's biggest galvanized washtub and proceeded to scrub away garage grease and dirt. By the time Jane came downstairs, he was sitting with his stocking feet propped against the open oven door. She was glad he had opted to stay home instead of going to Bedlam to play pool, as he often did on Saturday night. But she was puzzled by his worried expression. After all, it was Saturday, and despite the weariness of the week, they were free to enjoy a peaceful evening and a day of rest. Yet, she could tell by the frown on his face that he had something on his mind as he looked about the kitchen.

It was a drab, poor kitchen that no amount of scouring could make attractive. The oil lamp cast a yellow light over the table area, leaving the rest of the dingy little room in uneven shadows. The plain urn-shaped lamp was made of thick clear glass, but its chimney, narrow at top and bottom, ballooned into a fat middle decorated with delicate chalky etchings. A pewter sugar bowl, with matching salt and pepper shakers, cast shadows on the table. Even in the dim lamplight, ugly cracks scarred the smoked-up whitewashed walls. Near the lone window was a heavy dark gateleg table, which once belonged to Snow's mother. It was handmade, and circles, like anklets, were carved near the rounded bottoms of its stubby legs. The top of the tablecloth had been scrubbed until its once-brilliant flowery pattern was barely visible; at each corner the cloth was cracked, exposing a coarse, tan under-fabric. Two dull brown chairs with high runged backs were pushed under the table. Similar chairs stood against the wall on either side of the dark brown cupboard containing dishes, glasses, and odds and ends. Its lower insulated compartments served as the storage place for food (there was no icebox). That piece of antiquity, too, had been Snow's mother's. In one dark corner stood a tall white stool. A big rocking chair was near the black, wood-burning stove, its cooking surface spaced by four lids. Splintery floorboards bordering the ragged linoleum had been scrubbed almost white. Wide gaps between the boards exposed ground-in dirt which time had cemented there. Under the table and behind the stove were small unblemished patches of shiny blue and gray linoleum, but most of the floor covering, worn to a motley gray-streaked dull rust color, bore imprints of uneven floorboards. Nothing about the room was bright, nothing beautiful.

After pouring homemade dandelion wine for them and pulling the rocking chair close to the stove, Jane eased her body into it, rested her head against its high back, stretched her legs, and sighed.

"Been sitting down here thinking about how I won't miss nothing around this old place if we ever do get away from here," Snow declared.

"Think we really going get it, Snow?"

"Hon, I just got to think so. Ain't it what we been doing without all this long for?"

"I know that, Snow, but what about the money? We ain't got . . ."

"Just got to get that loan, that's all. Put it with what we got saved up, and we ought to have enough for down payment," Snow said slowly, as if trying to convince himself. "If old man Colton's halfways fair, ain't no way in the world for him to ask more'n Lawyer Newman says for that place, not the shape it's in."

"Sure hope you right, Snow. I know how much it must mean to you—say nothing about myself. It's nobody around here as anxious as me to get their own house, don't matter what shape it's in. I still can't see how on earth anyone's got nerve to move out and leave all that mess! How soon you think we can move if things turn out right?"

"Hard to say. Could be about a month or two, if we lucky."

"Well, sooner the better for me," Jane said patting her stomach. "I'd sure rather tackle all that dirt and mess now than have to worry about it after while. Closer we get to the time for the baby, less I'll be able to do."

Snow took his time, inhaling the tangy aroma of the wine before answering, "Reckon that's nothing you got to be worrying about. You know good and well I never let you do nothing that's against you. What I going start now for?"

"Sure'd like to get all settled down 'fore it's my time. Don't care how you look at it—it's a whole lotta work to get done in that house," Jane fretted.

"Well, Old Lady, s'pose we cross that bridge *if* we get there. I figured you'd be all excited just thinking about moving, 'stead of fretting about it."

"Snow, please don't get me wrong. I'm not even thinking about fretting. Just want things to work out, that's all. Far's being excited, to tell the Lord's truth, I'm scared to get too stirred up. Scared something might go wrong."

"Yeah, I been feeling the same way. Guess if things work out like we hoping, we won't hardly know *how* to act, huh? If we'd get in there soon, I believe I can get most of the painting and papering outen the way 'fore it's time for the baby. Ben promised to gimme a hand with painting."

"Mom stopped by to tell me old Miss Mullins got a real nice bedroom set to sell, washstand and everything. Think we ought look into it?"

"Couldn't hurt none to look; go see what you think. How much Miss Dell say it is?"

"I'm not quite sure. Find out tomorrow, though. If it's half nice as Mom says, we ought put it in the front bedroom—*if* we lucky enough to get the house," she added cautiously.

"Just hope Mr. Colton 'll settle for what we can scrape up for down payment."

"Don't worry no more about it right now, Snow. If push come to shove, I'm almost sure Mom can lend us enough to make it up."

"Reckon she can," Snow agreed without enthusiasm, "but I'd rather not do it like that unless I just can't help it."

"Course, that's up to you," Jane replied. "Anyway, it's nothing in the world we can do about it to next week, so let's try'n put it outen our mind for now. Want a little more wine? Sure turned out better'n I thought it would."

Without comment, Snow held out his glass. She poured the pale amber liquid and put the bottle in the cupboard. In the lamplight her smooth brown skin glowed, and the soft sheen of her hair, plaited loosely in two long braids, haloed her thin face. He felt good to see her looking and feeling well again after the past few months, when she had complained about one thing or another almost daily.

"Why you looking at me like that?" she asked without glancing up.

"Like what?" he teased. "How you see how I'm looking and you way over there?"

"You know how you looking," she answered, pretending to be straightening things in the cupboard.

"Ha!" he teased, grinning. "Maybe I'm just thinking you giving me a whole lot of this wine—good'n strong, too. And maybe I been wondering why all a sudden you feeling so frisky. "

"So that's wha'cha thinking, mister?" Jane fussed. "Well you got another think coming. Just sit right on back and rest your feet against that stove. I'd stay down here now if it nearbout killed me just to keep my eyes open! We going sit in this kitchen to you're not fit for nothing but sleep when your head hits that pillow."

"Aw, com'on, Hon," he said. "You can't take a lil kidding? It's time to call it a day anyhow. Let's finish our wine upstairs."

"Guess you not even going bother to lock up," Jane reminded him. "Don't tell me you all that anxious."

"Yes ma'am! I am all that anxious," he mimicked while locking the door. Then he went ahead with the lamp, lighting her way up the narrow stairs.

◆

Momma wondered whether she ever would see the entire kitchen floor of the "new" house on Fourth Street at one time. As soon as they finished getting up piles of plaster and trash in one area, more seemed to materialize. When the pantry was swept clean of debris, the floor itself was so filthy and grease-stained that the mere thought of scrubbing it clean tired her more than she already was. For weeks they worked, day and night, trying to clear out the junk-cluttered rooms.

After several cartloads of trash had been hauled away, and my father shoveled the last of it from the kitchen, plastering was done. They whitewashed the kitchen and painted the woodwork. The other rooms were papered. Windows had to be washed before the floors could be scoured and covered with new linoleum: a pattern of maroon, blue, and gray squares for the kitchen, and a beige and brown design for the dining room. The old bedroom matting suf-

Adele, ten, standing in her flower garden beside the family's Fourth Street home

ficed for their room and ours. They selected a new rug with a pretty green border and center motif for the front bedroom.

"So much to be done," Momma fretted. "Don't see how on earth we going get things halfway straight by fall."

But although Poppa must have had similar doubts, he assured her everything would be just fine. Being children, free of the burden of moving, we found the move from Bank Street to a big house on that great long street to be a wonderful adventure. Too young to be concerned about the worry and drudgery involved, we happily told school friends, who lived across town, about the nice big house with two porches—our new home.

Our house, the third building from the unpaved intersection of Fourth, Bank, and Linden, was one of four buildings owned by blacks at that end of Fourth Street. Our cousins owned the house to the left; the family on the right owned the corner store, too. While two or three houses across town at the other end of Fourth Street were owned by blacks, all the others were owned and occupied by whites.

The newly purchased dwelling was a six-room frame house with a yard on three sides and an unpaved sidewalk edging the front steps. A second porch made a welcome addition. The yard to the left had the same kind of hard-packed gray dirt as the one we were leaving on Bank Street. But the narrow strip of yard to the right, sheltered from the sun, had moist, black soil with tufts of grass and weeds sprouting in shady corners. In time, that spot became my flower garden, boasting zinnias almost as tall as I. Behind the house on a fair-sized plot were an ancient cabin and a woodhouse. The lot, big enough for a vegetable garden and chicken yard, was fenced off on the back and sides. To the right of the backyard was the dilapidated and filthy outhouse.

The fact that they had inherited the overloaded toilet as part of the purchase did not ease Momma's embarrassment when Ned Barnes came to clean it out. Ned, an elderly man who eked out a living by cleaning toilets and hauling away manure and junk in his rickety horse-drawn wagon, was not one to hold his tongue. Without removing his dirty work gloves, he stood by the pump mopping sweat and dirt from his face and drinking water. I sat on the step listening as he complained, but I was poised to dash indoors before he went back to bring that loaded wagon out to the street.

"Janie," he said, "Ah done clean out many a tarlit, man and boy, long 'fore you was ever thought 'bout, and Ah swear 'fore God Almighty Ah ain't never come across nary mess like this in all my borned days. Biggest, baddest load of 'do' Ah ever seen, Ah swear!"

Wiping his mouth on a limp shirt sleeve, he told Momma he'd have to charge seventy-five cents, instead of the usual fifty.

"Janie, Honey," he said, "if 'twas anybody 'cept you, Ah'd charge 'em a whole dollar. They still be getting off cheap!"

"I'm cert'ny sorry, Mr. Ned. Won't be that way no more, not long's we're here," Momma promised.

We called the log cabin behind the house the "old kitchen." That relic of the past was made of wide hand-cut boards shaved free of bark and blackened with age. A deep uneven carpet of green moss covered the roof. In sections the moss rose and swirled and curved with the richness of a finely contoured Rya rug. Black gaps marked areas where weather-worn shingles, swollen and crumbly, had rotted and blown away. All that was left of the chimney was a shiny broken-off brown pipe around which a few bricks still clung. The old kitchen had no windows, just a thick slab of half-hinged door, leaning inward at each end of the building. Inside, heavy rough beams at ceiling and sides matched the dark, oily floorboards, hand-cut and thicker than the palm of a giant. The room was cluttered with all kinds of debris. And whenever a driving rain came, the moldy contents located nearest the doors were drenched. Warped covers curled away from wavy yellowed pages of musty books. A humpbacked trunk, like those in stories of treasure hunts, and a tall bureau with many drawers invited us children to explore. But their contents were, with few exceptions, junk fit only to be thrown in Ned's wagon and hauled away. An indescribably bad odor permeated the old kitchen. It assailed the nostrils and lodged there, just as it clung, even after its removal, to even the smallest item salvaged from the old building. And whenever it rained, that dank, musty odor of age and neglect seeped into the open windows of our house, spreading its hateful stench even to the farthest room.

After months of intense work, the family was sufficiently settled in the new place for my parents to take stock of the dent they had made in the endless list of things to be done. They were proud of what they had done. Then came the crowning touch: a brand-new carpet. After laying the brightly flowered carpet and rearranging furniture, Momma and Poppa called us in to admire the front room. Although the living room set was bought new a year ago, it looked so much better in our own parlor than on Bank Street. The three-piece suite—settee, rocker, and armchair—had seats and backs upholstered in taut brown imitation leather. Chair arms and legs were of slender curved, highly lacquered black wood, which also bordered the cushioned backs. The settee was placed in an alcove to the far right of the door. The armchair sat between the side window and the organ, facing the sofa.

The organ, inherited after Mom bought a piano, towered almost to the ceiling; it was ornate and darkly impressive. Its upper section—above the slanted panel where the hymnal rested—was divided into a number of little balcony-like niches, which flanked the long mirror-backed center case, complete with glass shelves and a little glass-paned door that locked. On the shelves, Momma had arranged family photographs, along with a picture of Stephen Long (their late revered school principal, stabbed to death by white men), figurines, and other bric-a-brac. Catercornered on the left side of the organ were the rocker and a low cane-topped stool.

Between the front windows, my parents placed their special treasure, a brass Victorian lamp attached to its own stand. It was given to Poppa by "Miss Madge," for whom he had worked during the years when he was growing up. To me, that lamp was prettier than any other, including the red and gold one on Mom's piano or the fancy ones seen through the windows on Market Street. Standing nearly five feet from the floor, that impressive antique was the "crowning glory" in our new front room.

From the clear glass chimney that rose above the globe to the tiny brass feet that dug into our new carpet, I adored everything about that lamp. And that included the shiny spiraled post and curved leg supports; the marble-topped stand and the smaller replica near the bottom, both edged in intricately designed brass; the ornate brass filigree designs that encased the font (the receptacle containing kerosene); the golden mesh collar between the lamp top and the brass flange onto which the globe was secured.

Most of all, I cherished the large opaline globe with its delicate floral etchings. I used to think that globe possessed magical powers, especially during my teenage years of discontent. Then I would close myself inside the front room and read, imagining that I lived in a "True Story" world. But that was short-lived. The globe afforded a calming release from my frustrations. Something special happened when I gazed deeply into its windswept peonies, their magnificent petals swirling wildly apart and the scalloped edges of their pregnant buds unfolding in the wind. Long stalks amid wide, curling leaves were entwined with florets on thin, winding vines. I felt blessed as my eyes rested on those delicate sketches and colorings—the palest of pinks, glowing shades of rose and wine accented with traces of taupe—all reminiscent of works by the old masters. That priceless lamp—willed to me by my father—is still the most beautiful lamp I have ever seen or ever expect to see.

To the right of the door, on a mat of metal, was the gleaming black chrome-trimmed coal stove with a door pane of isinglass and a thick black pipe, ringed like a stout wrinkled neck, jammed into a metal-collared hole in the wall below the mantel. On the white mantel, a brown wood clock struck the hour. On both sides of the clock stood fragile bisque figurines in pastel dresses with bustles. In the middle of the room, facing the mantel, was a narrow dark brown table with a lower shelf, on which were arranged an illustrated copy of Paul Lawrence Dunbar's *Life Among the Lowly* and worn copies of *Little Lord Fauntleroy* and *Adventures of Tom Swift*. The table itself was draped with a white lace-bordered, embroidered linen runner.

Whatever a visitor noticed first—the finely patterned lace curtains, the huge brass-framed farm scenes high on the wall, the organ, the lamp, or the bright new rug—the family believed he would be favorably impressed.

"Hon," my father said, "I'm right proud of how it looks in here. You sure got them windows looking good. Ain't seen none around town can hold a candle to 'em."

"You don't know how good it makes me feel to hear you say that, Snow. Almost walk my legs off trying to find curtains like I want but didn't cost too much. These best I could do. But just look at that rug! Ain't it some pretty? Sure am glad we settled on it, even if it costed more'n we can afford."

"Yeah, Hon, me too," he agreed, "and since we getting that dining room set, we going be pretty straight. Good thing Miss Dell told you about them bedroom things, too."

"I'm so glad we this near straight. Won't need to be worrying about things not looking right when folks come around to help and all after the baby," she confided, sounding worried.

"Now just don't go starting worrying, Hon. Doctor says ever' thing's going along fine. Won't be much longer now. Tell you what I'd like to do more'n anything else right now, and that's put running water in here. Would make a mighty big difference, especially with the baby coming."

"Sure would be real nice," she admitted, "but we just got to make out, Snow, to we better able, that's all. Can't do ever'thing one time. Besides, it's not going to kill us to make out with the toilet and pump a while longer. It's not like we been use to anything else anyhow."

We children were happy in the new house. At first, it was scary to live a few doors down the street from one cemetery and to look upon another one from upstairs windows. Before long our fright gave way to the fascination of the long street with big trees. To us, it seemed as if the street, which stretched farther than one could see—far across Market Street, past "Bedlam," on to the railroad—surely must reach all the way to the end of the world. The houses on either side of our house were similar to it in size and construction. But two doors up the street was a big white house with porches on three sides, even a porch upstairs. It sat well back from the street and was skirted with a spacious green lawn with a paved walk leading to the front porch. It was an attractive dwelling, suggestive of leisurely afforded comfort. It was a place of mysterious goings-on, whose owners were said to be bootleggers with a still out in the country.

In contrast, the view directly across from our house was worse than what we had left behind. Unlike most houses on the opposite side of Fourth Street, the two across from ours faced Third Street, exposing their rears to our front. In one yard, rusty scrap metal, heaped in huge piles, rose up to the second-floor level of the house. The Hymans, a middle-aged couple and their five children, lived there. Zack Hyman sold scrap metal. A big, open barn, fencing in part of the Fourth Street end of the property, sheltered an old truck and more scrap iron. Separating the other side of that junky yard from adjoining property was an assortment of low buildings. The frame house itself, with its dark brown shingled exterior, was drab and damp looking, as if it were being continually drenched in summer storms. The family's cow roamed among the overgrown weeds in the yard, munching contentedly and dropping fresh steaming mounds upon her dried up waste.

Next door to the Hymans was a small white frame house. Its tiny back porch was high off the ground; steep steps led down to the yard, where the woodhouse stood near the toilet. Every morning the tenants walked past the toilet and emptied their slop bucket onto their garden. That well-tended, richly nourished garden with its wide green rows was the one thing of beauty directly across from us. In most other respects, however, the houses in the area were far different from those we had left on Bank Street. To us children, running to meet Poppa on his way home from work, the modest houses we passed and the people in them belonged to a totally different world.

5 · Cherished Family Memories

A world in sacred silence waits again.
No other word save holy shields the scene.
Listen . . . listen to angels' circling wings.

For Marie, who was just starting the first grade, school was just around the corner from the house on Fourth Street, while for Henry and me school was two blocks up Bank Street. Our parents were happy that the three of us were getting along satisfactorily in school. They were especially pleased that Henry, after having his adenoids and tonsils removed, was showing a marked improvement in his work. It was during the time of Henry's illness that my teacher decided I was being "held back" and promoted me to the next grade. Then, whether wisely or not, the new teacher decided that I belonged in even the next higher grade. My parents were a bit confused, but pleased, about the speedy promotions. Being in a class with older children made me feel uneasy because many classmates treated me like a baby.

Marie's teacher reported that she was doing just fine. This was especially welcome news to Momma. Initially, every morning Marie had put up a battle to return home with her. Once she actually slipped away from school, crossed the street, and rounded the corner to our house. Momma, washing clothes in the side yard when Marie sneaked inside the gate, wiped the suds from her hands and forearms and gave Marie a sound spanking. Then she ushered the truant, tears and all, around the corner and delivered her to a surprised Miss Williams. Never again did Marie steal home from school.

Although our parents were pleased with our progress in general, the unchanged conditions of the schools worried them. Even after Poppa finally managed to get a meeting with town officials, who could have done at least something about the inequities, nothing followed their promises of "We'll see what we can do for you, Snow."

Having begun school younger than the usual age and then having skipped grades, I acquired the distinction of being the youngest and smallest pupil in my class. Fortunately, this distinction did not present problems among the students. The girls, all at least a few years older, spoiled me with benevolent, big-sisterly affection, while the boys paid me little or no attention. However, one fall day things took an unpredictable turn. Mrs. Locks always left a responsible student "in charge" when she was out of her classroom. On that afternoon she left her youngest student in charge, and an unexpected situation developed. No one could figure out just what did happen to me that afternoon. I had been in charge many times without anything out of the ordinary happening. Perhaps it was the teacher's chair (as a rule the student-in-charge took a seat up front). But on that day Mrs. Locks told me to sit at her desk. Oh, the power of that coveted position! The monitor's job was to write the name of anyone who talked or did not study. But the moment the door closed, books always were pushed aside. Conversations started, and assorted objects—the worst being sloppy spitballs—whizzed through the air. A few boys darted about the room, risking being caught if the teacher returned earlier than expected. They always showed off, bullying smaller boys and even kissing a few girls, who made a pretense of not liking it when they did.

On that particular day, however, nothing so dramatic happened. Maybe everyone remembered Mrs. Locks's no-nonsense mood, or it could have been the impending spelling test. Whatever the reason, nothing much happened, just some talking, rather subdued talking at that. Suddenly, perhaps because Mrs. Locks might return to the sound of voices or perhaps because I was seated behind the desk, I shouted, "Stop all talking right now!"

For a few uneasy minutes all talking ceased. I was glad because I never wanted to turn in anyone's name. As I looked around the room to see that everyone was studying, I noticed Kate. Kate

Wright was one of the largest, smartest, best-liked girls in the room. She was sitting with an elbow propped on her desk, resting her face against an open palm. The pressure of her palm against her cheek stretched her face into what looked like a distorted grin, but no one seemed to notice until I said, "Sit up, Kate!" Students, who either had been studying or pretending to study, looked up to witness a confrontation. A wise person would have dropped the matter then, but something seemed to compel me to show the class that I could make Kate comply.

"Sit up, Kate!" I ordered, trying that time to sound exactly like Mrs. Locks.

"Ginny, you know I'm not doing anything," Kate responded, exasperation marking her words. She looked straight at me. She did not move.

"If you don't sit up, I'm going take your name," I threatened.

Lucy Coates, seated in the row next to Kate, eyed me with disgust. She was a good student, almost as large as Kate and equally capable of taking care of herself, both in and out of the classroom. Her voice was angry when she turned to me, "Why don't you leave Kate be, Ginny? She ain't doing nothing, and you know good and well she ain't! You try to be too smart, that's what! Some people get big headed just 'cause they left in charge. Ain't nobody like that going be in charge of me!"

"You tell it, Lucy, while I pats my foot!" shouted Carmen Brown above a consensus of mutterings.

I looked nervously from one classmate to another and saw in each direct stare a kindred expression. For the first time in my life, I was ashamed of my actions. I wanted to run from the room and never stop running. At that moment Mrs. Locks returned. Not a word was spoken. Or written.

The next day things went on as usual. But I waited on edge for someone to bring up what had happened. After the last lesson for the day, Mrs. Locks returned the papers from the big spelling test. When she announced that only one student had spelled all one hundred words correctly, I hardly glanced at the big red "100" before shoving the paper inside my composition book. All around the room excited students asked each other, "Wha'cha get on your'n?" Instead, I pretended to be busy drawing a circus clown, but his smile wouldn't stay in place. On the way home, Kate showed me her nearly perfect paper, on which she had failed to capitalize the "n" in "Negro."

"Ginny," she asked, "you the one made a hundred?"

I nodded. Although I had been too ashamed to look at Kate all day, I looked up into her eyes and said, "I don't deserve no hundred."

"Wha'cha mean? You didn't cheat, didja?"

"No! I never cheated none, Kate. You know I wouldn't cheat. But, I was mean to you yesterday, and you my friend."

"Forget it, Ginny," mumbled Kate.

"Kate . . ." I groped for words, "I don't know what made me act like that. You didn't do nothing for me to—"

"Forget it, Ginny!"

After an uncomfortable silence, I told her, "I don't want be left in charge no more."

"Why?"

"Just don't want to. That's all."

Neither could understand the other's feelings; I couldn't even understand my own. So we walked the rest of the way home without talking.

Since for two days I had been upset, I feared my mother would suspect something was wrong. There was little chance of my hiding anything from her. I tried to think of something convincing to say when she questioned me. I was ashamed to let her know how I had treated Kate, and after getting by the day before, I knew what to expect by the time I got home. However, when I stepped inside the kitchen, Momma barely glanced at me—just told me to change clothes and wash the dishes piled in the dishpan on the back of the stove. When I came downstairs, she still didn't appear to notice anything wrong. Later, she didn't intervene even when we argued over whose turn it was to fill the woodbox and water bucket. When she spoke, her voice sounded strange and tired, "We going see who makes most noise when your father's home." But when he came in, she didn't tell on us. We ate supper without any fuss and did our homework. Then, although Momma always went up with us to hear our prayers, we went quietly upstairs under Poppa's supervision.

At lunchtime on the following day, my hop and skip came to a halt midway between the gate and kitchen steps. A stranger flung open the screen door and threw a pan of dishwater toward the woodpile. She glanced at me before letting the door slam. Standing at the foot of the steps, feeling as if I must have turned into the wrong yard, I heard the gate open and Poppa cleared his throat.

"Hey, Honey, why're you standing out here?" Poppa asked.

"Poppa, it's a mean old woman in our house. What's she doing in there?"

"Ain't no mean old woman, Ginny; that's Aunt Sally. She's going help your momma a lil while. Got something nice to show you."

"What, Poppa?" I asked, momentarily escaping the uneasy feeling.

"Com' on in," he said, holding the screen door as I slipped in under his arm. "You'll see."

The stern-looking old woman, dressed in a white shirtwaist and dark skirt that touched the floor, was busy warming up food Momma had cooked the day before. She replaced a front stove lid, laid the lifter down noisily, and mumbled about not being able to keep the fire going and take care of things upstairs, too. While Poppa doctored the sluggish fire, Henry came in with Marie. Both stared at the stranger in our kitchen.

"I believe the fire's going be all right now, Aunt Sally. Children, speak to Aunt Sally," Poppa said.

"How you, Aunt Sally?" we said, still staring, as the old lady sucked in her toothless gums and grunted.

"This here's Henry, Aunt Sally, and this's Ginny and Marie," he told her. "They going upstairs to see the surprise that come while they been in school. Let's go, children."

No one said a word. The house seemed quieter than ever before. In silence we passed through the dining room and hall. But the steps squeaked noisily as we tiptoed up to the landing, where we huddled together in the bedroom doorway.

"How you feeling, Hon?" Poppa whispered.

"About well's I can expect, I guess," came the weak reply.

"Brought the children to see the surprise," he told her, smiling broadly.

Momma roused up so she could see us. She groaned and whispered, "Hey, Children. Now, I want you all to behave yourself and mind Aunt Sally, you hear?"

We nodded as we stood gazing at the little mound beside her in the bed. Raising herself up on an elbow, she turned back the blanket from a tiny pink face framed with damp black curls.

"Come see your new baby sister. Com'on," she urged. We crept closer to the bed and gazed at the baby.

"Can you see her?" asked Poppa. "That's lil Emily. Wha'cha think of her?"

"I think she looks like a lil doll baby," I whispered.

"Yeah," agreed Henry, "she's cute."

Noticing that Marie did not come close to the bed, Momma held out her hand and coaxed her. She patted her and tried to get her to talk: "You going help Momma take care of the baby, Honey?" But Marie, feeling deposed as the baby in the family, sulked and turned away, her big eyes brimming with tears. Seeing that nothing would be gained by pursuing the matter further, Poppa sent us back to the kitchen, where we tried to eat what the old lady set before us. But even after he joined us, we shared the unsettling feeling that, although we knew we were at home, we were in a strange house.

Within weeks, things began to settle down again in our home. Our parents repeatedly spoke of all we had to be thankful for. The baby was healthy. We were living in the home that would be ours in time. They were almost through paying for the secondhand dining room set of massive oak furniture with a thick round table on a base as stout as a tree trunk, cane-bottomed chairs, a high sideboard with drawers, and a large cupboard area and shelved mirror at the top. They had stocked the woodhouse and coal bin, and we looked forward to the best Christmas ever.

✦

My mother used to say the second-best part of Christmas—after the joy of seeing the expressions on our faces as we gazed upon our presents and Christmas tree—was the planning and preparation for the holidays. Even after Henry came home puffed up with hateful wisdom, boasting that there was no Santa Claus, she was determined to make the magic too marvelous to be exchanged for the educated tales told by schoolmates. Then, as we grew older, she felt knowing the truth could not destroy our early visions of the miraculous beauty of Christmas, even with what little they could manage to buy. Accordingly, a few weeks before Christmas she proposed means of cutting expenses.

"Don't give me one thing for Christmas, Snow," she repeatedly told Poppa. "Let's just save up much as we can to get some of what the children's hinting for and maybe some more ornaments for the tree."

"Well, you know you going want something, too. How you going feel when the girls start bragging about what all they got?" he asked.

"What girls you talking about?"

"Ever' one of 'em—Daisy, Minnie, Virgie—you know just well's me."

"Well, Sir," she said, "I just wish you'd tell me what any of 'em's got, or's likely to be getting, that's half much as I already got. Here I got a good husband and four nice children and living in my own house, too! Think they can beat that? Anyhow, I believe that gift part of Christmas is for the children, except for rich folks. And we sure ain't about to be pretending to be nowheres near rich."

"All right, Old Lady, you had your say. We going do like you want," he conceded. "More'n likely, we get a whole lot more'n rich folks get outen Christmas anyhow, just making it good for the children."

Preparations started long before December. Momma shopped, searching for bargains in toys and necessities. Poppa priced train parts, air rifles, and decorations for the tree and house. From time to time they brought in "Christmas things" camouflaged among bags of groceries. Larger items, including the tree, were slipped through the living room window or front door at carefully chosen moments. Since the living room was seldom used in summer and unheated and closed up in winter, we had no idea of the Christmas treasures locked inside that frigid room—not until we had outgrown the mystery of Santa.

For the actual preparations and decoration of the house and tree, our parents had their own special routine. Everything was left to be done on Christmas Eve, after some very excited children were supposedly in bed. It was then that the magic began to work in the little gray house on Fourth Street. The tall cedar tree had to be mounted and decorated. Glossy handmade holly wreaths, trimmed with clusters of red berries, had to be hung at sparkling clean windows. Toys had to be assembled. As we later learned, every Christmas it seemed that there were too many things to be done in too little time; every Christmas they somehow managed to do them all. And when their tasks were done, the whole downstairs, cedar-scented and bright, was transformed into a world of enchantment.

For us children, Christmas Eve was the longest night of the year. Supper was over earlier than usual; dishes were washed, dried, and put away without the slightest disagreement among us. Kitchen table and stove gleamed from thorough washings and polishings, and the broom stood propped in a corner of a just-swept floor.

Letters, folded in the shape of envelopes, were addressed to "Santa Claus, North Pole" and placed on the dining room table, where Santa would see them when he sat down to rest and enjoy the homemade goodies Momma always set out for him.

After once again pointing out the solemnity of the occasion, Momma cautioned, "You children want Santa Claus to come here tonight, you better go sleep soon's you get in bed; he's got plenty more to see about besides you. And you know you ain't been but so good nohow. Now, just lay up there and talk if you want to; maybe you'll find out how it feels to get nothing in your stockings but a switch."

"That's right, Hon," Poppa joined in. "I'll be dogged if I'm going be hollering upstairs to them ever' time you turn around. If Santa ask me how you been behaving, what'cha want me to tell 'im, Henry?"

Gulping nervously, Henry blurted, "That I been good."

"Good!" exclaimed Momma. "And all that fighting in the school yard—just look at that lip all busted open."

"But, Momma," Henry cried, "Moonie he hit me first. Ask Miss Brown. Ask BoBo and Charles. They seen him hit me right there on my head. I never even touched him, not to he hit me."

"Better had been that way, Mister," Poppa warned. "I don't never want hear of you starting fights. Of course, somebody hit you first, you got take up for yourself."

"I know one thing," interjected Momma. "You all best get up them stairs, and you better all be in bed by time I bring Baby upstairs."

After kissing us good night, Poppa issued a final warning. "Now, I'm telling you, don't let me hear no fuss up there, understand? "

"Yessir, good night," we chorused in a near whisper.

◆

Humming contentedly, Jane lifted the baby from the crib and settled down in the rocking chair to get her ready for bed. Soon she began talking softly to her.

"You talking to Momma, Honey?" she asked, smiling down into the big dark eyes that seemed to search her face as the little mouth cooed.

"What's this baby trying to tell Momma? You going smile for me? Com'on gimme a big smile. Don't be so stingy. There! That's Momma's sweet Baby, 'deed 'tis. You going be good and sleep so Santa Claus'll bring you something nice? Now Snow, where you think we ought start first?"

"Better make the fire in the front room 'fore anything else," he replied. "Time enough to get their things out after Baby's asleep, don't cha think?"

Jane nodded as she rocked. Then, ever so softly, she half sang and half hummed "Silent Night." It seemed as though she had forgotten that there was anyone else in the world, so absorbed was she in the infant at her breast. Snow stood watching them as he often did. But that night, in the lamplight and shadows, he saw them in a manger scene, mother and child with a halo-like glow about them. He started to speak to try to express his feelings, but he didn't know how to say anything so beautiful.

"She 'sleep?" he whispered instead.

"Nearbout. Still sucking though. Can't hardly hold her eyes open. There! Believe she's gone now." She eased her breast from the parted lips, which immediately began sucking again.

"Snow," Jane whispered, "hand me a diaper off'n that pile. She's soaked this one that quick."

After changing Emily, she flung snow-white diapers over her shoulder and went upstairs. Pretending not to hear the whispers, which stopped the moment her foot touched the stairs, she laid the baby in the cradle and tucked her in. She turned down the lamp and took it into the children's room. Not a sound could be heard.

"No need pretending you 'sleep," she said as she placed the lamp on the dresser between the white iron double bed and Henry's single one. "Could hear you talking the minute I set foot in the hall all way downstairs."

"Not me, Momma," said Henry. "It's them."

"Momma, I was just 'bout 'sleep," Marie spoke up, "but Ginny keep pulling all the covering off'n me!"

"Ain't doing no such thing. Just look at this lil bit of covering on my side, not even enough to cover me up," I cried.

Momma turned up the lamp and noted the blanket hanging almost to the floor on one side, while not quite covering the other side of the bed.

"Leggo that covering both of you!" she demanded. Then she straightened the blankets and tucked them under on both sides.

"Now," she said, "if I have to come in here again, you both going be good'n sorry!"

"Momma," I called, "she's already starting pulling some— right now!"

"I'm not neither!" shouted Marie.

"You shut up that noise 'fore you wake that baby up, Marie. Pull that covering once more, and I'm going take you downstairs and burn your behind up, you hear me?"

"Yes'm," came the sullen reply. "You didn't say nothing to her. She pulling it same's me."

"I saw where all the covering was. So just hush up. Don't want hear no more about it—on Christmas Eve, too. Maybe you think Santa Claus's *got* to come here. Way you carrying on, you ought'n get a thing but a lump of coal in your stockings!"

Sighing audibly, she leaned over for our good-night kisses before turning down the lamp and setting it on a stand near the door between the rooms.

In the front room, the odor of burning coal assailed Jane's nostrils. The room, no longer refrigerator cold, was cozy, the fire snapping. Snow had brought the brass lamp with the mantled light from the dining room, and everything stood out in exceptional brightness. The tree, mounted on its stand, lent its fragrant cedary aroma to the air, and the wreaths were up. After taking one look at the holly-dressed windows, Jane grabbed her heavy sweater from the hall closet, dashed out to the porch, and didn't stop until she reached the street. There she stood, as if spellbound, gazing up at her front windows dressed in lace and holly wreaths, all aglow in bright lamplight. Snow, wondering what she was about, propped the stepladder against the door and followed her.

"Snow, come look from down here," she called. Standing in the cold, they marveled over the way the house looked all dressed up for their first Christmas in their own home. Grasping her shoulders, he pointed to a big bright star.

"Look, Sweetheart," he said. "See that big star all to itself? Make you think about the way shepherds followed the star when Jesus was born, don't it?"

"Cert'ny does," she agreed. "Ain't it big, though? And the sky's so black, except for them teensy twinkles. Ever'thing so quiet. It's just different, that's all. It's something about Christmas Eve—not like no other night."

"It's the truth, Hon. Something about it all right. Wonder what people who don't believe in the Bible or nothing feel like on a night like this?"

"Lord knows," she replied. "Guess they don't think nothing about it."

"I know one thing," he warned, "you better get in the house outen the night air. This kind of cold'll go right through you."

They closed the door. Jane straightened the wreath and stood looking from front door to living room to stairway to hall. Then she asked Snow where she should get started.

"Guess best thing's to get this tree trimmed," Snow replied. "Once that's done, I'll get their things out—wait a minute!"

He crossed the room, reaching the hall just in time to see the tail of a flannel nightgown disappear from the stair landing. By the time he had reached the children's room, a master performance, complete with loud snoring sounds, was in progress.

"You just lemme catch somebody outen bed again, and they won't have to worry about what they going get. Maybe we ought just tell Santa Claus don't bother about coming here," he threatened. Without another word, he strode from the room.

"Get after 'em?" she asked, smiling.

"Wish you'd seen 'em," he chuckled, "pretending to be fast asleep. Don't reckon they going get outen bed no more. Lord knows when they going sleep, though."

When the last string of tinsel was tossed onto the tree, the trimmers stood back admiring their handiwork.

"That's just about the prettiest tree I've seen in my whole life!" he exclaimed.

"Listen to that man bragging about his own Christmas tree, wouldja?" teased Jane. "Sure's nothing bashful about him!"

They laughed together the way children do when they're just happy to be so happy.

Upstairs, we children tried hard to keep quiet. The excitement was unbearable; sleep was impossible. At least, that's the way it had been so far. Even when we counted sheep, whispering the numbers all the way to one thousand, it didn't help. Only Marie was able to doze off now and then. The slightest noise was cause for pushing back the covers, inching up to the window beside each bed, and peeking out into the darkness, hoping that Santa would be there. Once Henry got up sufficient courage to creep all the way to the stairway, where a telltale squeak summoned rapid footsteps from downstairs. After that narrow escape, there was hardly a whisper to be heard. So, far into the night, two pairs of eyes were squeezed shut and two pairs of ears strained to hear some sign of the visitor, anything at all, above Marie's snoring.

In the dining room, Snow and Jane sat down to rest and read the children's letters to Santa as they munched on Christmas cookies and sipped potent wild-cherry wine. Then they began arranging each child's presents on and close by the chair onto which Snow had hung the biggest, longest cotton stocking he could find. The filling of stockings was something they especially enjoyed. First, into each stocking went a big, beautiful apple, an orange, and a tangerine, giving the stocking a triple-globe shape at the foot. Following the luscious fruit came an assortment of candies and nuts, the likes of which none of the family would see until Christmas came again.

Although they enjoyed dipping into mounds of flawless English walnuts, pecans, Brazil nuts, almonds, and hazelnuts, Snow and Jane delighted most of all in dividing the array of candy among the stockings, leaving out enough to fill the glass bowl on the sideboard for company. So much beautiful candy— rock candy in shapes of animals and Christmas items; multicolored hard candy with fancy designs through crystal centers; satiny looped candy ribbons; peppermint pinwheels and canes striped like barber poles; pastel French creams, walnut topped or fat with delicious fillings; coarse-sugared gum orange segments and green spearmint leaves; Jordan almonds like tiny Easter eggs; coconut squares layered in pink, white, and chocolate; thin bittersweet nonpareils; shiny peanut brittle; pink and white squares flavored with bits of black walnut; assorted chocolates—everything imaginable to please the palate at Christmas!

When the last stocking was filled, the last bit of clutter cleared away, the last presents rearranged again, and the last toy put together so that it really worked, the weary parents climbed the stairs and, already half-asleep, fell into bed. In a few hours daylight would flood the room.

Just as she was dozing off, Jane felt a tugging at her back. Then, a whisper.

"Is't time now? Can we go down?"

"No! You better get back in that bed and go to sleep, else you won't have one thing in the morning!" she warned as the sound of feet scurrying across the cold floor was drowned out by snoring.

◆

Back in bed, Henry and I lay wide-eyed, afraid even to whisper. After what seemed like many hours, the last stars winked away. Shadows became familiar forms in our room as the two of us lay listening to the rhythmic rise and fall of intermittent snores. Gradually, light edged the curtains. If nothing went wrong, we thought, surely Santa must have come and gone. Cautiously, we eased out of bed, crept through our parents' room, and tiptoed down the creaking stairs. Each step brought us closer to a magical world.

We stopped at the foot of the stairs and gazed into the living room. In the corner opposite the door, a giant green jewel adorned in Christmas finery sparkled in the early morning light. Frosty designs, gold and silver dust, and glittering stones accented colorful balls of all sizes, in both shiny and deep, dull tones. Little bells of gold and silver, along with a tiny red one, tinkled at the slightest jarring movement. Several new brightly colored oblong ornaments pointed on either end—their scooped-out center inserts lined with silver, creased like pleats in crepe paper—hung in prominent places. The little old Santa Claus that returned every year smiled out amid fragile-winged angels. Green branches, scalloped with prickly golden ropes, were showered in tinsel. And at the very top of the tree, a handsome silver star glimmered. A miniature manger, nestled in folds of velvety, sparkling snow, glowed beneath the tree. For a few moments, in spite of the long-awaited treasures we hoped to find in the dining room, we both stood in awe, staring at that marvelous sight.

"Oh-h-h look at it!" I exclaimed, grabbing Henry by the arm.

"It's pretty, ain't it?" he said, pulling free. Enthralled by the beauty of the tree, we padded eagerly down the hall to the dining room.

"Hot dog! Lookit here, Ginny!" Henry called as he lifted a long, shiny rifle from his chair. "It's almost same as one's that shoots real bullets. And I got this ukelele I ask for and some what I didn't even ask for. What you get?"

"A pretty doll baby and clothes for her, a jigsaw puzzle, a story book, and coloring book and watercolors," I told him. "And look at my new raincoat and hat to match."

As I talked, my mind raced: "Wonder if Henry was looking? But he's been working on his gun—ain't paid no mind to nothing but that." Yet, I knew I couldn't be certain. Henry could have seen me try on the other hat, the one Santa had left on Marie's chair. No problems with the coats. They were identical.

But my hat, which had a narrow brim all around, was a rather loose fit while Marie's had a brim like a boy's cap with elastic in the back. A perfect fit! I pretended to believe Santa must have mixed the hats up; however, I knew which hat was on my chair. So, after shifting my eyes in Henry's direction, I switched hats, feeling sure no one could know the difference.

"Momma! Poppa!" I called from the stairs. "You all going get up and see what we got?"

A muffled "Humph?" came from somewhere among the pillows.

"Merry Christmas!" I cried, bursting into their room no longer bridling my excitement.

"Merry Christmas, Ginny," Momma murmured sleepily. "Was Santa Claus good to you all?"

"O-o-oh, Momma, just wait'n see! We got ever'thing. Even Baby's got presents."

"Well, it's nice Santa Claus left what you want. See if it makes you all better children."

With a groan, Poppa turned over, half glanced in my direction, and quickly laid an arm over his eyes. Too late—he knew I'd seen him.

"Merry Christmas, Poppa," I said softly.

"Mer' Christmas, Ginny," he mumbled, without raising his arm.

"You all coming to see what we got for Christmas?"

"We coming down 'fore long, Honey. Play with your things to we get up. Let Momma and me rest a while."

"Merry Christmas, Momma! Merry Christmas, Poppa!" Marie shouted from the doorway between the bedrooms, as she rubbed sleepy eyes with one hand and clutched the slop bucket with the other.

"Merry Christmas, Honey!" Poppa mumbled.

"You just waking up? Going take that bucket down 'fore you see what Santa Claus brought you?" Momma teased.

Wide awake now, Marie set the bucket back into our room and turned to me, "Let's go down! Henry's already down there!"

"I done seen my things. Your'n, too," I informed her.

"See, Momma," Marie cried. "They wouldn't even call me!"

"Did so call you—told me to leave you alone," I cut in. "Come see. We got ever'thing!"

Our parents had watched us for several minutes before we even knew they were downstairs. Henry saw them first. Jumping up waving his rifle, he shouted, "Merry Christmas, Momma 'n Poppa! Merry Christmas!"

"Come see my things," urged Marie, who was tucking an infant doll in its miniature crib.

"Mine, too, Momma 'n Poppa. Ain't she pretty?" I asked, holding up a rosy cheeked doll with painted-on brown hair and long-lashed blue eyes that opened and closed—eyes that reminded me of Henry's blue alley, hard and cold; eyes that—until I first stared, up close, into a pair of living blue eyes—I had believed could be found only in a doll's head. In my little world, even gray-eyed children often were subjected to scornful taunts such as "Gray-eyed greedy gut! Eat the whole world up!" or to being called "Cat Eyes." We were used to seeing an occasional pair of gray eyes, but not eyes so strangely blue.

"My!" exclaimed Momma. "Both of 'em's just pretty's can be. Guess I'd had a fit if Santa Claus ever left me something like that when I was a child. Snow, that's a mighty fancy looking gun he brought Henry."

"'Deed 'tis. Son, you better had know where to shoot that gun—I'm telling you right now. If I hear one word about you shooting where you got no business, you won't have no more gun. That clear?" Poppa asked sternly.

"Yessir, I won't shoot it nowhere lessen you say it's all right," Henry promised.

Sniffing the new rubber scent of the rain outfit, I strolled around the room, no longer concerned about the deception since no one had noticed anything, and called their attention to my prized outfit.

"Um hum. Fits real nice," Momma observed before turning to Marie. "Put your'n on, Marie, and see if they all right. Ginny, com' ere—believe Santa got something mixed up."

She removed the hat from my head, gave it a cursory check and said, "Thought so. This one's to Marie's coat. Gimme that hat offen your chair, Marie. This here's your'n, Ginny."

"B-but, Momma," I stammered, lying, "that's the one was with my things. It belongs with my coat."

"Ginny," she explained in a patient voice, "Santa Claus got a whole lotta things to remember. He's bound to get something mixed up once'n a while. Now this here's your hat, and that's Marie's. So don't let me hear no more about it."

Eyes downcast, I took the hat, wondering whether Momma suspected what I had done. But how could she know since it was Santa who brought the gifts?

Cousin Bill—who looked a lot like Santa Claus with his robust belly, twinkling eyes, and ruddy complexion—and his wife stopped by to wish everyone a Merry Christmas. Within minutes the aroma of perking coffee, mingling with that of hot sausage and slab bacon, drifted through the house. Christmas morning breakfast was special. The family sat down together then, just as we always did for dinner. We had buckwheat cakes with homemade preserves and syrup, spicy fried apples, bacon and hot country sausage, and eggs laid by our hens. Yet it was hard—in spite of frequent reminders—to hold ourselves in check long enough to eat a hearty breakfast. After breakfast, the day, for the most part, was ours to enjoy and share with relatives and friends. Later, when we finally came in to stay, there would be supper. Some time ago, Momma decided that it was a waste of time to prepare a special dinner on Christmas Day, when our only interest was our presents; besides that, we were far too excited to sit still even for

Christmas dinner. So we always had Christmas dinner on the following Sunday.

As soon as breakfast was over, Poppa took Henry out to let him practice handling his new rifle. When he returned, Momma, having bathed, dressed, and fed Emily, was straightening up the kitchen. She paused to ask for Henry's whereabouts.

"Left him out front with Junior," Poppa replied.

"Think he ought have that gun out there, Snow?"

"I believe he's going know what to do with his gun, Jane," he assured her.

"Just hope you right, that's all," she sighed.

Marie and I, waiting to be allowed to go down Mom's, played on the floor while Henry played outside. An hour passed before he burst into the kitchen.

"Where you been all this time, Henry?" Momma asked.

"Playing with Junior. I seen his presents," he volunteered.

"Who told you to go in there?" she demanded to know.

"But, Momma, he asked me to come see what he got for Christmas."

"I don't care what he ask you. You been told time and time again not to go in that house, Mister Man!" she fussed. "I got a good mind to . . ."

"Hon," Poppa cut in, "I can't see no harm in him going this one time, since it's Christmas. Henry, don't go nowhere else unless your mother says so, hear me?"

"Yessir," Henry said, grateful for the intervention.

Still fussing to herself, Momma took the baby upstairs.

"What Junior get for Christmas, Son?" Poppa asked, trying to minimize the discordant note.

Brightening up, Henry replied, "He's got a great big sled and roller skates, and I think that's all he's got to play with. He's got a new suit and a whole lot of clothes, but he ain't got nothing like our things. I feel right sorry for him."

"Don'tcha be feeling sorry about what Junior got," Poppa said. "They can get anything they want without thinking about it. Same's that fancy new school they talking about putting up for white children while . . ."

Suddenly Uncle Ray, Momma's brother, fumbled with the doorknob and shouted "Merry Christmas!" He jerked open the door and stood on the sill, waving his hands and grinning.

"Hey, Ray, Merry Christmas to you, too!" Poppa greeted him. Noting his brother-in-law's slight unsteadiness, he exclaimed, "Great day in the morning! You mean you started celebrating already?"

"T-tis the s-season t' be jolly, Snow. Whee-ee!" Ray shouted, with an elaborate bow as he doffed his cap. "Where Jane at? Gotta wish her Mer-ree Christmas."

"Sit down there, boy," Poppa coaxed. "She'll be down in a minute. How about some good hot coffee?"

"Coffee! You offerin' me coffee? Where your Christmas spirit, man? You want gimme sump'n? Gimme a swaller of good old John Barleycorn and jus' . . ."

"Shut up, boy!" Poppa said, jokingly. "You going drink this coffee so keep your shirt on. You know good'n well it don't take but a teaspoon of whiskey to make you drunk."

"Drunk? W-who's d-drunk?" demanded Ray, mustering an air of injured dignity. "You might *think* I'm drunk. Here, I'm s-so-ber's a j-judge. Ain't this sump'n? I comes in here fulla Chris-Chris'mus s-spirit jus' t' get insulted."

"Now, wait a minute, Ray," said Poppa, choosing his words. "You know right well nobody's aiming to insult you. Shucks, boy, it's Christmas. Com'on drink a cup of coffee with me."

Ray, still sullen, started to speak, but didn't. He gulped down the strong coffee. When Momma came down, he had sobered up considerably, even went to see our presents and tree.

After exclaiming sufficiently over our Christmas joys, he returned to the kitchen. We listened to them reminisce about Christmases when they were children, when hip-deep snow covered the countryside and when each of them was lucky if he got even one toy, instead of the "bounty" we children had come to expect.

As for our parents, their happiness was found in the warmth that flowed throughout our home, along with our boundless joy, as we gazed upon the tree or played with a favorite present. They declared it made all the scrimping and even the arguments about what they could not afford of no consequence. At least, it must have seemed so at the time. But they could not ignore, even on such a happy day, the persistent rumors of hard times ahead. They had known nothing but hard times, and they wondered what difference hard times would make to people who never wanted for anything. Everybody everywhere was talking about it. Even poor children knew something bad was coming, something called "the Depression."

6 · Mount Zion

The churchbell's call
jars a door
where hinges creak
reviving other days and things
unburied but ignored—
considered past.

Throughout the Great Depression years—when banks were folding all over the United States; when millions of families were being wiped out financially; when newspapers were headlining suicides of the bereft; when breadlines were lengthening in big cities; when men were working for fifty cents to a dollar a day—the worsening state of black poverty was simply taken for granted. Neither recovery programs nor the "We do our part" slogan addressed the growing needs of black people, many of whom already had done their part without even token recompense. Therefore, blacks were left to carve out a means of survival—one that demanded extraordinary determination, stamina, ability, and dreams of a better life—all fortified by the same religious faith that sustained our ancestors. It is that priceless part of our heritage that ties us to the faith of our fathers, to the church, and to the belief that with God on our side, we shall overcome.

During that time, I was blessed with two "second homes"—Mom's and Mount Zion. Our grandmother's home and our church were vital parts of my childhood. As children, we knew we belonged to Mount Zion Methodist Church, and Mount Zion belonged to us—a perfect relationship. We hoped that this euphoric state would last forever; however, the euphoria waned abruptly one late-summer evening.

It was hot and windless that August night. The air held an uneasy stillness. Far off in the distance a heavy rumbling—no lightning, just an ominous jarring sound—echoed, died down, then began again. Momma stepped outside the kitchen door and looked toward Mount Zion, speaking half to herself, "Looks like it's going storm real bad afterwhile. If Mom don't get here 'fore it starts, you all won't get to go."

"O-o-oh pul-eeze, Momma," we begged.

Mom had promised to take us to the big revival at our church. None of us had been to a revival. We were so excited about going that we had been good all day. If we misbehaved, we knew Momma wouldn't let us go. From what we had heard, the revival would be even better than peeking in the Hall on nights when the "Holy Rollers" beat tambourines, danced holy dances, got "happy," shouted, fell out, and rolled on the dusty floor.

All week we had been listening to talk about how the guest evangelist was "settin' the old church on fire." Even Uncle Tim, who everybody knew was a seasoned sinner, had been on his knees. He didn't go through a conversion though, but they were scheming to lure him back before he cooled off so the lady preacher could work on him some more. Uncle Tim must have got wind of it somehow because he disappeared and nobody laid eyes on him again until after the evangelist had left town. Nevertheless, some of the church leaders reminded Uncle Tim of the fate of sinners. He listened. Then in his usual unhurried way, he drawled, "Ah 'preciates you all aworryin' 'bout my soul. Ah knows Ah'm a poor sinner. Reckon Ah going know when the spirit do move me to join up. But Ah feels this way: long's Ah don't do nobody no harm and tends to my own business, it be bigger sinners than me right in the church." Shaking his head slowly, Uncle Tim aimed a probing stare from one to the other. The church leaders, some visibly embarrassed, mumbled about praying for his soul and departed and didn't trouble him again.

So, having heard several versions of the ways the Holy Ghost was shaking up the town's sinners, we eagerly awaited the evening's "entertainment." When Momma overheard our whisperings, she scolded, "You all better had behave yourself tonight or you going hear from me when you do get home. You not going to no circus, mind you. If Mom comes back here saying you all been carrying on—poking fun and laughing when somebody gets happy—I'll fix you so you won't be able to sit down for a week! What you need do is ask the Lord to take some the meanness outen you."

"Momma?" Marie asked.

"What? "

"Suppose Henry make me laugh?"

"Henry knows better'n make you laugh!"

"He say he's going to," Marie answered, stealing a sly glance in Henry's direction.

"Henry?" Momma called, fixing stern eyes on him.

"Didn't say no such thing, Momma," Henry grumbled.

"A revival's no place for giggling and carrying on. You forget it, and I'm going work on you right. And when I get through, your father's going give you some more!"

Soon we heard Mom out front and ran out to meet her.

"Hey, Mom!" Momma called. "You not even coming in for a minute?"

Leaning against the pump box, Mom sighed, "No-o-o, Honey! Tired as Ah am, all Ah needs do is sit down, and church won't see me none—not tonight. We best be going. Don't want be late. Thought Ah'd bring Mame; she wanted be with the others."

"Got a good mind to keep 'em home here, Mom, because I don't know how they going act what with people getting happy and . . ."

"What ails you, Jane? Think Ah'm not capable of makin' them children behave when they with me? Goodness sake! Let 'em come on, and stop holdin' me up!"

Our somber little procession turned onto Oxford Street and headed for Mount Zion. A few young men standing by the church steps spoke to Mom, "Evening Miss Dell. How you this evening?"

"Evening boys. Ah'm right smart, thankya. How you all?"

"We fine. Thankya."

Inside, everything was hushed. They had just finished singing "I Shall Not Be Moved" and were waiting for the spirit to move someone to start another hymn. Looking proud, Mom led us into a row near the front of the Sunday school room where dozens of tan wooden folding chairs were arranged in a semicircle before the platform. I slid well back into the chair, so it wouldn't tip over, and turned to gaze around the room. Everything seemed strangely different at night. Naked lightbulbs cast creepy shadows about, especially in one corner. That was where caskets were placed whenever a funeral followed Sunday services. Remembering the big gray casket that was there one Sunday during Sunday school, I decided not to look back there again.

Because we had arrived early, only about forty persons were seated near the front of the room. Ned Rollins, the choir leader, sat, whirling from side to side on the squeaky, claw-footed piano stool. He wiped sweat from his glasses with a white handkerchief, then used it to blot his bald head. From somewhere in back, a lone man began singing—slowly, intensely, softly—almost as if he were singing to himself:

> And I could-n't hear no-bod-y pray, O Lord,
> I could-n't hear no-bod-y pray, O Lord,
> O way down yon-der by myself
> And I could-n't hear no-bod-y pray.

One by one, others joined in. Then Bertie Adams began to solo a stanza so they could get it going right—the way it was meant to be sung with each soloed line backed by a chorused "Couldn't hear nobody pray." As hands clapped and feet patted to the beat of Brother Rollins's piano, Bertie sang out, "In the val-ley," and the congregation answered, "Couldn't hear nobod-y pray . . .!"

> On my knee-e-es—
> Could-n't hear no-bod-y pray.
> With my bur-den—
> Could-n't hear no-bod-y pray.
> An' my Sav-ior—
> Could-n't hear no-bod-y pray.
> O, Lord, I could-n't hear no-body pray . . .

As they rocked and swayed to verse after verse, a steady stream of worshipers filed into the Sunday school room.

Heads turned when Reverend Waller ushered the evangelist to the platform. They knelt in prayer before their chairs and took their seats as the last chorus of "I Couldn't Hear Nobody Pray" ended amid loud" A-a-mens" and "Praise His Holy Names." I was fascinated by the evangelist. Sister Clara, a solemn looking, stout, middle-aged woman, was dressed all in white. She reminded me of the Angel of Mercy in a picture book at home. Soft white material framed her face and cascaded about her shoulders. Her robe was long and full with flowing sleeves. And she was tall and stately, almost as tall as Reverend Waller, who towered over most men in our church.

Dignified and elderly, he stood looking over his congregation. Below the harsh lights, the top of his head shone like polished ivory.

"Don't know who started that hymn," he said, "but Children, it sure sounded good—mighty good. I've got a feeling we will hear somebody pray here this evening and, praise be to God, He's going to answer our prayers."

"Amen!" chorused the congregation.

"Just put yourself in the hands of the Lord," Reverend Waller continued. "Let Him have his way with you as His handmaiden brings His gospel to you. If you are saved, thank God. Ask Him to keep your feet on the straight and narrow path. If you've been putting Him off, put Him off no longer. Tomorrow could be too late!"

Abruptly, he stopped as if he had been reminded of his purpose—to introduce Sister Clara. He said quite simply that after last night's meeting, she needed no introduction, and the "Amens" rang out. Sister Clara stood, nodded to Reverend Waller, and greeted the congregation with, "It's good to be here. Praise the Lord!" Then for the first time since her entrance, she smiled, a beautiful, loving smile. There was not a sound in the room. Everything seemed hushed, both inside and outside, where the only visible movement was the flickering light of fireflies through the open windows. The sound that broke the silence flooded the room. Sister Clara was singing, her strong, deep contralto flowing out into the veins of the people, as they gave themselves over to the words and music:

Ste-e-al a-waay, ste-e-al a-waay
Ste-e-al a-waay to-o-o Jee-sus.
Ste-e-al a-waay; steal away home
I ain' got lo-o-ong to sta-a-ay here.

With palms outstretched, she invited the congregation to join
in the chorus. Already humming softly, they sang out, each one
singing as if his own moment for stealing away had come. They
swayed from side to side with the music. Some faces were pained;
others were so serene that the singers appeared already to be moving away to some glorious promised land. After leading a softer
chorus, Sister Clara raised one hand; a loud punctuation of
"Amens" followed the final note.

"Yes, Children," Sister Clara smiled as she spoke, "I'm going
to steal away from here—away where there'll be no more trials
and tribulations. No more sickness and pain. No poverty and injustice. Oh, yes, I'm going to steal away to Jesus! I know where
I'm going, and, as the old spiritual says, 'I don't feel no ways
tired—I know that my Redeemer liveth,' and He's promised to
come back after me. Praise God!"

Her voice broke. She gripped the sides of the lectern and gazed
upward, speechless for a moment.

"Amen! Amen! Praise His Holy Name! Do, Jesus!" they cried
until she could continue.

"The question you better ask tonight, every last one of you,"
Sister Clara shouted, "is *where am I going*? I know we like to sing
'Where Shall I Be When the First Trumpet Sounds,' but you don't
need to worry so much about that—nothing you can do about
that anyway—as about where you'll be *going*. Hear me, Children!
Sure as you're born—makes no difference where you are—one
day, one day you're going to steal away from here."

A woman jumped up screaming, alternately throwing out her
arms and flinging them around her body. She jumped, flailed her
arms, and screamed until, near collapse, she was lowered into her
chair, where members fanned her until she came around.

"This may be your last chance before God strikes you down!"
the evangelist continued. "He struck the dearest on earth to me,

and as sure as my Lord is writing all the time, Brother, He's coming back—Praise be to God—but I don't worry. I don't worry because I know, I know, yes, I do know my mother and father are waitin' for me in Glory, and I'm packin' up and gettin' ready to meet them there. What a day of rejoicing that's going to be, Children! Tell me you'll be there. He's coming, you know, whether you're ready or not. The old spiritual says 'green trees abendin'; poor sinner stands atremblin'.' Don't you feel the tremor tonight, Brother? Are you fighting the power God has over your soul? Don't fight Him! Hallelujah!"

"Preach the word! Preach the word!" urged an elderly sister, clapping her hands in ecstacy.

"Damnation awaits the sinner. Instead of everlasting life, his fate will be with the cursed one he has served. According to the word: 'The devil that deceived them was cast into the lake of fire and brimstone where the beast and the false prophet are and shall be tormented day and night forever and ever.' Do you want to be tormented along with the devil you're serving? Are you willing to be cast in the lake of fire and brimstone? Just think on it—to be tormented day and night for all eternity. Jesus, do have mercy!"

Her voice settled to a whisper, then gradually rose louder and louder: "So I say to you, Brothers and Sisters, don't worry about *when* you're going to steal away. Don't worry about *where* you'll be when that first trumpet sounds. No, Lord, what you'd better settle right now, before your lips are sealed in death forever, is the question of which way you're headed: up to join with all the Heavenly Host or down to the lake of fire and brimstone forever. Jesus! Jesus!!"

Clasping and unclasping her hands, she descended the steps and pranced back and forth along the platform's base. As she moved, she shouted—half speaking, half singing—with hardly a pause between exhortations except for sharp audible gasps when she became winded.

"Sinner," she called, "come home!"

Panting, Sister Clara dabbed her brow and peered into our troubled faces. Tears fell onto her hands. Without another word she lifted her face heavenward and sang:

Softly and tenderly Jesus is calling
Calling for you and for me.
Patiently Jesus is waiting and watching
Watching for you and for me.
Come ho-o-o-ome . . . come ho-o-ome . . . ye who are
weary come ho-o-ome.
Earnestly, tenderly Jesus is calling
Calling, O Sinner, come home!

"Come to Jesus!" screamed a woman behind me. It was Lessie Green, who "got happy" every Sunday and often fell out unconscious. Two ladies fanned her; all the while her body jerked spasmodically and her head rolled from side to side. Suddenly she bolted upright, flinging her arms, and cried, "Do, Jesus . . . " over and over. She soon calmed down, leaned back in her seat, and looked about her. On her face was the smile of one who has just discovered the secret everyone hopes to find. In the meantime, her cries had been taken up by other old-timers. Frightened by all the commotion, I moved closer to Mom.

From far back in the room, it came, barely audible at first, sounding as if it were rising from the floor. Gradually it grew intensely louder, a man's voice, trembling as if he were in agony. It was Rob Gwynn, head lowered, eyes closed, kneeling before a chair on the dusty floor. He gripped the chair back as if it were a person who might answer his pleadings, if only he held it hard enough. Rocking slowly back and forth, he appeared to be unaware of his surroundings. Tears bathed his face, distorted and terrible looking, as he sang the same words over and over, sounding each time more desperate than before:

Forgive me, Lord, and try me one more time.
I'll be yours, Good Lord, if you'll be mine.
If I falter if I sin, let me rise and try again.
Forgive me, Lord, and try me one more time.

"Help him, Jesus," a man cried out. "Help him."
"Speak to him, Lord; speak to him," cried old Zeke Jones.

And all the time, Rob continued to sing those words, over and over, even after someone got up to testify.

"Praise the Lawd, Children, Ah knows my Savior cares!" It was Aunt Mary, the oldest member of the church, slowly getting to her feet. She leaned heavily on her cane as she quoted words from her favorite hymn. Although tears glistened in her eyes, her dark, wrinkled face was calm. Sucking in her toothless mouth she looked from one familiar face to another before continuing her testimony:

"Seventy-five years ago last winter the good Lawd laid His blessed hand on me, Children, and Ah ain't never stop aleanin' on Him. Ah knowed hard times and troubles 'fore most you'uns was even thought 'bout. Yas, Lawd! Sometimes it seem like the sun got loss somers up there, but Ah ain't never stop atrustin' in Him. And He seen me through. Praise His name! Ah done live longer'n most. Ah seen Him move in His own ways. Ah done feeled His hand in mine, Children. Ah feeled it when they took my first-born out to Hall's Hill—Lawd, do have mercy—and my last! And Lawd, Ah feeled it that dark night—when white mens haul my poor innercent brother outen the house and hung him. Lawd, have mercy . . . "

Her voice broke, but she drew herself upright, looked around, and continued. "Ah feeled it last winter, Lawd help me, when they took poor old Henny out to Hall's Hill. Old like me, she were. Now she gone to Glory and they ain't nobody old like me left herebouts. Children, Ah'm weary . . . lonesome, too. But He say He ain't never going leave me alone, Praise Gawd. He's got His hand in mine. Ah feels it, Children, and Ah'm ready to go. Ain't nothing here fer me to stay fer. My Father done promise me a mansion in the skies, and Ah'm ready to journey on. Mongst you pray fer me, and Ah pray fer you. Pray to Him, Children. He care fer His own. Glory Hallelujah!"

Waving a bony hand, she sank into her chair. Then she leaned her snow-white head against the crook of her cane and sobbed aloud.

Several persons were moved to testify after Aunt Mary. Some started favorite hymns; others quoted from the scriptures or gave accounts of what the Lord had done for them. The singing lowered and Sister Clara spoke as gently as a mother coaxing her reluctant child to take his first step, urging the unsaved to give their souls to Jesus.

"Jesus is waiting for you," she said, "tonight. Not tomorrow. Who told you you've got tomorrow? He suffered and died on the cross for you. How can you turn your back on Him now? Tell me, Children, what are you waiting for? Don't wait young people! Don't wait gambler! Backslider! Thief! Adulterer! Judas! Don't wait, no matter what your sins: though your sins be as scarlet, He can wash them white as snow!"

The entire scene—Sister Clara's passionate preaching, Aunt Mary's stirring testimony, folks everywhere getting happy, all the singing and amening—mesmerized me. I was engrossed in watching Rob Gwynn, who had moved to a seat across the aisle. Someone began singing "For You I Am Praying." Others joined in, and Rob dropped to his knees, lifting and lowering his head until it nearly struck the seat of the chair. His face depicted the worst kind of suffering as he cried hysterically. I had no idea what compelled him to carry on that way. I certainly felt no compulsion to act like that.

Meanwhile, Moses Hull jumped up shouting and ran crying down to the mourner's bench. He fell into a heap and knelt between two class leaders. The hallelujahs echoed through Mount Zion as everyone prayed and awaited the next convert.

Suddenly, Mom's hand rested on my shoulder, startling me.

"Ginny," she whispered.

"Ma'am?"

"Don't you all think's 'bout time you joined church and give your soul to the Lord? You almost old enough to answer for your sins now, you know," she said.

I didn't know what to say, but I did know we hadn't come to the revival to join church. To me, things seemed all right as they were. We went regularly to church. This always had been our church. Anyway, I hadn't thought much about answering for sins, except maybe when I'd been punished for "telling a story" or something like that. And the only time I worried about where I was going after I died—couldn't imagine dying anyway—was after Reverend Waller preached about hell and all that fire and brimstone. Then for days I was afraid even to go upstairs alone in the daytime. I wondered if my mother and grandmother and aunt had talked about our joining church and perhaps decided it all without telling us. Whatever the case, we never had the chance to decide. Mom drew us together and whispered, "Now, Children, 'mongst you get ready to go up and give yourself to Jesus. It's about time you do." That said, she rose and shepherded us to the mourner's bench as more hallelujahs rang out.

Although dazed by the turn of events, I later recalled being sung and prayed over for so long that I almost went to sleep before we were allowed up from the mourner's bench. Being children, we would not have had to stay down so long, but everybody was so busy singing and praying Moses through that they probably never thought of how tired we were. Besides, they knew that time spent at the mourner's bench couldn't hurt anyone, even innocent children. So they sang on and on. They sang and prayed and prayed and sang until Moses saw the light. It seemed an age before the shouting ended and, half asleep, we stumbled homeward.

In bed, I continued to hear echoes of loud clapping and singing. I continued to feel the jarring of stomping feet shaking my body. Over and over, I heard snatches of one piece they had sung—one I couldn't remember having heard before, or since. But the echoes bouncing through my head left words that have lingered through many decades:

> Across the river of Jordan
> In the Garden of Eden
> There stood a Tree of Life
> All in her bloom, thank God, all in her bloom.

◆

The next morning Momma talked with her newly converted children about our responsibilities as church members:

"Now, you *got* to behave yourself," she warned. "Ever'thing you do from now on'll be recorded in the Book on High."

After Henry and Marie had gone outside, each trying to act sanctified and holy, I sat thinking and watching my mother.

"What's matter with you, Ginny?" she asked.

"Nothing," I replied. Then, deciding to talk, "Momma . . ."

"What?"

"When I get older," I confided, "I'm going get a religion of my own."

"What're you talking about, Ginny?" she asked, eyeing me with concern. "You just got converted last night. Sometimes I don't know what in the world to make of you!"

It worried her that I was upset—she could see I was—just at the time when I was supposed to be "easy in my mind." She waited for me to say more, for she knew I would.

"Momma, what I mean's I want to get my own religion. We went down there last night 'cause Mom told us to," I explained.

Sighing, my mother shook her head and gave me a long, puzzled look.

There was something else I would not forget about that morning; it was what my mother said after I described Rob Gwynn's actions as he sobbed, prayed, and moaned on his knees.

Having given all the details, I said, "Momma, I feel so sorry for poor Mr. Gwynn."

"You feel sorry for him, do you?" she asked.

Her cold tone shocked me. How could Momma, who had sympathy for just about everyone and everything, have no sympathy for that poor man, as pitiful as he was on his knees crying?

"You would pitied him, too, Momma, if you was there. He just cried and cried."

"He needs to cry," she declared.

"Why, Momma? Don't you like Mr. Gwynn?"

Momma leaned wearily against the washboard and gazed into the tub, where suds sparkled and popped among steaming laundry. She sighed and turned to me.

"Ginny," she said, "don't worry no more about Mr. Gwynn. I'm going tell you why. But it's something that you can't talk about, not to nobody. Hear me? They say he was mixed up in the murder of one of the nicest men anywheres around here."

"He *was?!*" I cried. "Why ain't he in jail then, Momma?"

"Jail! Humph!" Momma grunted. "Ginny, honey, you too young to understand; you'll know soon enough. Child, it was a colored man they killed. They don't bother none, not long's it's colored killing colored. If it'd been a white man they killed, they would strung 'em up and forgot all about 'em long ago. Yes, Lord, Rob Gwynn got something to cry about. And crying ain't near enough for him. So you just stop worrying, and say no more about what I just now told you. Hear me?"

"Yes'm," I answered soberly.

But in spite of my mother's bitter words, for days afterward I found myself wondering whether God would answer Rob Gwynn's prayers. I recalled Sister Clara's promise: "Though your sins be as scarlet, He can wash them white as snow." I remembered, but I could not understand.

7 · A Father's Challenge

Sing me a troubled song . . .
echoes of slavery's lashed-on pain
and fears of a tomorrow nobody knows
drowned in today's shocked sorrow.

Preachings and teachings can be sources of confusion for children, especially when decisions are made for them—instead of by or with them—as Mom did for us at the revival. However, my confusion did not affect my feelings about Mount Zion. That beautiful old church still was another home to me. It was my belief that even children should be allowed, with guidance, to make certain crucial decisions, and matters of religion belong in that category—a conviction that has not wavered through the years. While being shepherded to the mourner's bench did not harm us, it just might have helped strengthen us for troublesome times ahead. And troubles we children could not have imagined soon swept throughout the country. Suffering woes of the Depression, plus all the deprivations of segregation, our family faced some of life's gravest tests. It was a time of trouble—a time that many of little faith did not survive.

Poor people wasted no time standing around banks and offices discussing how "bad" times were. It would have been useless to exchange views on the difference between having next to nothing and having a shade less than next to nothing. They had no need to listen to employers' constant complaints. They already knew what was not in their week's wages, what was not on their tables at dinnertime, what was not on their children's backs and feet.

One day Momma delivered two heavy baskets of expertly finished laundry to Prissy White, who dropped change into her hand and complained, "Jane, you all must eat my soap and drink the bluing! I declare, it's gone before you get it. Maybe you all don't realize it, but money's getting scarce. We're going to start cutting corners. Susie doesn't charge Mother near as much as I'm paying you for this little bit of laundry. I'll let you know what I decide."

Momma was furious. She said it was all she could do to keep from emptying both baskets onto the muddy ground and stomping dirt into every laundered piece. She wished she could stand over Prissy and make her pump water until all the pots and buckets were full, lug them into the kitchen, hoist them onto the hot stove, bend over steaming washtubs and scrub out her own dirt on a washboard until her knuckles were raw. Then that was just the half of it; she'd empty tubs and refill them for rinsing and bluing, hang out the laundry to dry, bring it in, and sprinkle it. Then let Prissy stand near the hot stove, trying to handle heavy flatirons. The mere thought of Prissy's struggling with that heavy, smelly wash made Momma smile in spite of her anger. "Them clothes would look just like the devil," she declared, "and so would Prissy! Got nerve to tell me, 'Maybe you all don't know!'"

At supper Momma started talking about Prissy, but the worry in Poppa's face must have stopped her. Ignoring the lone hamburger left on the platter, he pushed his chair from the table, saying, "Supper's good, Hon."

"Sure you got enough Snow? It's another hamburger, if you want it."

He shook his head, "Give it to 'em."

She forked the hamburger into three pieces. Henry and I gobbled ours, but Marie minced at hers until ours was gone, after which she made a production of enjoying what we no longer had.

"Guess I better get on 'cross town and see what's what over to Pop's," Poppa said. Poppa's stepmother had been ill for some time. "Miss Nannie's not doing no better, I hear. Sounds like her mind's getting bad."

Grabbing his jacket and cap from the nail on the kitchen door, he felt in his pocket, then told Marie to bring his Chesterfields. After lighting up and inhaling deeply, he said he'd get back as soon as he could.

Momma always said there was something eerie about being alone in the house at night. As relieved as she was when we were in bed and she could have a few moments' peace and quiet, she never felt at ease when no one was around. It was different in the daytime; then she was too busy to think anything about it. Besides, she was used to being alone in the day. At night the whole world was different—dark, quiet, and lonely.

As she sat waiting for Poppa, Momma thought about his father, Caleb Holden. Long years after Poppa's mother died, Grandpop married Nannie Turlington. They lived in an old house across town in Bedlam. Grandpop worked hard until he was in his seventies when severe asthma attacks wore him down. Things worsened when Miss Nannie suddenly became very sick.

Later that night, Momma finally heard the anxiously awaited signal: Poppa clearing his throat as he opened the gate. He looked so tired and worried as he hung up his jacket that she hated to ask how things were at his father's. Just as Poppa feared, Miss Nannie was bad off.

When she no longer seemed to know who or where she was, Miss Nannie's daughter and son-in-law came to take her to their own house up in Delaware. Grandpop watched helplessly as they lifted Miss Nannie into the car, cranked the engine, and drove off. All the while he had tried to get his wife's attention, but if she heard him or realized he was there, she did not respond.

My parents knew that Grandpop could not keep up with tending to the house and paying rent by himself. And what a lonely house it would be without Miss Nannie. Momma graciously suggested that Grandpop come live with us. Poppa said he wouldn't come, that we children would get on his nerves, and besides, Grandpop was convinced that Miss Nannie would be coming home after resting up for a while. But Momma insisted that they'd just have to make Grandpop understand. The only thing Momma asked was for him to do something about his chewing and spitting, especially around the stove while she cooked. Grandpop would spit right in the woodbox if nobody was looking, she said. They implored and suggested, until tired of trying, that he either move in with them or agree to live with someone in town who might need a boarder. Grandpop resisted at every turn. He was too stubborn to move from his own place and too optimistic that Miss Nannie was coming back to him. And Poppa dared not make decisions for his father.

But soon enough, decisions were made for us. Just a few weeks later, Miss Nannie died and they brought her body home. The small procession bore her slowly out to Hall's Hill, the wooded, unkempt graveyard at the edge of town. They buried her beside Poppa's mother as Grandpop, chin quivering pitifully, shed tears over their graves.

Snow Holden's father, Caleb, late 1800s

Whether it was an act of providence or timely good luck, the family that rented half of a small, double house behind ours moved out. Since it was clear that Grandpop never would be satisfied unless he could live by himself, Poppa rented the three rooms for him, although he could not afford the extra expense. They cleaned up the place and moved him in. Realizing that times were difficult for his father, Poppa tried to overlook the old man's peevishness and constant complaining. My parents hoped he would adjust to his loss and to the new situation. Meanwhile, they did all they could to help him. Gradually, Grandpop began to speak of "his house" and to take pride in puttering around the place fixing it up. Even more encouraging, he had not suffered a serious asthma attack since they moved him. Of course, he never would admit he was better, but that fact was evident by his appearance and actions.

After a few months of adjustment, Grandpop seemed much improved. He began doing light janitorial work in the canning factory. Poppa had been skeptical when his father first spoke of his plans to get a job. However, the doctor said the light work would provide Grandpop with much-needed activity, as well as pride in being partly responsible for his own support. Still Poppa was apprehensive, afraid his father would overexert himself, but he soon realized the doctor was right. Just to watch his father unpack a bag of groceries bought with money he had earned was ample proof. However, on one extremely hot day, Grandpop swept too long after having been told not to work outside in the burning sun. A packer found him drenched with sweat, trying to raise himself from the ground where he had fallen, his long-handled broom on the ground beside him.

Caleb Holden was never quite the same again. It seemed as if he sweated out his very spirit that day.

♦

Meanwhile, still inspired by Reverend Waller's call to action, Snow continued to petition town officials to consider improving the conditions of "colored" schools. Although the city council members were constantly putting him off, he was determined to haunt the mayor and anyone else who could initiate some changes in the colored schools until somebody did something. Meeting after meeting had been set up and postponed for one flimsy excuse or another. One time a member of the city council reportedly remembered a previous engagement. The meeting was canceled. Later, the officials reportedly had not received necessary materials from Snow Hill, the county seat, where matters of education were handled. There was also a series of ailments, which reportedly incapacitated first one then another council member. But as regularly as a meeting was postponed, Snow requested a rescheduling. Finally, an afternoon arrived when there was no cancellation message left for him at the garage. So after washing up and changing after supper, he left for the long-postponed meeting.

The door to Mayor Andrew Turner's office was unlocked; after knocking and waiting a while, Snow turned the knob and stood in the doorway of the dimly lit room. A gooseneck desk lamp with a green shade threw an arc of light over the impressive mahogany desk, on which several ponderous legal volumes were propped between brass bookends. A few dark ladder-back chairs were arranged in a semicircle opposite the desk with its heavy swivel chair, and a dark bookcase against the wall accented the room's somber atmosphere.

As he waited alone, Snow thought of the special church meeting Reverend Waller called after the firing of Miss Blaine. He remembered those who had remained after the meeting—men who had sworn to stop talking about the school situation and to start doing something about it. Each man recruited several others and they held meetings in their homes. But their enthusiasm lasted only until the first scheduled meeting with the council was postponed. This time, however, he had not received a message of postponement, so he spread the word to each man. Yet he waited alone.

It was almost eight o'clock and the meeting was scheduled to begin at eight sharp. He began to wonder if the council members really would come or if this would be another disappointment. In a way, he felt that those white men were no worse than his own friends who had said they would stick with him, then reneged. They declared they weren't about to let white folks make fools out of them, especially since everyone believed that the town council would not take any action anyway.

Wondering where to sit, Snow settled on a position midway along the semicircle of chairs set up in front of Turner's desk. A few minutes later, the mayor arrived, and the two men exchanged friendly greetings. Then, Snow expressed his hope for positive results from the meeting.

"We'll see what we can do for you, Snow," Turner said, while busily thumbing through a pile of papers on the desk. "Thought George and Lora and the others'd be with you. They are coming, aren't they?"

"Can't say for certain, Mr. Andrew. Guess they been ready so many times before they don't believe's going be a meeting. You think Mr. Ed and them's coming?"

"Far as I know, they are; here's Ed now."

After a bit of idle talk, the mayor got to the point: "Snow, suppose you tell us what's on your mind. Maybe you ought to start by letting us know the main things you people are concerned about— things you've been discussing in all those meetings I hear you've been having."

"Yeah," Ed chimed in mockingly, "tell us some we ain't already heard."

Aiming a sharp glance in Ed's direction, Snow said, "I don't know what you been hearing, but we are concerned about the kinda school our children got to go to, same's you'd be if you were in our place. All you got do is look at the colored school, then look at the white school. It's no way anybody can help seeing what's wrong, and that's a whole lot."

He paused, looking from one red face to the other, then continued: "Another thing, our children got no chance to go beyond ninth grade, don't matter how smart they are in their studies. It's a whole lotta things just ain't right, Mr. Andrew; that's all 'tis to it. But that's two of the worse. We been reading about that school bond issue, same's you all. It's going be fine for white children. What's it going do for our'n? Me, I got three in school and one home. And every day of my life I hate to think my children's got it no better'n I did when I was coming up. Right down to the same old broke-down schoolhouse!"

He paused again, waiting for one of them to speak, but they eyed him in silence. Unfolding a newspaper clipping, he continued: "Got this outen the paper; it's about the school bond issue. Now, what I'd like to know's this: what on earth would they be writing if they'd stop and give a second thought to them two old buildings with them broke-down nasty outhouses our children got to go to? Mr. Andrew, you and Mr. Ed both would have a fit if your children had to go there a single day. Go look at 'em. See for yourself."

"We don't need to look at them, Snow," said the mayor, "we'll take your word for it. Let's see that article."

Turner began reading the article. Then he turned to Ed, "You see this, Ed? It's an editorial from the *Worcester Democrat*. Listen to this part: 'So deplorable are the material school surroundings of our boys and girls that the buildings are used as examples of the very worst that could exist. Worcester County is at the very lowest depths of school deprivation. They are show places of backwardness and an insult to modern advancement . . .'"

"Hm-m-m, they sure put it down in black 'n white, didn't they?" Ed mumbled.

"The important thing is that we've let things get so bad our own editors could write about them this way," the mayor lamented.

"One thing certain, Andy," Ed said, "that bond issue's going to free right smart money for school improvement. We got to make sure we get our share. Then we can make some real changes. How that sound to you, Snow? Snow!"

"*Sounds* good all right," Snow replied slowly. "I got no quarrel about how it sounds, but it's going take whole lot more'n good-sounding talk to help our children. And if the truth be told, that editor wasn't even talking about colored schools. He's talking about your white schools that's just like a palace alongside of our'n. Shucks! They want to write something? Let 'em write about what happen to Fred Wilson's boy, Wilbert. I'm sure you all heard about that. And before that poor lil boy got all messed up back of that old broke-down toilet, you couldn't find a child smarter'n him anywhere around here. Wilbert ain't been right since that day."

"Snow," the mayor cut in, "I'm afraid I've got to agree with you, at least for the most part. I'm sorry as you about the Wilson boy—anybody'd be. We are going to look into things and get something done about them. You have my word on that. Of course, these things take time. Can't get everything done at once, but we can start."

"Glad to hear you say so, Mr. Andrew. This'll help folks believe it's worthwhile to try and get together, and I'm right sure I can get the fellers out to a meeting soon's you say."

"Can't see the need for that just now, Snow," said Turner. "Better wait till I see what I can work out with the council. But you can always stop by if you want to talk with me about anything. Meanwhile, I'll see what steps we can take."

"Thankya, Mr. Andrew, for the meeting and for your promise. We going be waiting—praying, too."

"I won't let you down, Snow, not if I can help it," the mayor assured him.

For the next several days, buoyed by the meeting and Mayor Turner's promise, Snow contacted the other men who he hoped would be sufficiently encouraged by his news to meet and work out plans of what they, with the mayor's backing, could do to improve the schools. As usual, some muttered that nothing would come of it. Never had. But a few renewed their pledge to stick together and do all they could. One thing was certain: nothing had stirred up the black community as much as Snow Holden's meeting with the mayor—not since the firing of Miss Blaine. Everyone eagerly waited.

◆

Time on the Shore seemed both stagnant and fleeting. Days turned to months, early summer picking turned to preparing for Christmas, school years came and went. In spite of steadily worsening conditions as the Depression wore on, nothing could smother the enthusiasm of students like Henry and me who were graduating from elementary school, which in Worcester County in the 1930s went through the seventh grade. During commencement practices we sang over and over, "Tis May the month of flo-o-wers, of golden sunny hours . . ." and other songs Mrs. Henderson had selected for the commencement program. At last the day came when the class walked in pairs from school to Mount Zion for a full rehearsal. Boys lined up on the stairs to the left, girls to the right. When Mrs. Henderson struck a resounding chord on the piano, we entered the sanctuary with a step-stop-step cadence and marched up the center aisle to the front pews. There we stood, girls on the right side and boys on the left, until everyone reached his seat. Kate Wright and I, class valedictorian and salutatorian, were seated on the platform. After repeated seatings and risings, we finally managed to sit in unison on signal. We rehearsed that program until everyone was weary of it all—even of thoughts of commencement and entering junior high school.

By graduation night our house was filled with confusion as Henry and I prepared for the ceremonies. Poppa groomed Henry while Momma fussed with my curls and white voile cape-collared dress with dainty ruching scalloping the skirt and a bow tied in back. When everyone was dressed, the family listened to the final practice of my speech. After thanking the "wonderful parents" for their many loving sacrifices and the "wonderful teachers" for their patience and diligence in keeping our feet on the "rugged road to education" and steering us onto "learning's path," I told how "puffed up and happy" we were to be graduating from elementary school. Then came a rather lengthy discourse on the folly of letting one's education go to one's head that ended with the time-worn:

> There is so little learning in the wisest of us
> And so much wisdom in the dullest of us
> That it isn't fitting for the best of us
> To talk about the rest of us.

Looking expectantly at the critics, I asked, "Did I do all right?"

"You done just fine, Honey," Poppa said. "Just say it half that good and Poppa'll be real proud. Course I'm already proud of you both."

"'Deed so," Momma seconded.

Walking home after the exercises, our father told us, "You children make me real proud tonight. Now all you got do is keep on same's you been doing and we going do all in our power to see if you can't go all way through high school—college, too if it's anyways possible."

"I'm going try to do the best I can, Poppa," I promised, as did Henry.

✦

May was a short school month on the Shore, and as soon as most Shore black children could distinguish between ripe and unripe strawberries, they were taken with grown-ups to pick berries. Strawberry pickers left home very early, often before sunup. Farmers transported them in trucks and horse carts to fields a few miles out of town. Pickers knelt—sometimes sat—to fill boxes, which were placed down seemingly endless rows, until we had picked enough boxes to fill a long traylike carrier with a handle running lengthwise. The filled carrier, holding several boxes, was then taken to the packing stand, where pickers were paid a few pennies a

Laura Jane Holden, "Momma," and Dorothy Emily in front of Fourth Street house

box. Smaller children picked along with adults. We worked in the hot sun all day for a little change, stopping only long enough to sit in the shade and eat lunch. Picking continued, whenever weather permitted, until strawberry season ended. It was tiresome, back-aching work to kneel, squat, or bend up and down long rows day after day. Yet, we children, who enjoyed playing in the clean, sweet-smelling fields for as long as we could after lunch, were sorry when the season was over. We missed the daily excursions under Mom's supervision.

Late spring gave way to summer, and life for many Shore children was a time of carefree days; others worked in the fields as seasonal crops ripened for harvesting. For Marie and me there were household chores to be done. Henry's jobs were mainly in the garden and yard. After lunch was over and jobs done, we usually went down Mom's unless we were being punished. In that case, we stayed wherever Momma told us to or sat in green woven rocking chairs on the front porch. When the hot sun flooded the porch, we played behind the house, in the old kitchen, on the side porch, or sometimes under the house where it was dark and cool.

When we played under the house, we crawled the length of the building, looked through the latticework which closed in the area below its front and sides, and peeked at passersby. Oh, the exploring expeditions that went on far under that house! All kinds of old, unusual things were found there. Once Marie found a two-headed doll, with a black head at one end and a white head at the other. But even the lure of hidden treasures did not ease my fear whenever we moved too far under to see light from the outside. Constantly glancing back to the light, I was frightened by the thought that something might happen to prevent our finding the way out. The others laughed and called me Scaredy Cat. At times, after crawling a few yards in, I would turn back. One hasty exit, however, did not deter me from returning the next time the others went, even though I knew I would lie awake at night shuddering with thoughts of the awesome darkness under the house. Lying in the darkened bedroom, I likened being far under the house—too far to be able to see light—to being buried in a grave.

One afternoon Mom took my cousin Mame and me to Hall's Hill, the colored cemetery. It was always a treat to accompany Mom on long walks in the country. She told such fascinating stories as we hiked. As we skipped along, Mame asked Mom to tell us a story, the one about the boy who returned from the dead and took his mother to the graveyard. I protested—that story was scary.

"It's a terrible story all right," Mom agreed, "but it's supposed to learn you a lesson. See, that mother never done nothin' to make her son behave hisself. Just let him do anyways he want to. Growed up to be a real mean man, forever acussing and fighting and bothering people. Well, one night he got in a bad fight, and a man cut him to death. Cut his throat from ear to ear! His poor old mother cried and grieved and pined for him for a long, long time. One night, they say, she cried herself to sleep. Way in the night something waked her up. She looks up and there's her son standing by her bed. All bloodied up he is, with head thrown back and throat cut wide open. She calls his name, but he won't say a word. Just keeps staring and beck'ning for her to go with him.

"'Peter,' she begs him, 'say something, Honey. You want me go with you?' All he done is beckon her to come. So she gets up, and he takes her straight to the graveyard.

"'Peter,' she says, 'why you want bring me here?' And then he open his mouth and says something for the first time.

"'See this tree, Maw?' he asked her, and she nod her head. 'This here's a big, tall tree,' he tells her. 'Ain't no way I can bend or break this tree, can I?'

"'No, Son,' she answer.

"Pointing to a lil puny thing, he says, 'Now, lookit this tree. I can bend this one, can't I?' The mother nods, watching him grab the lil tree and break it in half. Then holding the tree in both hands, he turn to his mother. 'Maw,' he says, 'if you done me like I done this lil tree and bent me when I was a boy, I wouldn't be in hell tonight. Why didn't you bend me, Maw?' he cried. 'Why'd you send me to hell? It's all your fault! You ought be right here with me!'

"Then he starts hollering and his mother starts crying. He raised the tree high in the air and come down right on his poor mother's head and busted her brains out right there in the grave-yard. And that's the story," Mom concluded with a deep sigh.

"Brr-rr," I grimaced, "that's sure one creepy story. Mom, nothing like that didn't really happen, did it?"

"Ah hopes not, Sugar. But it's some awful things happens in this world. My mom told me that story. Her mom told it to her. Said it happen right out in this very same graveyard," Mom said pensively. "Could be it's just a story. Never can tell though. Just might happen that way. We can stop talking about graveyards, Children. We're here now."

The clay bank crumbled beneath our feet as we climbed up the spongy uneven slope to the graveyard. Here and there a few tombstones were the only marks of distinction between the grave-yard and the rest of the unkempt woods and the nearby junkyard. Total silence was shattered now and then by the shrill call of a bird or the eerie swish of wind through the pines. We stayed close be-hind Mom, treading uneasily on the deep carpet of brown pine needles covering long depressions and crusty holes.

"Lemme see," Mom said to herself. "This here's old man Drummon's lot and over there's the Webbs'—onliest one all chained off like that, with fancy tombstones and all. Yonder's the Waters', and Clarence's just lil bit pass their'n. Com'on, chil-dren."

Carefully, we picked our way through the brambles, past sunken graves until Mom stopped abruptly. Mame and I saw nothing, not even a depression in the ground. But Mom said, "Here 'tis, children." For a long time she stood leaning against the rake handle, staring at one spot. We still couldn't see how she knew that that unmarked spot was the grave of her long-dead hus-band.

"Poor Clarence," she murmured over and over, shaking her head. "Poor, poor Clarence."

Then, as if suddenly realizing she was not alone, she glanced at us, pulled on big cotton work gloves, and told us how we could help clear off our grandfather's grave. We worked steadily until the lot no longer resembled a briar patch floored with layers of brown pine needles. Each time we unearthed a sunken white-washed rock, I feared the next object the rake struck might be part of a skeleton, half-exposed in its last resting place by the junkyard. But, although bleached bones reportedly had been seen protruding from the clay bank, we unearthed only rocks, which we used to mark the grave of Clarence Dickerson, Mom's husband and our grandfather, who died in a train accident before Mame and I were born.

What a relief it was to gather up the tools, fill the tow bag with dried pine needles to be used to smooth the surface of flat irons, and make our way out of the graveyard. With every trembling step, I feared what would happen if the spongy earth beneath us gave away. What awful thing would our feet touch? Bones? Worms? A grinning skull? Fat black bugs? What horror in that wilderness of a graveyard lay waiting to rise up before us? During the long walk home, Mame and I were solemn. Mom tried to take our minds off the cemetery by telling tales about the families living in houses we passed along the way. At Sixth and Bank, Mom put some pine needles in a paper bag for Momma and told me to tell her she might see her later.

When I reached home, Momma was sitting down ironing—she was pregnant again and standing bothered her. Several dresses, still warm from the iron, hung behind the door. A half dozen expertly ironed men's shirts lay in neat rows on the kitchen table. Balls of sprinkled clothes were piled in the basket. She looked up wearily and asked, "See Marie and Emily out there?"

"Yes'm, they on the front porch. Mom said she hopes you feeling better, and she might come down after supper. You want me do something?"

"Think you can peel some white potatoes without peeling them all away?"

"Yes'm. How many you want me to peel?"

"I'll tell you when to stop. Peel a big onion with them, Ginny. How was your walk?"

"The walk—it was all right."

"What's matter then?"

"Nothing, I don't guess. Maybe it's because we went to Hall's Hill. That graveyard's bad looking. Don't look nothing like ones around here."

"These graveyards are white, Ginny. They got enough money to pay somebody to keep them looking pretty all the time. Ain't like out to Hall's Hill," she said matter-of-factly.

"But why'd colored people have to be buried way out there by the junkyard, Momma? It's awful bad in that graveyard. Hope I'm not going be buried in no graveyard like that."

"Honey, you won't know no difference, not when you're dead," Momma said gently, "and I don't think you ought be worrying about being buried nowheres. If God's willing, be a long time 'fore you need be thinking about dying. Now go peel them potatoes so's I can get them on the stove."

After supper, Momma—weary from hours of ironing—settled down in the dining room rocker. Once we children finished cleaning dishes, we dashed outside to play just as Mom arrived. She visited briefly with Momma, who was too tired to be much company, then reappeared in the yard just as Poppa came through the gate, clearing his throat as usual. Mom stopped him.

"Snow," she said, "you seen them buildings they moved in the school yard?"

"What buildings, Miss Dell? First I heard a word."

"They great long old buildings with all the windows to one side," Mom chimed in. "It's two of them. Just moved the other one yesterday. Nothing but old portables from the white school 'cause they ain't goin' use 'em no more."

"So that's all they going do, huh? If that don't beat all!" Poppa exclaimed. "Last thing they said was that—since they can't build schools for both white 'n colored same time—just soon's they get finish with the white school, they plan to do something about our'n. And that's what they doing? Somebody ought go see Mr. Andrew about this. Even if I got to go by myself."

"Snow, Honey, don't get yourself all riled up about this," Mom urged. "Right now, you got all you can handle. Your father sick and Jane feelin' more tired and poorly. Don't let that school add to your worry. Them buildings a whole lot better'n what's already there. You know well's me them white folks ain't about to give us much of nothing they got use for, let alone no new school. But them buildings better'n nothing. Lord knows it's time they done something."

"I know what you're saying, Miss Dell. Course, I haven't seen them portables or nothing, but it just don't set right with me, for us to get no more'n what they're through with. And if we keep on being satisfied with their hand-me-downs just 'cause they're some better'n what we got, Lord knows we'll never get nothing!" he declared bitterly, banging his fist on the gate post.

"You probably right, Son," Mom agreed. "Cert'ny can't be noways right for these children not have no better schoolhouse then when Ah was a child. Here we payin' taxes same's them, and what we gettin' for our money? If it's somethin' Ah can do, Ah'm ready'n able. Ain't never been afraid to stand up to no ornery crackers. You know that, Snow!"

"Sure do, Miss Dell," he replied. "Let's wait'n see what they got to say about what they doing. Then we can figure out our next move."

Poppa checked on Momma and left to walk out with Mom before stopping to look in on Grandpop.

Momma said she spent the rest of the evening resting up in the dining room. Eventually, she hoisted her body from the rocking chair and walked slowly to the kitchen to take her medicine before climbing the stairs. She fell immediately to sleep, but soon was awakened by a child's cries.

"Who's that crying?" she called.

"It's me, Momma."

"Ginny, you sick or something?"

"No'm. I'm scared. Something's looking in our door."

"Ain't nothing in that door, Ginny. You know I would see if anything's there and I'm laying here looking right in there," Momma said, trying to convince me.

"But I seen it standing there, Momma. I'm scared. Can't I come in there with you?"

"All right, com' on in here."

"I'm scared to come by myself," I cried, too afraid even to peek out from the quilt over my head.

Grunting as she got out of bed, Momma came to the door.

"Com'on outen there, Ginny," she said. "Ain't nothing in this door but me. Uncover your head and com'on."

But all I could do was beg her to come get me.

"If you can't come with me standing right in the door with this lamp, I'm going get back in bed. I do, and you can cry your head off. I'm not getting up no more—don't feel like no foolishness!"

"I-I'm too s-s-scared, Momma. P-p-please c-come over here," I pleaded.

She had just left the doorway when Poppa returned and found her sitting on the side of the bed.

"What's matter, Hon, feeling bad?" he asked anxiously.

"Not no worse'n usual—Ginny, she got me up. Must been having a nightmare. Woke me up hollering and crying. Says she seen something standing in the door—got me feeling all nervous. Even after I got outen bed and went to the door, she wouldn't walk from the bed to the door. So I let her stay there!"

Henry and Marie, undisturbed by the outburst, slept soundly, but I was huddled far down in the bed when my father came into our room and whispered, "Ginny, Poppa's in here with you now. Take the coverin' offen your head."

"I'm 'fraid, Poppa," I whimpered.

"Ain't nothing to be scared of, Honey," he said. "You think Poppa'd let something happen to you and I'm standing right here? Let's get this coverin' offen your head so you can get some air."

He turned back the quilt from my face, but I was afraid to open my eyes. When he did persuade me to look at him, I turned away from the door. Nothing he said could convince me to look in the doorway and see nothing was there. For a long time he sat on the side of the bed trying to calm my fears. Finally, I told him if he went to bed, I would try not to be "too afraid."

I promised I'd try, but before he reached the doorway, I had pulled the quilt back over my head. Even efforts to focus my thoughts on the thrill of now being in the eighth grade did nothing to lessen my fear of what I believed to be lurking in that shadowy doorway.

8 · Poppa's Tears

My first death,
blurred through Poppa's tears . . . and mine
chased me, the child, outdoors . . .
to our backyard;
as spasms spattered vomit on fall ground
brown leaves defined the antonym of life.

In the 1930s on the Shore, high school started in the eighth grade and, for white students, went through the eleventh. However, most black students in Pocomoke City, only attended school through ninth grade. Families that could afford the room and board—and that could afford not to have another person work to support the family—sent their children to Snow Hill, the county seat, to finish tenth and eleventh grades at Snow Hill Colored High School. Even as a small child playing pretend school in the house on Bank Street I knew that I would "graduate" after the ninth grade and start to work. But with that prospect only two years away now, the idea of the favorite thing in my life coming to an end began to worry me.

The first day of high school was even more exciting than usual. In most cases, instead of new clothes to show off, there were carefully mended hand-me-downs worn by pouting children whose poor mothers despaired of explaining that they had no money to buy new clothes. However, hand-me-downs did not dull our excitement on that first day. New students came from nearby areas such as Unionville and St. James, where there were no high schools. Many children who lived on opposite sides of town had not seen each other since the close of school in May. We made the usual comments and speculations about the teachers, especially new ones. But what interested us new high schoolers, even more than the new principal, was the long portable building—really two buildings connected into one—that was our "new" school. The portable was better than the old school, but even the white-wash job did not change it into anything more than it was. Nevertheless, that was more than black students in Pocomoke ever had before.

Most students from rural areas had come from one or two-room schools. The old square school, the portable unit, and the little manual training building represented a big change. Few, if any, thought about the big new brick school on Market Street, with its beautifully landscaped grounds that whites felt belonged to them as naturally as they felt blacks were destined to be excluded from it. To them and their parents, the idea that black children should have—not to mention share—facilities even remotely similar to theirs was unthinkable. Town officials had planned a model school just as they were in the process of planning a "public" library—for whites only.

After the first weeks of school, our household settled down to the usual daily routine. It was a good thing, too, because that September proved to be a time of crises for our whole family. Momma kept getting more and more tired daily. She rocked for hours in the dining room every evening.

I only added to her strain. My recurring nightmares, often disturbing my parents' sleep, caused serious problems. I remember holding out my hands, fingers spread apart, and telling them that worms had been crawling between the fingers, that I could feel them squirming and see them disappearing under my pillow. One morning, following a restless night, I tried to describe the crawling sensation to my mother as I held out my hands for her to see. She gasped in horror: the skin between the fingers was parched and peeling! She was still upset when Poppa came home for lunch. That evening we went to the doctor. Following the examination, he asked what had happened to upset me. When Poppa traced the trouble to the trip to the cemetery, the doctor shook his head and ordered, "Don't let her go again. She's high strung enough as it is!"

He gave them some salve to rub on my fingers before bedtime and prescribed some pills. A few nights later I awoke with the feeling that I had heard someone else screaming and crying for help. I lay back down, wondering what I must have been dreaming. Then I heard my father on the stairs and called him.

"Go back to sleep, Honey. You just dreaming, that's all," he said, pulling the door almost closed.

Next morning, when he came to get us up, he sounded strange.

"You children get your clothes on and be quiet so you won't wake Emily up and worry your mother. You know she ain't feeling good. Got something to show you when you're all dressed."

"Bet I know," I mumbled, slipping on a dress. Momma lay in bed with her arm around a small white bundle. She looked sick, but she managed a wan smile and whispered, "You all got a lil brother. Want see him?" For several minutes we stood at the foot of the bed. No one said anything. Then I edged around to Momma's side. Henry and Marie followed. She turned back the top of the soft white blanket, revealing a puffy red face. The baby's eyes were tightly closed, and Momma stroked his slick black hair with one finger.

"Wha'cha think of your new brother?" Poppa asked. "That's lil Buddy."

When I said, "He don't look like nobody here," Momma raised herself up to look down on him. "Give him time to get his eyes open. Maybe you'll like him better then, Ginny."

"I like him all right," I replied indifferently.

"Me, too," Henry spoke up. Marie looked from the baby to Momma and said nothing.

Shortly after Buddy was born, Grandpop ventured outdoors—first time since his setback. From his account of that venture, we learned that he put on his heavy old coat over a long-sleeved undershirt, flannel shirt, and bib-topped overalls. Then he went down a step at a time until his feet rested on the ground. The earth felt good beneath his feet, but his head was light. So he eased down on the step. There he stayed until he decided he could make it to the outhouse.

Breathing heavily, he leaned on his cane and slowly made his way to the toilet, where he sank onto the seat until he could find strength to raise himself up and get his pants down. Outside again, he crept over and leaned against our back fence. He peered at what was left of the garden and fussed at the mean old rooster strutting about the chicken yard until he saw Emily running toward him.

"Hey Grandpop!" she called.

"How do, Baby."

"We got a new baby!" Emily announced.

"Aye-uh."

"You want see him?"

"Baby," he wheezed, "Ah ain't got that youngun to study 'bout!"

Perhaps he felt the new baby was taking away attention he needed. Anyway, without another word he turned and shuffled back to his open kitchen door. Inside, flies crawled around the half-filled bowl of lumpy oatmeal he hadn't been able to finish. He slammed the door behind him and almost fell into his rocking chair. And there he sat wheezing and staring at nothing. But he said he was thankful that he had made it to the outhouse and back so no one would have to "carry out" after him. A few days later Momma was in the kitchen nursing the baby while Emily played outside on the steps. It was one of those unmatchable end-of-summer/early-fall days, bright with sunshine and with just the right zip in the air. Momma heard voices outside and thought Emily was talking with her imaginary playmates, but she soon realized that voice belonged to Grandpop.

"Mr. Caleb!" she exclaimed. "What are you doing out? How you feeling?"

"Just tolerable, Daughter," he replied, backing up to the top step. "How you?"

"I'm doing pretty good. Feel like coming in? Be more comfortable then setting on them steps—want you to see the baby."

"Got catch my breath first, Daughter."

"Well, well! Look who's out avisiting—Caleb Holden! How you feeling?" Miss Anne called from behind her screen door. "Thought that sound like you."

"Guess I better not complain none, Anne," he said. "Ah seen better and Ah seen worser, Ah reckon."

"Mr. Caleb," Momma called from the kitchen, "feel like coming in now?"

"See if Ah can make it, Daughter," he answered, half rising and holding onto the step.

As soon as Grandpop had settled down inside, Momma held the baby so he could see his new grandson. As he squinted down at the infant, she said the stern expression of his face, lined and gray stubbled, softened, and his cloudy eyes sparkled. He did not move to touch Buddy, just nodded his head and smiled.

"He's a fine looking youngun, Daughter," he said. "Mighty fine."

"I'm glad you like him, Mr. Caleb. We thankful he com'ere all right. Got some healthy lungs on him. You ought hear him when he's hungry," she said joking as she laid the baby in his crib.

For several days following that visit, Grandpop appeared to be improving. His asthma attacks were less frequent, and when he did have one, it was less severe. By taking his time and pausing to rest every few yards, he was able to walk the length of his block. He was resting on his cane at Gray and Bank Streets one day when a schoolmate and I passed. The moment he saw me he smiled, and I stopped to ask how he was feeling.

"Ah'm tolerable, Daughter," he replied. "Coming home from school, eh?"

"Yessir. Bye," I called back.

When I caught up, Lillie gave me a hateful look and asked, "What's that old white man doing talking to you and calling you 'daughter'?"

"That ain't no old white man, Lillie," I protested. "That's my grandfather."

"Him? Humph!" Lillie grunted. "Sure don't look like no colored man to me!"

"But he's my grandfather, Lillie!" I told her and waited for her to say something. Instead, we reached my house before either one of us said anything. When we parted, instead of the usual tag game, there were strained "see yas." And I was confused because that was the first time I had heard anyone refer to Grandpop as "not looking colored"—the first time I was made to face a different kind of prejudice.

When I rushed into the kitchen, Momma looked up from her patching and immediately sensed something was wrong.

"Hey! Now, what's ruffled your feathers, Child?" she asked. After relating the incident, I said, "She's got no business talking like that about my grandfather!"

"Well, Ginny, Lillie didn't know. You can't hold that against her. I'm sure she didn't mean no harm; so you just try'n forget it, hear? After all, she lives way out Quinntown. Ever'body out in the country don't know Mr. Caleb," she explained.

"Yes'm," I replied. But deep down inside I knew I never would forget Lillie's reaction and the way it made me feel.

The world seemed to change overnight from brilliant sunshine and blue skies to gray clouds dribbling on brown leaves blown by bone-chilling winds. As the days grew short and cold, Grandpop grew weaker and less sure of himself. On one damp, cold day after Poppa had cautioned him to stay inside, he crept back to the outhouse. When finally he made it back to the kitchen, he said he couldn't get warm. The fire, left unattended, had died down, and he wasn't able to get it going again. Exhausted, he slumped into the overstuffed chair by the stove. Even the dregs of lukewarm coffee didn't help. Huddled in the old chair, he waited for his son. And so Poppa found him, when he came home for lunch, shivering by the cold stove.

It was impossible to say, the doctor warned, what to expect. Grandpop was extremely weak and dangerously near pneumonia. One thing was certain: he must not be left alone. My parents found a young man named Carl to look after him in the daytime; Poppa stayed with him nights. The arrangement worked fairly well, and for a while it seemed as if Grandpop would again lick his infirmities. But another severe cold weakened his frail body. For days, he coughed uncontrollably. Then one night as my father dozed by the sickbed Grandpop sat up abruptly:

"Snow," he said, "tell Nannie to sit down. Ain't no need her standing in the door that-a-way!"

Poppa was startled but tried to sound calm. "Pop, you know it's nobody in here but me and you."

"Well!" exclaimed Grandpop. "Never thought Ah'd live to see the day you'd dispute me, Boy! Guess Ah don't know what Ah see with my own two eyes. All you got do is look and see for yourself."

Reacting to Poppa's request to check his temperature, Grandpop ranted, "Ah do nothing of the kind! Think Ah got a fever just 'cause Ah says what Ah see? Go home! Ah ain't needing nobody 'cept Nannie nohow."

After that outburst, Poppa told him he wouldn't bother him, that he wanted to stay in case Grandpop needed something. But it was a rough night.

By morning he was so much worse that Dr. Hull stayed twice as long as usual, and for the next several days and nights Poppa hardly left Grandpop. He took care of him as one would care for a baby. Then, one bright Sunday morning, Poppa was surprised to see that Grandpop seemed to be himself again. He got up to relieve himself, washed up by himself, and ate a good breakfast, after which he asked:

"Snow, what you doing over heah in the daytime, Son?"

"I been staying with you, Pop. You been real sick. Thank the Lord, looks likes you going be all right now."

"Poor Snow," he lamented. "Ah wouldn't for the world cause you all this trouble, not with all you got on you a' ready. How Jane 'n baby? And Ginny, she still upset?"

"They all doing all right, Pop. So don't be worrying about nothing. Just getcha strength back and get better. We all going be glad about that."

"Do the best Ah can, Son," he promised. "Now, why don't you go 'long home a spell? Ah'm doing all right."

"If you sure you going be all right, I'll see if Carl can stay with you while I put in some time down the garage. Been missing lots of days. Sure you going be all right now, Pop?"

"Way Ah'm feeling right now, Son, 'tain't no need of paying that boy to stay with me. You got enough on you 'thout that."

"Now, I'm not about to leave you by yourself, Pop. If I go, you got promise me you won't get outen bed to I get back."

"All right, Son, Ah'm going do like you say," he promised.

There was no making up of all the time lost from work. Even before Grandpop's relapse, there had been another cut in pay, and to make matters worse, Poppa had to put in even more extra time on Sundays. Things had reached the point where it was impossible to pay all the bills—only a few dollars a week for house payments, Grandpop's rent and doctor's bills, the new baby, groceries, clothes—more and more bills and less and less pay. For the first time he could remember, Poppa later admitted, he really felt discouraged; there seemed to be no way out. He couldn't talk with Momma about the way things were; she might try to take back the washings, and she needed time to gain her strength. He had to believe that God would see him through; otherwise, he didn't see how they could make it, especially since Grandpop's sudden "recovery" had lasted but a few hours. He grew steadily worse and needed constant attention.

After a distressing night, Poppa said he got up from the lumpy, overstuffed chair and stretched, thinking he must have dozed off near daybreak. Throughout the night Grandpop had been raving one moment and moaning miserably the next. Reluctant to leave him after such a night, Poppa prepared to get him cleaned up for the day. The aroma of coffee perking seemed to arouse him. Although he did not speak, Grandpop's eyes followed Poppa's every move. His response to Poppa's asking how he was feeling was that he didn't "rightly know—just bad all over."

His iron gray hair bristled like a crew cut. Gray stubble covered his sallow face. Dark furrows above thick eyebrows lined his forehead. His eyes, vague and cloudy, were fixed upon the heavy dark quilt that covered his bed. Although he had not smiled for weeks, his once-stubborn mouth gaped as he struggled to breathe, so that he appeared to be grinning. Overall, he was but a ghost of the man he used to be.

Sometime around noon Momma sent me to check on Grandpop and take him a bowl of soup. I pushed the door open slowly. There was no sound in the room. Hoping that Carl was in the front room, I called him. No answer. So I turned to my grandfather and called him softly at first and then louder, "Grandpop, how you feel?"

Sprawled on the bed, with most of the covers sagging to the floor, he was neither wheezing nor snoring, but his mouth was open. I set the soup on the stove; again I called. No response. Over and over I shook his shoulder, trying to wake him. Once I thought I heard him grunt, but that was all. Frightened, I ran home and had just begun to tell Momma what had happened when Henry burst into the kitchen.

"Momma," he panted, "Carl says—Carl, he said something's wrong with Grandpop. Said he went home a minute, and when he got back . . ."

"What!" cried Momma.

"Where's Carl now?"

"Gone after Poppa," Henry said.

Poppa said he knew the moment he reached his father's house. Yet, he shook him and called him over and over as if expecting an answer. Poppa fixed the pillow so that his father's head looked more comfortable and straightened the blankets, all the while shaking and gently calling him. Dr. Hull came and left in a few minutes, and Poppa sent for old Gene Phillips to do what must be done. Then, for the first time since entering the room, he looked about him at the curious people, who had done nothing to cheer up his father during his long illness, crowded into the little room. Without a word, he left the house. Not until he walked into his own kitchen and met the look in Momma's eyes did he cry for his father. He crossed the room, fighting to control himself.

"Poor Pop," he blurted, voice breaking, "I done all I could for him. Stayed there all them days and nights so he wouldn't be by hisself. Paid Carl to stay with him. And he left him there to die all by hisself—all by hisself."

He cupped his hands over his face. Tears trickled through his grease-stained fingers. Momma, helpless and saddened, dropped her head to the table and sobbed. We children stood in awe, looking from father to mother. Suddenly I ran from the kitchen; I leaned against the old kitchen door. Bewildered, I struggled with a strange surge inside me. I clutched the door with both hands when the first spasm shook my body. Then the vomit came in gushes until nothing came up but the sound of retching, leaving me drained and sick as never before. Through the death of my father's father, I suffered my first death.

They laid him out in the front room of the little house. Everything was prim, scrubbed clean; everything was in its place as it never had been while he was alive. On the gray felt-covered casket was a metal plate engraved with the words REST IN PEACE. And Grandpop lay in the casket's cold silky whiteness. His hair, that once had curled and waved so handsomely, was crew-cut straight. His skin had a waxen pallor, but the deep lines of his forehead looked the same, as did the thick moustache that drooped over the corners of his sullen mouth. After the first night came and went, Poppa, realizing that his father would never again be alone, locked up the house and went home to bed.

While Poppa was out taking care of business, Momma and Mom sat talking about Grandpop and the funeral arrangements. We children played quietly inside. As Mom was leaving, she said, "Think Ah'll go look at poor Caleb. Want go with me, Jane—but you ain't been out yet though . . ."

"No ma'am," Momma replied. "I'd rather not look at him anyhow, not less'n I just can't help it."

"Ginny? Marie? You all want go see your grandpop with me?" Mom asked.

After a few moments' hesitation, I decided to go, but Marie continued to play with her doll. Had I been wise, I would have done the same, but I probably thought it was all right to go, since Momma didn't object.

When Mom opened the door, the hush engulfed us. We walked through the kitchen to the front room, I close behind her. Mom stopped beside the casket and stood gazing down on Grandpop. I moved closer to her, uncertain of what to expect since never before had I been as close to the dead as at that moment. The room held an air of strangeness, and a fear such as I had not known before gripped me. It was unlike that brought on by a nightmare or what I felt when a dog got after me or when I saw something frightening like a snake. An overwhelmingly chilling sensation seemed to dictate speaking in whispers in that shrouded room.

Mom stood shaking her head, saying, "Poor Caleb, poor old Caleb," as she smoothed her hand over Grandpop's forehead. Impulsively, I reached out and touched his brow but quickly snatched my hand away. What I felt sent shivers through me. The wrinkles in Grandpop's forehead felt like the ridges of a cold washboard. The experience imprinted its memory on me for a lifetime. As we closed the door behind us, another memory surfaced: I thought of the afternoon Mame and I went to Hall's Hill with Mom and helped her clean off the grave of my other grandfather in that dismal cemetery, where they soon would bury Grandpop.

9 · *Wayne's Tales*

*So many times
the dream was cursed—
could it survive the dreaming?*

For our people, the Depression only intensified deprivation that was widely considered to be a normal way of life. Nevertheless, in spite of circumstances, we continued to plod onward. And within our everyday experiences dwelt segments of a people's history in Maryland, especially on the Shore, with its many customs and prejudices.

On Saturday nights we took baths in the kitchen because it was warm in there in winter and not quite as sweltering as other parts of the house in summer. Winter or summer, until we ourselves were grown enough to do so, no one was about to lug a washtub and hot water upstairs for our baths, then bring it down afterward. So every Saturday night after we finished with supper dishes, Marie and I arranged to take baths near the rear end of the kitchen stove. We placed three or four chairs so that their high backs fenced in a small area; over the chair backs, we draped an old lounge cover, along with large pieces of clothing, for privacy. On a stool between us, Momma placed a little galvanized tub partly filled with hot water. Seated on opposite sides of the tub, we soaped washrags and scrubbed ourselves, smoothing on sweet-smelling Palmolive suds. Such was the weekly "bath-all-over" routine for the cold season. In warm weather we bathed separately in big washtubs, usually in the afternoon. When we could do so without fussing, each washed the other's back. Generally, we did a quiet, thorough job because we knew if Momma intervened, more than backs would get scrubbed until it hurt.

Then one particular Saturday night we bathed together for the last time. We soaped washrags, as usual, and scrubbed busily while our parents talked, Poppa resting his stocking feet on the open oven door and Momma rocking contentedly near the front end of the stove. Our weekly routine ended abruptly when I was twelve. Marie suddenly noticed my slight signs of puberty and questioned me loudly within earshot of our father. Years passed before I could accept as innocent curiosity what, on that Saturday night with Poppa sitting close by, was the most embarrassing moment of my young life. Had I given any thought to that possibility, the incident might have been avoided. An earlier experience should have alerted me to the dangers involved in sharing grown-up secrets with Marie.

That realization came the day I first heard, from older classmates, their version of where babies come from—complete, unabridged, with all the terribly fascinating details. I could hardly wait to get home and tell it all to Marie. As we sat on the front steps, Marie listened, her big eyes widening with surprise. She didn't say a word until I finished talking. Then she looked straight at me and said, "I don't believe that! Bet they made it all up."

"No, Marie, it's the truth," I assured her. "Even Kate says it's what happens."

"I don't care who says so. Bet they telling a story," Marie snapped before she jumped up and ran into the house as if pursued by demons.

I was confused by Marie's reaction, but I could understand why she did not believe it: all along, the "stork tale" had been gospel for us. Perhaps the girls' story was harder to believe because they made everything about it sound nasty. Nevertheless, it was the most fascinating thing I'd ever heard. Sex perplexed and frightened me. I was even afraid to ask my trusted grandmother about it. Later that afternoon my confusion deepened. It was obvious that something was wrong—Momma's tone of voice revealed that. Puzzled, I wandered out to the porch where Marie pretended to be absorbed in dressing a pock-marked doll she had left out in the rain. Actually, she was waiting for me.

"Ginny," she said flaunting a see-what-you-get look, "Momma told me to tell you to talk about what you know about and leave what you don't know about alone!"

I swallowed hard but said nothing. How could Marie do that? How could she go tell Momma the secret things I told her? For a long time I sat clutching the arms of the chair. I didn't rock, just sat and thought. What worried me even more than Marie's tattling was my mother's sending her message through Marie instead of talking directly with me. I was miserable and almost wished she had beaten me rather than send Marie to tell me.

Shortly after the bathing incident our parents began making definite plans to put in running water. At the mere mention of that marvelous convenience, Momma paused at whatever she happened to be doing, shook her head, and smiled. What a difference it would make in our lives. Nevertheless, Poppa knew they could afford only one fixture at a time; they decided what was needed most was an indoor toilet. So until the toilet was paid for, there would be no sink in the kitchen, no relief from the struggle on freezing cold mornings with the balky frozen pump, no lightening of Momma's housework. Therefore, we would continue to lug bucketfuls of water from the pump outside to fill pots on the stove until there was enough for family washing and the laundry Momma took in, as well as for cooking, bathing, cleaning, dishwashing—everything. Until they were able to afford a kitchen sink, the old pump would have to do, but at last we would have an indoor toilet.

The end of the hall outside the front bedroom was partitioned off for the new addition. The toilet turned out to be a squat, dark, ugly, unlidded, wooden-seated flusher with a tall galvanized water tank against the wall. Whenever the user rose from the seat, it literally popped up beneath him, often splashing him with water. While flushing, the toilet made an embarrassing, metal-grunting, water-swooshing racket that could be heard throughout the house, even outdoors at times.

Momma hated the appearance of that flusher. She swore that if she couldn't have a nice white enamel commode with a lid covering it, she'd almost rather have the outhouse. It bothered her to think of how long she had waited for that one convenience only to get such an unsightly toilet. But Poppa picked it out to save money. He had to do that, and she knew it. Still no matter how dissatisfied she was, she admitted that it was a relief to be rid of the slop bucket from our room. It was good to be free from walking out back on bitter cold, pitch-black nights with only a flashlight to find the way to the outhouse. No longer would she be worried by one child's fussing because he had to go out and sit with another on an urgent night call. It would not be soon, she knew, but Poppa had made her a promise: one day she would have a real bathroom with gleaming white fixtures, not just a partitioned end of the hall containing an ugly flusher and a stand holding an old-fashioned washbowl-and-pitcher set. As things were, it was amazing that he managed to keep up payments on everything as well as he did. We all accepted the fact that we would have to keep clean and make do with the pump, just as we had done all our lives. We had the toilet—something very few blacks in Pocomoke had at that time. And we all knew Poppa was doing his best.

✦

The excitement of high school—new people, a different building, a busier schedule—soon dulled. Things seemed much the same as they had been in grade school; at least, that's the way students who had expected a great difference felt. There were differences, such as taking home economics or manual training twice a week, but nothing dramatic. Glancing out at squealing, frolicking elementary schoolchildren, we secretly missed the old recess periods. Study periods replaced recess fun.

After the first few weeks, new students from rural areas with such vivid designations as "over-the-river" and "down-the-neck" were as much at home as if everyone had been classmates since first grade. We looked out for each other, missed each other during prolonged absences, visited each other, played together, and got crushes on each other. Everyone knew who was stuck on whom. Boys bragged about their sexual exploits; girls listened and were fascinated. Some feigned embarrassment, and others actually were embarrassed with ample cause. Older girls tried to impress one another with their knowledge of the facts of life. Frequently one would shush another, pointing toward me, whom they considered to be too young for their talks. One day when this happened, Kate objected, "You all ought stop trying to keep Ginny from knowing what's what. It's time you stop treating her like she's a baby. Bet when you was her age, you knew just much as you know right now. Anyway, 'tain't no need of shutting up ever'time like she's not never going know nothing. Might's well tell her now."

After that, they talked more freely and explained things they knew I didn't understand. Many choice discussions went on during study periods, as everyone pretended to be working and quickly shifted to difficult assignments whenever the teacher came within earshot. Usually the conversations centered around personal experiences, especially when the girls talked among themselves. What excited us most, though, was any discussion including boys, especially Wayne Waters. Wayne was a handsome boy who already sported a mustache and whose favorite topic was sex. According to him, most of his exploits were with older girls, women even. Kate observed that that part of Wayne's tales was probably true, since any schoolgirl would be a fool to mess around with him, knowing he'd be sure to broadcast it all over town. Nevertheless, the students liked to hear Wayne tell tales that probably would have shocked many parents.

One of Wayne's favorite tales, not about himself for a change, was about Big Jim Buck and a new woman in town. Her name was Lovy. Big Jim—a tall, dark, and handsome lover man—claimed he could get any woman in town he wanted. And few who knew him were likely to disagree. Lovy was an ordinary looking, light-skinned woman with long black hair and an hourglass figure. She was pleasant, kindhearted, talkative, and tongue-tied. The story, as Wayne told it, was that Big Jim, who was used to being chased by women, had a thing for Lovy and was after her like bees swarming around honey. And in the telling of an incident involving those two, Wayne left few details for the imagination.

One Saturday night, Big Jim called on Lovy at the house where she worked and lived. Lovy's "people" were out of town for the weekend, so she had the house all to herself. Instead of washing up in a tin basin in her room, that night Lovy filled the tub and laved herself in the luxury of her first tub bath since she'd been working there. After drying herself, she dusted her glowing body with her madam's best powder and splashed on matching cologne. When Big Jim knocked on the door, Lovy met him in a red satin embroidered wrapper. Big Jim flourished a bottle; for a while they sat talking and drinking. Soon Lovy was sitting on his lap.

"Girl," said Big Jim, "you sure smellin' some good tonight. What's that smell so go-oo-od? Make me just want kiss you all over, and that ain't no lie!"

"O-oh, Big Jim," purred Lovy.

"I be damned if 'taint the truth," he swore. "How about we stop wastin' time—when your folks comin' back, Sugar?"

"Not t-t-to Sunday night," replied Lovy with undisguised relief.

"So, what we sittin' down here for? What we waitin' for when— where your room, girl?"

"S-s-sin th-th-the attic," Lovy blurted, jumping up from his lap and drawing the wrapper around her. She bolted the front door and cut off the lights. When she turned around, Big Jim was standing there with outstretched arms, and Lovy walked into them, snuggling against the steel of his body.

"Guess they got some back steps up to that damn closet you sleep in," he whispered into her ear, but Lovy took his hand and led him up the wide carpeted front stairs, ignoring the narrow, winding bare steps leading up from the kitchen. They put the bottle and glasses on her old bureau and forgot them. Big Jim kissed her hard and long as they lay on the narrow cot. He kissed her until she gasped for air. When he freed her lips, he teased her breasts until she cried and moaned for him. He stroked her thighs until his hands met to fuse their passions. For Lovy, the world was but the two of them, straining into each other until they were left helpless, spent, and at peace. When she opened her eyes, she smiled to herself. She could not remember ever before having been com- forted by the sound of snoring, but at that moment everything about Big Jim gave her a good feeling. She tried to shift her body without wak- ing him, but the snoring stopped and his arm tightened around her. Looking up, she saw that he was watching her.

"Smatter, Sugar?" he asked.

"Nuttin . . . tain't nuttin madder, Big Jim," whispered Lovy.

"Want some more?" he grinned, fondling her and kissing her forehead.

"G-g-g-guess we bedder not," Lovy said slowly.

"Why? What you scared of, Baby? Com'on," he whispered, smoothing his face against her breast and caressing her.

"N-no, Big Jim," she said, stiffening in his arms.

Big Jim propped himself on one elbow and frowned. He blew a long sigh before speaking in a strained, puzzled tone, "Tell me what's matter, Sugar, somethin' I done?"

"No, Big Jim," cried Lovy, *"d-d-don't t-think nut'tin' l-l-like that."*

"Well, that's onliest thing I can think 'less you tells me what's wrong."

"Um scairt y-y-you goin' mess me up!"

"How come you warn't carryin' on like this lil while back?"

"Y-y-you got me so 'cited, Ah-Ah f-fergot."

"All right, Baby. Don't be worryin'. We ain't goin' do nothing you don't want," he said, reaching for her as he spoke. *"Tell you what—I'm just goin' pet'cha all nice and sweet like. Let's see, where I goin' start?"*

He kissed her breasts gently, then hungrily, pausing to ask, "That all right?"

"Es . . . 'es," Lovy panted.

Moving leisurely southward, he circled her navel with kisses then basked his face in the warmth of her belly as he stroked her thighs.

"Like that?" he asked.

"Es . . . 'es—Ooo, Big Jim."

Big Jim began to kiss her thighs, and she felt herself soaring high-higher-higher until she heard herself screaming out to him.

She heard him moan, but he didn't move, not even when everything within her let go. The only sound between them was a gasp, followed by an awful sigh. When Big Jim raised his head, he smiled sheepishly and pulled Lovy down so that her head rested in the crook of his arm. And so they slept until the church bells rang for Sunday morning service.

When Wayne told that story both boys and girls were speechless, almost as if someone had cast a spell over them. Herman was the first to speak.

"Wayne," he said, "you mean he . . . ?"

"Sure, he did. Least that's what they say," Wayne replied, matter-of-factly.

"I don't think I'd tell nobody if I done something like that," said Ray. "Besides, that ain't for me nohow. Nah!"

"Don't be so sure now, Ray," cautioned Wayne.

"You mean you . . .?" Ray began, staring at Wayne.

"Hell, no!" Wayne exclaimed. "I'm just saying can't no man say what's he going do when his love comes down on him. And that's a fact!"

"Humph," grunted Lizzie, "I don't think much of nobody who'd go out and tell anything like that."

"What's matter, Liz? Jealous?" Wayne teased.

"Not on your life, Wayne Waters!" Lizzie sneered. "And you ought just shut up because you ever' bit bad as Big Jim when it comes to mouthing off about ever'thing you do. Wouldn't be a bit surprised if you didn't make up half of what you forever bragging about anyways. So busy trying to make ever'body think you so much man!"

I did not understand much of what Wayne said about Big Jim and Lovy, and what I did understand embarrassed me. Noticing my discomfort as the others grinned, Wayne moved near me and said, "What do you think about all this, little girl? "

Blushing under his brazen stare, I mumbled, "Nothing," and moved to a seat away from the group. I opened a book and pretended to study, but all I could think of was Wayne's tale. After school, I caught up with Kate and asked her to tell me whether Wayne had said what I thought I'd heard, since I couldn't believe it.

"Is all what Wayne was saying . . . I mean, is that how people really do when . . .," I stammered.

"You mean do they do it?" Kate replied. "Sure, Ginny. I done told you it's just natural for ever' body to."

"That ain't what I'm talking about. I mean that *other* part."

"Other part? Oh, I know what'cha mean," she said with a grin. "Just don't pay no attention to ever' thing Wayne says. Most times he's just talking to hear hisself. Wants ever'body to think he's done so much. Let him keep on. I'll tell you this much though, it's a lotta different ways people can get some. Milly says it's like that old saying: 'Diff'rent strokes for diff'rent folks.' I don't know much about all that myself, and care less. So you sure don't need to, hear? Just forget about what Wayne said."

"Sure, Kate. But I just get tired of them laughing at me and saying how dumb I am."

"Don't be worring about them laughing, Ginny. Some of them laughing's wishing they didn't know so much right this minute. Besides that, they a lot older'n you anyway," Kate advised in her big sisterly way as we passed the manual training building and walked down Bank Street.

The manual training building, an old frame two-story house with one room on each floor, served as a woodworking shop for boys on the first floor and a domestic science (home economics) room upstairs for girls. There we learned the basics of cooking and home care. In sewing class each girl had to make a white apron and headband that we starched so stiff it could stand alone. We really enjoyed domestic science periods. Besides learning to prepare some foods we never had at home, we could eat whatever we cooked. Often there was enough for each girl to take home samples. Boys working with tools on the lower floor grew hungry as mouth-watering aromas drifted into the shop. Each hoped that he would not be slighted when samples were doled out.

On days when classes were not scheduled in the manual training building, some students used it as a trysting place. Several girls in our class had spent time there with boyfriends. Usually a friend served as lookout while his classmates upstairs hurriedly fumbled with sex. It was Kate who, in spite of her big-sisterly role, decided it was time for her innocent little friend to find out "what life was all about." Knowing that I liked Billy Townsend, who made no secret about his crush on me, Kate promised Billy that she would send me upstairs to meet him during study hour. While Kate pretended to be studying with me, she was informing me of the rendezvous she expected me to keep. She prodded me to ask to be excused. Although I said I was afraid to go, she told me there was no reason to be afraid. "After all," she added, "you like Billy, or I wouldn't tell you to go." Still I was afraid; at the same time, I didn't want her to be angry with me. And I did get tired of being called a baby by classmates. So I asked to be excused. However, the moment I left the room, I ran, not to Billy waiting in the manual training building, but straight to my grandmother's. Mom was seated on her high stool ironing; a big basket of sprinkled and rolled laundry waited on a chair beside her.

"Hey there, Sugar," she said. "What you doin' all out o' breath like that? You not sick is you?"

"No'm."

"Then sit down here'n tell Mom what's matter."

"I don't hardly know how to tell you, Mom," I said, looking nervously at the floor.

"Suppose you just go on and tell me, Sugar. Ain't nothin' you can't tell your Mom. Now, you know that."

I somehow got it all out, but I could not look at her. Sensing my discomfort, she put her iron aside and faced me.

"Com'ere, Ginny."

Brushing away tears, I went to her. She put her arm around my shoulders.

"Now they all going be laughing at me," I whimpered. "I get so tired, having 'em call me a baby. But I didn't want go up there like Kate said to. I was 'shamed."

"Listen to me, Ginny," Mom cautioned. "Don't waste nary another minute worryin' about what them children goin' say. And don't ever be doin' nothing just 'cause rest of 'em's doin' it. Learn one thing if you don't learn nothin' else: you got to think for yourself, Child. Long's it's somethin' you 'shamed of, you dassn't do it. You got plenty time for all them other things when you older. Right now you needs to keep your mind on school so's Jane and Snow can do for you like they plannin'! You hear me?"

"Yes'm, but what's I going tell Kate and them? They going tease me."

"Ginny," Mom replied, her voice almost stern, "you don't let what people say make no difference—not when you doin' what you b'lieve's right. Same's you didn't go up them stairs 'cause you didn't want, you got to learn how to not worry about what they thinkin' or sayin'. You understand what I'm tellin' you?"

"Yes'm. Mom, I'm glad I came over here."

"Me, too, Sugar. Just hopes you keeps right on like you doin'. Guess you know school's done been out. Better go tell your teacher where you been. Tell her somethin' happen, so you come over here, and Ah made you stay. Tell her Ah be glad to explain all about it if that's what she want," she said. "Now, run along. Tell Jane Ah'll stop by on way to choir practice."

"All right. Bye, Mom."

When I arrived back at school, the yard was deserted. I was glad because I did not want to face my classmates.

10 · "In This Free Land . . ."

Legrees nap lightly
in old grey towns.
Fierce crossed eyes stare
on dark low grounds.
Ears strain; lips ban
late wakening sounds.

At school the next morning—December 5, 1931—teachers had huddled together whispering or speaking in low tones, backs to the class. Instead of the scheduled class, we were given an extra study hour that extended well into the following period—something completely new to us. We could tell something was wrong.

"Hey, Billy," Henry called when Mr. White left the room, "you know what's going on?"

"Naw," Billy replied, "but sounds like something bad's happened."

"I don't see why they don't just tell us what's wrong and be done with it. We going find out sooner or later," interjected Bessie.

But no one told us anything. All morning we wondered—not whether something was wrong, but *what*. It was in the air, it was on the teachers' faces. Lunchtime came, and town students rushed home to tell about the strange morning at school. When I began to tell Momma about it, she just looked at me then quickly turned her attention to the biscuits she was taking from the oven. At that moment the gate swung open and I heard Poppa clear his throat.

"Children, Hon," Poppa spoke, looking at no one. He neither looked nor sounded as if he was on a lunch break. When he spoke, his voice was as strained as the lines around his mouth.

"You children, sit down and eat," he said. "Then it's something I got to tell you."

"It's something bad, ain't it, Poppa?" asked Henry.

"I said *after* you finish, Henry. I'm ready to say the blessing:
Dear Lord, make us truly thankful . . ."

I was relieved when Momma made no comment about the
food I had left on my plate. No one said a word. Poppa nervously
coughed a few times as if clearing his throat would help start the
words.

"Did you all's teachers tell you anything about what happen?"

"No, Sir, but we didn't do much the whole morning," I volunteered. "They been acting like somebody's dead or something."

"Well, what's happen's enough to upset anybody that's halfway human. You going be hearing a whole lot about it. It's awful
bad, but I'd rather tell you than have somebody else do it. They
lynched a man in Salisbury last night!" The words seemed to be almost choking him. "Lynched him right there on the courthouse
grounds."

"They did?!" we cried.

"In Salisbury, Poppa?" Henry repeated, as if Poppa must have
made a mistake. To us children, Salisbury was a "big" city—met-
ropolitan almost like Baltimore or Annapolis. A barbaric lynching
there was unimaginable. If that could happen in Salisbury . . .

"Why'd they lynch him, Poppa?" Marie asked.

"It's hard to tell, Honey. Doubt if they know theirself. They
just mean and full of prej'dis, that's all. Claim he killed the man he
work for, but Lord only knows what really happened," he added,
shaking his head.

"If he killed somebody, why didn't they lock him up? Why'd
they have to go and lynch him, Poppa?" I asked.

"Because he's colored, Honey. Just because he's colored,"
Poppa replied. "When you colored, they put you in jail all right.
Then they just soon's unlock the door so's they can drag you out
and lynch you. It's a terrible thing, but you got to know about it.
Now, you all go on back to school and keep your mouth shut
about all this. You want talk about it, wait to you come back home
here." Poppa's order and tone of voice intensified my fears. Even
as he spoke, I was desperately trying to drive from my mind
frightful scenes of broken bodies dangling from tree limbs. I had

"Maryland, My Maryland!" editorial cartoon by Edmund Duffy, *Baltimore Sun*, 1931

seen pictures in newspapers that made me feel sick, but news of lynchings seemed too far away to be really real. No more—not when the Salisbury courthouse grounds were only a few miles from home! There was no need for my father to caution me about discussing anything so horrible. Just thinking about it caused such a sickness to well up in my throat that I can compare it only to what happened to me following Grandpop's passing—my "first death."

In school, on the job, and in our homes, blacks tried to stop thinking, to stop wondering why.

Not for twenty years, years before I was even born, had a man been lynched in the state of Maryland. It did not take long for more news about the Salisbury lynching to circulate around Pocomoke. A black man by the name of Matthew Williams fell into a rage, who knows for what reason, and murdered his white employer—some said brutally. Unfortunately for him, folks were ripe for revenge. Some months prior, another black man had killed a white man—a murder that apparently went unavenged and, in the minds of white people on the Shore, lingered in the courts because of "intervening know-it-alls" in Baltimore. Still seething, and doubtful that justice would be swift, locals took the law into their own hands, dragged out Williams, and strung him from the nearest tree. Momma and Poppa always said killing was wrong, but I also knew that for those men in Salisbury to act as judge, jury, and executioner was just as wrong.

One evening we sat around the table listening to Poppa read the local paper's version of the lynching. He paused for a minute before turning to Momma. "Listen to this editorial, Hon. They actually got nerve to try and take up for them lynchers. Says here: 'If we ventured to give an opinion as to the cause of all this ballyhoo against the Eastern Shore, we, of course, would say that the occasion for the outbursts was the Salisbury lynching incident; but the real cause is the failure of certain individuals to size up the Negro character as others more intimately associated with the race.' Failure to size up the Negro character; what's that s'pose to mean?"

"It's awful, just awful," Momma lamented.

"Here's something else," he added. "'When in the midst of all the legal bickering, a second Negro killed his employer, it was therefore understandable, though none the less horrible, that he should have been lynched.' Understandable, eh? I don't see why they even wasting time trying to make 'tend they not to blame,' he muttered. "Anyway, they're going answer to a higher court— ever' last one of 'em. A judgment day's coming, and I hope they burn in hell. They all just alike. Not enough difference to tell one from . . .'"

"I know just how you feel, Snow," Momma interjected, "but it's still some good white people around here. Look at Miss Madge and her family, and them giving us this beautiful lamp and always treating you real kind."

"Yeah, it's got to be one or two good ones," he admitted, "but if push come to shove, they're not going do no better'n keep quiet. You ought seen 'em down to work day after the lynching, talking and grinning like it was funny. I come up behind 'em and heard that Jack saying, 'Well, that's one nigger we won't have no more bother with.' Grinning from ear to ear and all set to say some more when Steve seen me and give him a nudge. You ought heard that cracker change his tune, pretending he was talking about that accident on the bridge. I looked him dead in the eye and kept on by. Turned red's a beet.

"And, mind you, me and him been working together on old man Hill's car. After all his talk, that thing had the gall to ask me what to do with *his* part of the job! 'Snow,' he says, 'don't look like this here switch's going work out.' I didn't open my mouth. So he's standing there looking dumb, waiting for me to check it and show him what to do, and I kept right on up front to get a part I needed. Steve wanted start a conversation, but he seen I didn't want no talk with him neither. Got back to the car, and that dunce he's still standing right where I left him, looking simple's ever. 'Fore I could get back under the car, he says, 'Snow, you mind showing me how to fix this switch?' I told him he's s'pose to be a mechanic same's me. Here he can't do two cents worth work and ain't been there a year and still's getting paid more'n me."

"Don't care how you look at it, it don't make no sense. Did you help him, Snow?" Momma asked.

"Ended up doing the whole thing, same's usual!" he grunted in disgust. "Can't make sense, Hon. It's got nothing to do with sense. It's just in 'em, that's all. Look like to me they come here hating us. The other day Sid told me his little girl come home crying 'cause that old Boone boy bothered her when she passed him on the street. After he got up close to her, he says, 'My but you sure one black, ugly nigger!' Then he spit at her. Took all Lena could do to keep Sid from going after that boy. Course it's a good thing she stopped him."

" 'Deed it's the truth," she agreed. "And here that old freckled-face, ugly boy can't be more'n six or seven years old, and all ready he's . . ."

"It don't make no kind of sense," said Poppa, as if he were realizing all over again the uselessness of it all. "No sense atall."

It made no sense that now, added to the pitiful, depressed lot of Shore Negroes, was the curse of a renewed overwhelming fear: the aftermath of a lynching. Fear saturated our lives, and even we children felt the strange uncertainty that had invaded our world. Parents tried in vain to shield children from the gruesome details that were being circulated around town. Children brought tales to school—accounts of the horrors overheard in their parents' work places and discussed when their children were supposed to be sleeping. And I was not the only child whose "lynching nightmares" alarmed the restless slumber of many parents. Not even the thought of Christmas and holiday preparations overcame our fears.

✦

Soon into the New Year my father started petitioning the mayor for another meeting. As I recall countless barriers that beset my parents during these years, I marvel at my father's courage and persistence in his struggle to overcome limited educational opportunities for area blacks. Trials, frustrations, and occasional triumphs were kept alive through his frequent recollections. And I no more tired of hearing accounts of those struggles than I could cease to be amazed by his determination and bravery in that time and place. He told of the many weeks it took just to convince a few fathers to meet and discuss the school situation, and when they finally did meet, according to my father, they sat around our dining room table for hours and settled nothing. Each man had children in the ninth grade, the highest grade for blacks in Pocomoke. After discussing the children's need of a high school education, my father told them his plans to request a tenth grade for us: "They can put on the tenth grade," he said, smiling at their certain reaction to the rest of his statement, "unless they don't mind letting our children go along with theirs to tenth grade in that fine new white school. You men know well's me our children deserve just much chance to get a education as theirs."

"Course we know that, Snow," Chris spoke up. "Same's we know they ain't no more going put no tenth grade on than they'd give a second thought to letting a colored child set foot in their big fancy brick school. And they saying ain't even enough children in it to halfway fill it up!"

"I agree they're not about to let our children fill up none them empty seats," Poppa replied. "What I *don't* see's how you can make up your mind to what else they not going do before we even ask. Fellers, we not going get one thing unless we stand up for it. It's true, we never had no more'n ninth grade, but that's not saying we can't ever get no more!"

"What you saying makes good sense to me, Snow," said Floyd. "All us knows if warn't for you, we wouldn't even have them portables. I'm willing to take a shot at it. Don't care what we ask, they going be dead set against it, but it can't hurt none to try 'em."

"Then how about asking for a meeting with the mayor and city council so's we can tell 'em we got to have provision for our children to stay in high school?" my father asked. "It's plain as that."

"You going make arrangements for the meeting?" Bernie asked my father.

"If that's what you fellows want," he replied. "But this time I'm counting on you all to come once the meeting's set up. It's going take ever'body and then some to make 'em budge a inch, I tell you. Be a good thing if ever' one of us'd get two or three more to go along. After all, it's not just for us. It's for ever' Negro around here."

"You tell it, Snow," said George. "We going start right out rounding 'em up. Some's bound to be willing."

"Sure good to hear you talking like that, gentlemen," he said. "Least it sounds to me like we headed in the right direction. I'll let you know about the meeting. Sure glad we got this far."

And so they left, promising to stand together until something was done about the school situation. After locking the door, my father said he went back to the dining room, where he sat thinking about the challenges ahead. Hours passed and he had been unable to figure out a plan—one which the white men would not ignore and our people could believe in and be willing to fight for. Nothing he could think of promised to work both ways. As he gathered up his notes from the meeting, his thoughts became a prayer: "Heav'nly Father, please help me find a way to figure out what to do next. Help us to stand fast and know how to look out for our own. Amen."

Some time passed before Poppa met with the mayor—a meeting he often described to us.

At the first knock, Andrew Turner bade Poppa enter and greeted him with a friendly, "Morning, Snow. What can I do for you?"

"Morning, Mr. Andrew. I stopped in to see about setting up a meeting with you and the city council soon's you can arrange it."

"Something wrong, Snow? Any special reason behind you wanting me to set up a meeting?"

"We believe we got cause enough, Mr. Andrew. Since we got no way for our children to go pass ninth grade, we're asking the school board to make provisions so Negroes can get a high school education, too."

"Well, now," said the mayor, "that just might present a few problems, Snow. I don't have to tell you a lot of colored children drop out of school long before ninth grade. How you figuring on keeping them in school for the tenth grade?"

"I realize some drop outen school early, Mr. Andrew, but the last two graduating classes was bigger'n any we ever had. This year I hear the graduating class going be bigger'n that and—"

"That might be true, Snow," Turner cut in, "but somebody'd have to pull a lot of strings to even *begin* setting up a tenth grade for you people. And what's going to happen if the children don't attend? How're you going to guarantee they will? Any committee's going to want a lot of answers, and that's one of them."

"Well, I tell you, Mr. Andrew," my father responded, measuring each word. "Way I look at it, our children s'pose to have chance to go to school. This way they got no choice. That can't be right. Sure, colored children drop out 'cause most of 'em's got no choice, not if they want enough clothes to keep warm. Boys got to work to help put food on the table and fuel in the woodhouse. Girls, same. And don't matter how hard they work, they lucky if they get paid a couple dollars a week, working Sundays and all. We ain't had much of nothing all along, and Depression's took away most little we had. Spite all that, you going see a big change in how our people feel about schooling. They're going to school, and they're not going stop with no ninth grade neither. Here we got children wanting to go to school with no way to go. And right out there on Market Street's a great big new school I hear ain't nowhere's near full."

At that point, Turner cut in, promising to see what could be done about the "colored school situation." Then, as if confronted with shocking news, he exclaimed, "First time I ever heard a word about you people wanting a tenth grade, Snow!"

"Every'thing's changing, Mr. Andrew," my father told him. "Beats all, how anybody responsible can look at this situation and keep colored people—and it's a lot of us paying taxes— from getting their schooling."

To that, the mayor made no response; instead he told Poppa he'd try to have some information in about a week.

A week later, my father met the mayor on Market Street. Walking home for lunch at his usual brisk pace, he heard someone call his name and realized he had walked right past Andrew Turner, who was standing in front of the bank talking to Gerald Lewis, without seeing him. Turning back, he waited impatiently for the two men to end their conversation. Finally, Lewis moved on, and Turner told Poppa he had informed the officials of his request and of their predictable reactions: they could see no reason to go to a lot of trouble for nothing. And whenever Poppa talked about their reactions and his response, anger simmered beneath each word.

"Course, they going think same's they been doing all along, Mr. Andrew," he said. "But I don't see how they can talk about having to go to so much trouble, especially when they done nothing up to now. Far's that goes, the world wouldn't come to a end if they'd let our children go to tenth grade right out on Market Street, where's plenty . . ."

"Snow," the mayor cut in, "we'll work out something. I promise you we'll work out something."

"I sure hope so, Mr. Andrew. Fact is I'm counting on it. My children never gimme one bit of trouble, and I aim to keep 'em in school, one way or another. You decide when we can meet?"

"Could be we won't need to have a meeting, not just now anyhow," Turner replied. "I'm waiting for word from the Department of Education over to Snow Hill. They're checking with the state office. Soon's I hear anything, I'll contact you."

When Poppa got home, we children were eating lunch.

"Hey, Hon," he said. "Met Andrew Turner outside the bank just now. He stopped to talk about tenth grade. Says he's got to wait for word from Snow Hill and the state office, too. Course, you know good'n well they going try to get outen doing much as they can. Come telling me how much trouble they'd have to go to! You ought seen his face when I told him it wouldn't be no need of all that trouble if they'd just let our children go to tenth grade out on Market Street!"

"Snow!" Momma cried. "You didn't lose your temper, did you?"

"No, Hon, I didn't lose my temper. Just told him, that's all. Burns me up how they always doing so much for us when they doing nothing but cheating us outen what belongs to us while they doing everything for theirself and making us help foot the bills! Just mentioning our children taking up some them empty seats in the white school upset him plenty."

"I just bet it did! Guess they think colored children'd poison theirs. Makes no sense. Here they want us to cook their food, tasting in it much as we want, nurse their babies, and ever'thing else. But they scared to let the children learn together."

"Sweetheart, I keep telling you it's got nothing to do with making sense. It's that old prej'dis they holding on to."

As they talked, I barely managed to keep from blurting out questions about tenth grade. Once I did start to speak, but Poppa's stern "I'm talking to your mother!" glance stopped me. Before we were ready to return to school, Poppa issued a stern warning: "You children heard me say this before, and I'm saying it again. What you hear in this house is not for you to take outen here. Understand?"

It was the waiting that troubled my father most—waiting and not knowing what to expect, or even what could be done, if the board decided against adding on the tenth grade. We knew how hard he tried not to worry about the rumors being circulated around town. Several neighbors warned him and advised him to leave well enough alone. They said nobody in his right mind would go around town saying Negro children ought to be allowed to go to white schools. No need to try to turn the world upside down. Even men who had sworn to stick together and work for the additional grade backed down, saying, "We been making out with no more'n ninth grade all this time, and we can just keep on making out same's before." They were afraid of what white folks might do. They pretended that the handful of students likely to go on to tenth grade wouldn't be worth all the trouble white folks would give them in return. Still Poppa tried to get them to stand together and fight for their rights, but only a few elderly friends offered encouragement.

Throughout the rumors and all, Momma stood by him, even encouraging him in spite of her own fears, until after what was described as the scare of a lifetime. It all began with a warning from a woman Momma washed for. As Carrie Griffin sat at the wheel, watching my mother struggle to put the heavy basket of freshly ironed laundry onto the back seat of her old car, she raised her eyebrows above the smirk of thin tight lips and said, "Jane, Snow doesn't mind his mouth one bit, does he?"

"Wha'cha mean, Miss Carrie?"

Mrs. Griffin grimaced before replying, "Jane, now don't pretend you don't know how Snow's been running his mouth about things he'd best leave alone. I'd sure hate to see . . . Just talk to him, Jane. Mr. Griffin's right bothered. That's all I've got to say."

After Carrie Griffin had driven off, my mother said she stood by the roadside unmindful of dust clouds swirling about her. At that moment she knew she must do something. She would beg Poppa not to take further chances. But neither pleas nor tears worked. What did make a difference was a bone-chilling nightmare. Although I sensed that something had changed after that night, many years passed before Momma told me the dream. Then I fully understood the current of terror that flowed through our humble life along the Pocomoke River.

"Snow! Wake up!" Jane called, shaking him. "Somebody's banging on the door, and it's way pass midnight!"

Jumping out of bed, Snow pulled on his pants and ran downstairs.

A tall man, wearing a floppy, peaked-brimmed cap pulled low over his eyes, stood on the porch. In the dim light from the street-lamp, Snow could not see the white man's features, but he sensed that he was no stranger before asking, "Something I can do for you, mister?"

"C'mon outen there, Snow," ordered the man. "We going have us that meeting you been raising so much hell about!"

"How come you meeting this time of night? Mr. Andrew never said nothing to . . ."

"Damn Andrew! This here meeting's just between us. Now get moving. We ain't got all night!"

"Snow, what's matter—who's out there—somebody sick or something?" Jane called nervously from the stair landing.

"Better tell her something quick," warned the man, "unless you want us take her along, too."

"No, Hon, ain't nobody sick or nothing," Snow replied. "Man's got car trouble out on the Stone Road. I'm going fix it."

"Then whyn't they wait to it's light? How you going see how to work in the dark? If you going, take your jacket, Snow. And do be careful."

"Getcha jacket," the man said, "and hurry up."

Before leaving, Snow called up, "They going tow the car in, Hon. Now go back to sleep. Be back soon's I can."

"Make me real nervous—you going out this time of night."

"C'mon here, boy!" a man shouted from the car.

Snow closed the door but not before he heard Jane call his name again. After the noise of the motor faded in the distance, she heard someone calling her, almost whispering. It was Cousin Bill at his kitchen window in the dark. She rushed downstairs so they would not wake the children.

"Here I am, Cousin Bill, in the dining room."

"Something wrong, Jane? Where Snow go to?"

"Said he had go fix a car out on the Stone Road."

"That car it belong to them mean old Pilcharts," said Bill. "It's hard to tell what they up to."

"Then whyn't you say something, Cousin Bill? S'pose something'd happen to Snow," she cried.

"Thought Ah best stay outen it. Wouldn't help none for us both get mixed up with them ornery buzzards, but they ain't going bother Snow none. No need you getting all upset for nothing. Go back to bed, Jane," he muttered before closing the window.

Slumping into the rocking chair, Jane cried and prayed and rocked alone in the dark. Meanwhile, Snow sat between the men on the back seat. He could not see well enough to recognize anyone in the car. However, as they talked around him, he soon knew who each was. He knew also an overwhelming fear. He wanted to say something to them, but he did not trust himself to speak. For a few minutes they rode in silence. Then he heard himself asking in an unfamiliar voice, "You men mind telling me what's this all about?"

"Oh, we going tell you all right," Cliff Pilchart, seated beside Snow, spoke up. "We going tell you so good you ain't never going forget! Lenny, drive over the river."

"Yeah," agreed Lenny, heading toward the bridge, "that's the place all right. Folks says they's parts of that river they ain't never found no bottom to. Sure could lose a body real good in there."

"'Smatter, Snow? What you jumping for?" smirked Reds Hill, seated on the left.

Cold sweat trickled down Snow's back. He tried to answer Reds, but his voice failed.

"Now, don't be bashful, Snow," Rod Pilchart drawled from up front. "Looks like you not going have to wait to get this here school business straight once and for all. That's what you want, ain't it?"

Snow remained silent.

Lenny pulled off the road by the woods on the far side of the bridge where the ominous slapping of water against the Shore was the only sound in the darkness. Rod began to speak quietly, almost as if rehearsing lines. "Damn it to hell, Snow! You listen to me, and listen real good. You've caused more trouble'n you're worth around here, and we don't like it one bit! We oughta done this long time ago. Thought we'd wait and see just how far you'd go. Who the hell you think you are anyhow going around stirring up trouble, upsetting peaceable folks?"

"Answer him, nigger!" shouted Cliff.

"I'm not aimin' to stir up no trouble, Mr. Rod. What trouble you mean?" asked Snow, relieved to hear his voice, even though it still didn't sound natural.

"What trouble you mean?" mimicked Rod. "You know damn well what trouble! All that farting around town about letting niggers in our school—with white kids! That's what's the trouble, and you damn well know it!"

"But, Mr. Rod, I ain't . . ."

"No use denying it. We got it firsthand from white folks—some niggers too, mind you! Snow, don't you have sense enough to know it ain't a single nigger in town crazy enough to try to send their children to our school? We don't give a good goddamn about no school board. Course, they ain't crazy neither. Ever'body around here knows how things suppose to be here. And how they been all along's how they going

stay. Starting right now we're going learn you a lesson you better not forget. You see that river?"

"Rod," Cliff cut in, "I believe he knows we mean business. Right, Snow?"

"Yessir."

"Don't know if he do or no," shouted Reds. "Never did trust no smart-mouth nigger nohow. But he damn well better know if he come out with anymore that fucking mess he won't be doing no more talking—at all!"

"I don't reckon's going be no more trouble," interjected Cliff. "Snow's always been a pretty good boy. Just gets a lil excited now and then."

Then he turned to Snow and underlined their threats, "We don't want to hear no more foolishness about niggers even thinking about going to our school. Don't cause us to pick you up again. You understand me, Snow?"

"Y-yessir."

"This time we warning you," said Rod. "Won't be no other time. Understand?"

"Yessir."

"You damn well better had," blurted Reds. "Now get outen here whiles you still can, and crank up this goddamn car."

"And if you know what's good for you," Rod cut in, "you'll keep your mouth shut tight. Say nothing to a living soul. You say one word about tonight, and you'll be sorry to the day you die!"

When Snow stumbled from the car onto the uneven ground, his legs buckled. He grabbed a low-hanging branch and steadied himself until he could inch alongside the car to the hood. The first time he swung the crank he pitched forward losing his balance. The motor did not even sputter. Pulling himself up, he managed to swing the crank over and over again until finally the motor jerked to a deafening start. At that moment Lenny swerved the car, knocking Snow to one side, and steered toward the road, leaving him stunned on the ground as the taillight bobbed across the bridge and disappeared. Slowly he raised himself on his hands and knees and waited until he could trust his trembling legs. When he was able to stand, he leaned against a tree to get himself together.

Beneath his sweat-drenched clothes, a chill shivered his body. Staggering homeward, he prayed that he would be able to walk the distance. Each block seemed like a mile. But even as he fought to stay on his feet, his thoughts were troubled with what he could say to Jane. The instant he touched the gate latch, she was at the kitchen door: With effort he drew himself erect and tried to move with his usual stride. But she had sensed the situation, even before she saw his face and soaked clothing.

"Snow!" she cried. "What happen? What they do to you?"

He tried to tell her about the trouble he had repairing the car, but suddenly he began shivering violently. His teeth chattered so that he could not speak. And Jane knew. He did not need to speak. As she bathed his face and helped him out of the wet, cold clothes into dry things, she wept, hardly making a sound, but she could not stop crying. Even after he had drunk the strong, hot coffee, she stood beside his chair; cradling his head against the warmth of her body, and tears fell onto his damp hair.

Suddenly, amid all the agony, screams and shouting filled the room. Groping in the darkness and overwhelming sense of suffocation, Jane began to realize that the shouting was coming from Snow, and the screams had been hers. Even after she was fully awake, she sobbed over and over, "They could killed you, Snow. They could killed you!" After he finally was able to convince her that he had not left their bed, she calmed down sufficiently to relate the nightmare, every horrible detail. But nothing he said could convince her that it was no more than what it was—a terrible nightmare. Perhaps that might have been possible had he not known the unspoken truth: both believed the nightmare to be an omen.

◆

For the next several days, we heard very little about the school situation. But one evening as Momma expressed relief that for the time being there should be no threats about anyone's talking up the idea of blacks going to school on Market Street, Poppa said, "I can still keep on trying to get a tenth grade put on to our school, Hon. They not going bother me none for that." Aiming a worried glance in his direction, Momma made no comment. There was no use. However, he let about a week pass before mentioning tenth grade again. We were sitting around the table after supper. Balancing his chair back on its rear legs, Poppa spoke in a forced casual tone, "Saw Luke Jones today. Says he's aiming to let his boy and girl both come to school if we get that tenth grade. Boy's real smart. Been working at the sawmill going on two years now when he could been in school."

"It's good Luke's going let 'em go," Momma said, suppressing a sigh.

"No more'n a man oughta do. Makes me feel more like trotting all over the place trying to get people to see how much these children need much education as they can get," he fumed, stretching noisily away from the table.

"Supper's right good, Ol' Woman," he teased. "Think I just might walk out to Quinntown and make sure them folks not thinking about backing down. All we need's for that board to decide in our favor and then not have enough children to . . ."

"Snow, you know you too tired to be going way out there. Besides, it won't be too long before night," Momma protested. "How do I know some of them's not waiting to do just about anything to stop you, Snow?"

"I'm tired all right, Hon, but I best see Joe and them. I'll be back before dark. Don't worry, I'm not doing nothing they care about now anyway," he added on his way out.

"You going go don't care what I say, but I still wish you wouldn't," Momma called. The squeak of the gate was the only response.

Days passed. No word from the mayor, but Poppa was determined to be ready. He knew he had to talk again with all the parents he had seen and to manage somehow to catch up with the rest. Evenings after supper he walked from house to house in all parts of town trying to convince other parents to do everything within their power to keep their children in school, at least until their ninth-graders could complete tenth grade. During lunch hours he found parents who lived in rural areas but worked in town and pleaded with them. There were nights when, after a hard day's work plus several visits to parents' homes, he was too tired and discouraged to sleep. But determination kept him going.

One day Poppa received a message to stop by the mayor's office on the way home for lunch. Turner was waiting for him, propped back from his big desk, eyeing him with a quizzical smile. And, as I recall the description of that visit, both frustration and hope ensued.

"Well, Snow!" said Turner. "All ready for the news, eh?"

"What's the verdict, Mr. Andrew?"

"Looks like they're going to be good to you all, Snow; they've agreed to put on the tenth grade for you!"

"Best news I had in ages!" he sighed with relief. "And I sure thank you, Mr. Andrew."

"Don't thank me, Snow, not yet anyway," said the mayor. "Fact is, they put a sort of condition on the whole thing. They'll give you your tenth grade, but only if within the next two weeks you can give them a list of students whose parents sign a statement saying they will enroll their children in the class and keep them in school 'til the term's over. Do that, and you'll get your tenth grade. The list has got to have names of at least fifteen students, Snow."

"That many?" he questioned in dismay. "They sure not asking for much! They know how many's in the ninth grade, and who knows if all them's going pass? So where'm I s'posed to get a number like that guaranteed from?"

"I reminded them of that, too, Snow, but they say fifteen or nothing," Turner replied; then, after a moment's thought, he said, "Tell you what, Snow, it just might not be as impossible as it sounds. Our Clara's girl finished ninth grade last year, and she's been working for Al. Clara says the girl's trying to save up enough to go and live with her aunt in Philly to finish high school, but it'll be a long time before she can save that much. She'd sure be tickled if she could go to a tenth grade right here. More'n likely there's others in the same boat. I'd be glad to furnish you with lists of ninth-grade graduates for the past few years if that'll help."

"Sure would appreciate it, Mr. Andrew. Need ever' bit of help I can get. It's not easy, I tell you, trying to get folks that's counting on what little the oldest children can bring home to give that up, especially when they're not hardly making it nohow. If it wasn't for this Depression, it wouldn't be much a strain as it is. But I'm going get them names if it kills me!"

"That's the spirit, Snow," said Andrew. "You stick with it. Heard you been walking all over town trying to get straight for this."

"I'm doing my level best," Poppa assured him. "Got a ride outen town to one or two families, and a couple of times it was a car in the garage I could try out."

Fate must have stepped in to prompt the mayor's response to Poppa's predicament: he offered the use of his car to enable my father to contact parents in outlying areas, whenever he himself did not need it. That gesture was not forgotten; nor were the mayor's words of encouragement.

My father said he felt like running down Market Street shouting for joy, but the memory of numerous trips to pitifully poor, over-crowded homes; of near-illiterate parents' laments; and of arguments such as "too many mouths to feed and nuttin' comin' in" and "he's old 'nuff to be some help with farming" sobered him.

Word spread rapidly around town. For the very first time, there would be a tenth grade for blacks in Pocomoke if my father could get a specified number to make up the class. Several ninth-grade students' parents had signed the paper, but not nearly enough. A few ninth-graders would not be promoted. Some parents were not convinced that they should deprive themselves further, when already their children had received two or three times as much schooling as they. A number of students, anxious to be out on their own, still were undecided. So every night and nonworking hour Poppa tried to convince the unconvincible. By the middle of the second week, the list was short two names. That problem would be solved if some of the undecided previous graduates would make up their minds to attend tenth grade. But as soon as Poppa thought he had one problem solved, others popped up. To make bad matters worse, even some prospective ninth-grade graduates couldn't see much sense in staying in school instead of getting a job. They asked, "What difference is another year of school going make 'round here?" Parents who had sworn to sacrifice to the limit to keep their children in school backed down. But Poppa never gave up trying to convince students of what could be gained by staying in school, even for only one more year. They listened, or pretended to listen, but most doubted the wisdom of leaving their low-paying jobs and trying to subsist on less pay for part-time. My father understood their plight; perhaps that helped him to keep on trying. He knew there was very little in their lives to hold the promise that even an additional year's schooling would—or could—make a difference. Still his determination never wavered.

Another solution presented itself if Poppa could find room and board for two sisters whose destitute family had moved to a distant farm to work the land of a white owner. After several trips to the farm, Poppa persuaded the parents to consider doing without the help of their older girls during the school week. Finally, they agreed to enroll Edna and Bernice if they could find someone willing to support the girls through the school week for little more than their domestic services in the home. That problem was solved when an elderly Mount Zion couple decided to help the cause by taking them in. Then, almost miraculously, names of three earlier ninth-grade graduates swelled the list.

Whenever my father described his next meeting with the mayor, his every gesture reflected the relieved excitement of that memorable day. As he approached the office, he was conscious of a different feeling, different from any he had known since he first set out to get at least some part of what he knew belonged to his people. He carried that feeling into the mayor's office.

"Morning, Mr. Andrew," he said, reaching into his pocket. "Got a lil something here for you."

"Could tell that by your walk," Turner commented, accepting the sheet bearing the impossible number of names along with the parents' signatures. Some signatures were hard to read, barely legible, but there they were. The mayor scrutinized the list.

"Sit down a minute, Snow," he said. "You deserve a whole lot of credit for what you've done. I hope your people know how much they owe you."

"They don't owe me one thing," Poppa told him. "Long's my children's going be able to stay in school, I'm satisfied."

"Well, whether you think so or not," Turner emphasized each word, "they owe you a helluva lot. And I don't mind saying this whole town'd be a damn sight better off if we had more citizens like you—white and colored."

"I appreciate what you're saying, Mr. Andrew, and I won't forget all the help you gave me. Couldn't managed without it."

"Let's put it this way, Snow," said Andrew, extending his hand, "we helped each other."

As the two men shook hands, for a brief moment there was no room between them for the invisible barrier that was at the root of the struggle.

That September of 1932, Pocomoke's first black tenth-grade students were seated in the old ninth-grade homeroom with the principal. Everyone was happy to be back, especially those who had been out of school for a year or more. Our principal gave a short lecture on the responsibility of high school students—with emphasis on tenth-graders—to the school and community. He reminded us of our special obligations as the first tenth-grade class for Negroes in the history of the town. When he praised the man who deserved credit and appreciation, I looked down at my hands, but Henry grinned with unabashed pride.

◆

That unusual school year seemed to pass more quickly than any other. In spite of struggles with difficult subjects; long, tiresome rehearsals for special programs; the trauma of falling in and out of love; desperate crushes on teachers; and countless other incidents marking that final year, time passed too quickly. And once again, former ninth-graders turned tenth-graders were rehearsing for commencement. As soon as we had become used to being tenth-graders, we were faced with the end of the school year. And for most of the class it would be another kind of ending—the end of their formal education.

Long before we started practicing for graduation, Poppa began making inquiries about the possibility of the addition of an eleventh-grade class. The answer was unequivocal: "No!" There would be no such consideration, no further discussion of the matter. Even worse, it was announced without explanation, that the tenth grade would be discontinued at the end of the year.

So black parents who wanted their children to complete high school would be forced to make their own arrangements. They could travel daily to Snow Hill, the county seat, or to wherever else they could manage, if they had a means of transportation. How they got to and from school, in other towns or cities, was of no concern to the authorities. One thing was certain: if they completed high school, it would not be on Market Street or any other place in Pocomoke. Our parents did not know how they would manage. They could not afford to send Henry and me to school in Snow Hill and pay for our room and board. But they promised, with the help of God, to find a way.

Most black tenth-graders in town had no hopes of continuing their schooling. A few fortunate ones would stay with relatives in distant cities and attend schools, where they were certain to be demoted due to gross differences between our county schools and the sophisticated curricula of city schools. Still, in spite of discouraging odds in that time and place, some would make a go of it, all the way. And our parents were determined that their children would be among the few who did.

11 · *A Second Shame*

> *"Oh, thus be it ever*
> *when free men shall stand,*
> *between their native land and—"*
> *between the lines you hear:*
> *"Get back 'nigger!'*
> *Stand back black man!*
> *Stand back!*
> *Stand back!"*

For several months, nothing in my world seemed right. After long talks with my grandmother, I would spend hours shut up in the front room reading about "life" in *True Story* magazines and fantasizing a role in the most sensuous of love scenes. Summer nights, long after the only sound in the house was a chorus of snores, I would lie looking out on the darkness behind the corner store, which served as a dance hall on weekend nights, and listening to raucous noises and jukebox music. Frequently, the single bulb hanging over the back door of that building shone on men staggering and passing around a bottle, or on noisy lovers arguing and fighting.

One Saturday night I heard a woman screaming and a man trying to calm her. Suddenly the man cried out, "You missed me!" But the woman shouted, "You think I did, huh? Shake your head!" After that, pandemonium broke out with women screaming, people running, and automobiles racing away. Within minutes, the back lot was abandoned to the night, and the silence was broken only by cat cries in the darkness. By morning the story was all over town: Bob Cooper's woman had followed him and the town flirt to the back lot and confronted them. Lulu didn't waste time talking, but when she flashed the razor in Bob's direction, horrified onlookers, as well as Bob, thought she had missed him.

However, the moment he turned his head, blood spurted from his slashed neck. Luckily, his friends got him to the doctor within minutes, or he would have bled to death. A week later I saw "Mr. Bob," a kind, gentle man who used to give us pennies when we were little. His head was so swathed in bandages that he looked like a mummy. When he turned into our yard, I spoke, turned away, and ran upstairs. I cried, not knowing why, but I could not stop crying.

There were nights, too, when happy sounds drifted through the bedroom windows. The air was filled with laughter; voices were loud, but gay. Some Saturday nights live dance music wafted through the darkness into the little room where, caught in the confusion of early teen years, I yearned for the world outside, even for the gaudy magic inside the dance hall. That forbidden place was not, as Momma echoed her reminder, for "nice girls." Still the jukebox's groaning Bing's "Please, lend your little ears to my pleas" was but another reminder of the thrills I felt I was missing.

During those agonizing teen years, though, I probably would not have been satisfied, as my mother phrased it, "No matter what!" Because other girls in my class were older, they were too grown up for me, according to my parents. Except for my sister and cousins, no other girls about my age lived close by, at least where I could visit. Even if they had, I knew that my chances of going around with them were out of the question. Actually, there really was no suitable place of entertainment in the area for black teenagers. We had school, church, a minstrel show in town now and then, the circus every spring—a sad offering for the whole year. Older boys and girls bragged about good times in dimly lit beer gardens on the outskirts of town. I listened and felt cheated. Whatever was supposed to happen in teenagers' lives was not happening in mine. Although there were daydreams of intimate moments with Billy Townsend, they always ended with a doubtful "maybe this time next year."

There was a "white" movie theater downtown, but Poppa had laid down the law about that: he swore he would never set foot in the place or give his children one penny to go there because the enclosed fire escape served as the entrance for blacks, who, after climbing the fire escape, had to sit in the balcony. And Poppa kept his word; neither he nor Momma ever patronized that theater. However, he did not stop us as we grew older and earned change to pay our way. Too young to understand our father's wisdom, we could not see that his harsh words reflected the pain he suffered each time one of us climbed that enclosed fire escape to be blinded by the fantasies of a celluloid world.

◆

On our first day at Snow Hill Colored High School in 1933, Poppa pulled up to a boxy, frame building in Uncle Ray's little coupe. Poppa, Henry, and I sat for a moment, saying nothing. After a while Poppa spoke, "Well, children, here you are. Don't look much better'n what you just left to me."

"Oh, maybe's not all that bad," Henry ventured to find a bright side to the situation.

He probably felt just as apprehensive as I, but neither of us said anything as we stood watching the car disappear down the road. By the time Poppa got back to work, I hoped we'd be all settled in a homeroom. I thought of all Poppa would have to contend with in order to drive the thirteen miles between Snow Hill and Pocomoke City four times a day: beginning work extra early so he'd be able to leave and make the trip, then racing back to the garage to make up lost time, often through lunch hours, at day's end, and late night hours. With those thoughts came similar ones of Momma sweating over baskets of other people's dirty laundry, scrimping, making do, and doing without. And I began to appreciate more fully the kinds of sacrifices being made by our parents to keep us in school.

From the very first day, Snow Hill teachers and students made the commuters from nearby towns—Berlin, Stockton, Girdletree, and others—feel right at home. Perhaps they realized that life was somewhat harder for students who went to extremes to remain in high school. Our class was especially fortunate: the moment we met our homeroom teacher, the new principal, we fell in love with him, and we were glad that he was our math and biology teacher, too.

Rob Williams, a personable young man, was as enthusiastic about teaching as he was about almost everything. Frequently, he would interrupt himself in the middle of a lesson on the respiratory system and give a play-by-play description of the crucial football game, at Morgan College up in Baltimore, in which he had sustained broken ribs. Then after an impressive account of the meaning of school spirit and personal dedication, he managed to steer us back to the miracles of the human body. And we relished each word because he was the kind of teacher who made learning interesting. Although he joked with his students, he treated us as young adults should be treated, and we respected him. It took only one example of Mr. Williams's capable handling of the class "tough guy," when he got out of line, to convince all students that there would be very few disciplinary problems at Snow Hill Colored High School that year.

On the morning of October 18, a wonderfully crisp fall morning, Henry and I entered homeroom and I immediately sensed something was wrong. Our teacher sat frowning at his desk blotter. Several silent students sat in assigned seats. Ordinarily there would have been friendly conversations among students finishing assignments, standing around in small groups, or talking with Mr. Williams. But only the principal returned our greetings.

"What's matter with ever' body?" I asked.

"You mean you ain't heard?" cried Harriet Black.

"Heard what?" demanded Henry.

"Might's well tell you. They lynched a man in Princess Anne last night!" Mr. Williams blurted.

"My soul!" Henry cried. "What for, Mr. Williams?"

"Why do these people ever do any such horrible things, Henry?" asked Mr. Williams in a bitter, angry tone. "Son, you've been on the Shore all your life. You know what they're like down here."

Henry slumped into a seat and stared at his hands. Herman James moved beside him and said, "They saying the man attacked and beat a white woman in the woods."

"Then why couldn't they lock him up if he really did anything to her?" Henry protested.

"Oh, they locked him up all right. Locked him up then unlocked the cell, most likely, so they could get him. They hung him, then set him on fire!" Herman groaned.

Princess Anne was less than halfway up the road from Pocomoke to Salisbury. An angry mob lynched George Armwood, a retarded twenty-two-year-old black man, for allegedly assaulting an elderly white woman. Rumors circulated that one of the lynchers worked at a store in Pocomoke City. Horror, it seemed, was creeping closer to home. Girls wept. Boys were visibly upset. Although most students had arrived early, it was clear that nothing would be gained by attempting any class work that day.

When the *Worcester Democrat* came out, it carried the "Shore" version of the lynching. After supper, I read parts of it to the family. The headline read: "Negro Ravisher Hanged and Burned by Enraged Crowd of Shore Citizens."

"It's a lot you don't want to hear," I observed, "and I don't blame you. But listen to this: 'The negro was taken from his cell, a rope tied around his neck, was dragged to a tree, hanged, and an attempt made to cremate the body.'"

" 'Cremate,' huh?" Poppa grunted. "So that's what they got the nerve to call it."

"It's awful," Momma groaned. "And what makes it worse'n ever is Sue said her old boss was in on it. Come home with piece of the rope they used to hang that poor man with. Says he walked in the kitchen throwed it right on the table and said, 'That's a lil souvenir from that nigger's party!' Can you picture anybody doing something like that? Got no more feelings than that stove!"

"You dead right, Hon," Poppa said. "Just can't help wondering how much longer they can go on lynching us and going around bragging about it 'cause they know the law's not going touch 'em."

In history class, we secretly followed local coverage of the Shore's latest lynching. One headline, "Hearing in Princess Anne on Lynching," was followed by "Investigations Fail to Reveal Any Knowledge of the Real Participants: Actual Lynchers May Have Been Foreigners." A month later an anti-lynching bill was introduced at Annapolis, but the very next week the paper's banner declared, "Four Lynch Suspects Freed." A local editor, incensed by H. L. Mencken's criticisms of the Eastern Shore, wrote that the Baltimore journalist's initials stood for "Hellish Liar." Another *Worcester Democrat* editorial contained an excerpt which we discussed, horrified by what we were learning. In part, the editorial stated:

> One might suppose that on the Shore, it was the habit of people to intimidate courts, lynch prisoners, mutilate their bodies, then burn them whatever the accusation might be. It is true that lynchings have occurred here as in other states and will continue to take place. . . . Thousands of people in Maryland as well as other states think Armwood and his kind deserve no better fate.

For months after the Princess Anne lynching there were gruesome rumors of how the lynchers mutilated the body of their victim, how he was tortured but kept alive for the burning, how dismembered parts of his body were displayed for public view. We listened and lived in fear, knowing that the same element of society could come in the night and drag away our fathers, brothers, other relatives, or friends. White men lynched black men—innocent or guilty—and were confident that nothing would be done about their crimes.

But when less than two years separated lynchings in neighboring Shore towns; when the oppressed continued to suffer scourges of injustice; when my own mother watched townsmen drive past our home in a truck equipped with ropes for a lynching, faith in God and prayer fortified blacks to hold on. Some believed that the guilty, freed by a questionable system, would be dealt with in God's own time. As proof, they cited the fate of the murderers of Stephen Long, my parents' revered principal, who was attacked on the street near our house as his adopted child ran home screaming.

According to my parents, two white farmers had adopted a colored boy, Jerry, from the orphanage with the agreement that they teach Jerry how to work and keep him in school. Because Jerry was not in school, Mr. Long went to check on him; the farmers admitted their failure and promised to send Jerry when school reopened, which they did not. In passing the farmers on the street, Mr. Long asked whether they were going to send Jerry to school. The reply was affirmative, but one added, "But suppose we don't. What the hell's it to you?" After explaining that he was required to see that all colored children attend school and to find out why if they don't, he told them he would have to report continued absences. At that point, one man jumped from their buggy, shouting, "You'll never report us, you black son of a bitch." Reportedly, Mr. Long returned the epithet and threatened to call the law. He was stopped by stabbings. When onlookers finally got him to the doctor, the verdict was "There's no need to take him to the hospital; he's dying." Some folks tried, but he died before they could cross the Pocomoke River bridge.

The guilty men were locked up—even though witnesses were afraid to tell what they saw and knew—and there were trials involving Pocomoke City, Snow Hill, and Baltimore. Some folks believed that, in the face of a prejudiced court system that might have been lenient of the accused, God took over the case.

One man got sick and suffered like a mad dog. Another one had a nervous breakdown and said snakes were crawling on him. Courts wouldn't give them what they deserved, some said, but God sure struck them down.

"There's no need to take him to the hospital; he's dying." Just as the doctor pronounced the fate of one good man, Stephen Long, the courts reportedly decided the fate of one murderer: "What's the use of sending him to prison? He's dying." Still, no amount of physical suffering by the guilty can compensate for the pain of justice denied—a lesson many of us are forced to learn at a very early age.

✦

In spite of emotional wounds that left permanent scars, we eleventh-grade seniors knew a sense of fulfillment that memorable year. Our class boasted an unusual number of very bright students,

Adele, high school senior

many planning to go to college. After a moderate start, I finished with good grades; Henry did well, too, especially in mathematics. For the two of us, May meant the third graduation in three years. But this time graduation would be from high school (at that time students in our county school completed the required course load in eleven years).

Everyone was busy with preparations for graduation. I was excited about the class-night play, a mock wedding uniting Knowledge and Wisdom. Ken Walton, the handsomest boy in class, was the groom, and I, his bride. For the play, Momma borrowed a friend's white organdy evening gown, layered in soft ruffles from waist to hem. After turning up ruffles and taking in the waist, she laundered it, and it was the most beautiful dress I'd ever seen. "Momma!" I cried. "It looks like an angel ought to wear it. That's the truth!"

"Maybe one will," she teased, relishing my pleasure.

On the afternoon of class night, Henry and I went home from school with friends. Following the program and dance, Mr. Williams, who had begun to treat Henry like a buddy, would drive us back to Pocomoke. My friend, Flonnie, knew how to do hair and promised to fix mine. Although I knew my mother, who already had washed and twisted my hair to hang in long curls, would not approve, I rationalized that the occasion justified my having a totally new experience. In spite of Momma's repeated explanations that my hair did not need straightening, I yearned to see how it would look pressed and curled, as if it had been done by a beautician.

Immediately after dinner, Flonnie began the transformation. Each time a warm curl brushed my shoulder, I grew more anxious to see how my defiant venture would turn out. Flonnie had almost finished when she flipped the curling iron and lost her grip on it. The hot iron fell, striking a stinging blow against my cheek.

We doctored the burn. But the pain did not bother me nearly so much as the thought of the scar I would have for class-night activities and graduation. In the midst of the confusion, I remembered my mother and the fact that there would be no scar if I had not, knowingly, gone against her wishes. Still, neither conscience nor scar could dim the magic of that very special evening, when for the very first time I felt a bit grown-up. Most likely, it was the evening gown. After Flonnie finished with me, she told me to look in the hall mirror. I could not believe that the wide-eyed young lady staring back could be a reflection of me.

Too soon, the long-dreamed-about night ended. Riding home, seated between Henry and Mr. Williams, I wished the evening were just beginning, for I knew as soon as I took off the magic gown, like Cinderella, I would be "little Ginny" again. Nothing, however, could take away the memory of Ken's smile when he saw me all dressed up as a bride. Even Mr. Williams treated me differently, not just as Henry's immature little sister.

"Ginny," he said, "I'm certainly proud of you tonight. I hadn't realized what a fine young lady you're getting to be. That's the truth, and you look beautiful."

"That's 'cause Flonnie and them fixed me up and everything," I said shyly.

"Listen, Ginny, you're growing into a lovely young lady," Mr. Williams said. "You've got to learn how to accept a compliment. Any time you look and perform the way you did tonight, you deserve to be complimented. So accept it and say thank you."

"Thank you, Mr. Williams," I complied, and we all laughed happily.

When we reached home, it was too late for sleepy parents to listen to detailed accounts of the evening. Nevertheless, they roused up when we went upstairs.

"Have a nice time?" Momma asked from her pillow.

"'Deed we did. Best time I ever had, Momma," I declared. "Want to hear about it?"

"Better wait to morning, Honey," said Poppa. "Your momma's sleepy. And you all better get some sleep, too."

Stepping out of the ruffled gown, I could feel the magic of the evening slip away. For a long time I lay, unable to sleep, reliving moments of the evening and knowing that in the morning everything would be the same as before, that is, everything except the dark scar across my cheek. One touch of the good fairy's wand had created a romantic evening; it also had sown additional seeds of discontent in a young and restless mind. When, after graduation, I bade classmates and special friends good-bye, I felt sad because I knew it was unlikely that I would be seeing most of them soon, if at all. With Henry things were different. Until now, Momma's "It's different with girls" had sufficed.

Even though I felt left out, I realized that Henry was a few years older. Also, there wasn't any place around town where I really wanted to go. However, I was fifteen at last, and now a high school graduate. The idea that other grads were going out and enjoying themselves made me feel like someone forced to sit on the side lines and watch life whirl by. No longer was there consolation to be found in the fact that the other graduates were older.

My dissatisfaction intensified as unforeseen problems added to frustrations during the summer. Sulking from one uneventful day to another, I tried to think of things I would be doing when I no longer had to walk back and forth to work for the Mudds. For a week's work of cleaning and doing other menial jobs around the house, I was paid little more than change. However, even that pittance was more than I would have had otherwise. Didn't mind the cleaning nearly as much as I hated pushing my way through tall weeds and bushes in the backyard to their old abandoned, cobwebbed toilet. Mrs. Mudd had given orders that "help" was to clean, but not use, the bathroom. The outdoor toilet was for her "help." Resentful, but intent on doing what had to be done in order to save money for college, I plodded through the bushes and concentrated on the time when things would be better for us all.

Even if it had not been decided that I was too young to go away to college, my parents had first to see how they could manage to keep Henry there for one semester. It was understood that while they would make every possible sacrifice, each child was responsible for doing all he could to help himself get his education. Otherwise, fulfillment of the dream would be impossible. So Henry was enrolled in the Hampton Institute in Hampton, Virginia, under a work-study plan. I had to stay home, work, and save what I could for a year. Then, if possible, our parents planned to try to keep two children in college. Meanwhile, they made arrangements for Marie to live in Salisbury with an elderly lady who was so much in need of someone to help with the housework that she agreed to provide room and board for Marie in exchange for little more than her help with household chores. Although the high school in Salisbury was about twenty miles farther from home than Snow Hill's, there was no such offer from anyone in Snow Hill. So Marie finished high school in Salisbury, and Poppa did not have to make the four-trips-a-day run to and from Snow Hill for another year.

Nevertheless, our family often had to do without many bare necessities. While Poppa overworked and borrowed to pay the bills, Momma worried and repeatedly asked, "Snow, don't you think you're taking on too much at one time?" And his answer never changed: "We'll manage somehow, Hon. If we do all we can, the Lord'll help us make a way."

My father never stopped reminding town officials of the deplorable conditions under which black children were attending school, while out on Market Street white children were housed in a fine brick building. His stubborn refusal to accept the little they meted out was a major factor in the long-delayed construction of a modest frame building across town, in Bedlam, where blacks could at last attend a modern, well-heated school, a school that was named for the late, revered principal, Stephen Long. At least Emily and Buddy could be spared the indignities and deprivations which their grandparents, parents, and older siblings had endured.

In addition to the new school, plans were made for a county bus to transport black ninth-grade graduates the thirteen miles— far from the hallowed brick building on Market Street—to Snow Hill Colored High School. Poppa was relieved of some problems he had struggled with in order to see Henry, Marie, and me through high school. There would be nothing quite like that for his last two children and for any other Negro child in the area. And no one did as much to bring about those long-overdue changes in Pocomoke City as Snow Henry Holden.

12 · *Shadows of Discontent*

Again I conjure up
a brighter dream
and watch these embers
slowly ash and frost . . .

Over the years things change. Change often comes slowly, but it comes in small bits, even to the Shore. Some changes made deplorable conditions a little less so, but if the idea of equality in education or equality between whites and blacks in any other respect crossed the minds of area whites, it was only insofar as to what must be done to protect Shore towns and townspeople from any such ideas of an "outside world."

Throughout that year of discontent, it seemed as if nothing ever could be as bad as the way I felt, being deprived of what was an essential part of my life. Instead of the accustomed routine of school and cherished relationships with classmates and teachers, there were hateful chores at work for pitiful pay. It was lonely at home since both Marie and Mame were away attending high school. Noting my restlessness, my mother often lamented the lack of nice girls, or what she considered as such, in our part of town. Most of the hometown girls I had gone to school with were considered to be young women; several already had babies. And Momma's constant reminder was that she did not want her daughter "ending up that way." So I ended up, most of the time, at home alone.

There was one older girl, Lorna Gray, who visited me. It wasn't that my mother approved of Lorna as a pal for me, but she really didn't want me to miss the companionship of close friends. Besides, she had not heard anything too bad about Lorna, who lived across town with elderly grandparents, respectable members of Mount Zion. Most times it was Lorna who came to our house although now and then I visited her. We took long walks, played the Victrola, listened to the radio, and talked secretly about life. There was little else to do. When we talked, Lorna did most of the telling. She mesmerized me with details of her intimate experiences with men—not boys, because Lorna said boys didn't know what they were doing. If Momma had had the faintest idea of the experiences I shared through Lorna's colorful accounts, those visits would have come to an abrupt end. However, she did not know. So I fed on Lorna's experiences, and when Lorna felt like listening, I told her about my dreams of going to college and becoming a teacher.

One Sunday, in the lull of twilight, I walked partway home with Lorna after she had spent the afternoon at our house. Within minutes, silhouettes were swallowed in darkness, relieved only by the glow from windows and the arches of widely spaced streetlights. Crossing Market Street on the way back, I recognized Billy Townsend's loping walk. We met near a lamppost. He smiled, and my heart started hammering the way it did whenever he looked at me.

"Hi, little Ginny," he said, drawing me to him. The moment he touched his cheek to mine, I heard it—"Har-rumph!"

I immediately recognized the sound of a man clearing his throat. I knew it all too well. Jerking away from Billy, I stood watching a man stride down Fourth Street until he disappeared in darkness. The magic of the moment was shattered. Refusing to let Billy walk the two blocks home with me, I hurried away. I felt anger, first at my father, then Billy. But most of all, at myself, and I didn't know why I was so angry.

After second helpings of lemon meringue pie, the family relaxed in the dining room, looking at the Sunday paper, listening to the radio, and talking. My father, tired after a seven-day week at the garage, stretched out on the lounge against the wall.

"Tired, Snow?" Momma asked, gazing at the frown on his face.

"Right smart tired, Hon," he answered. "Wouldn't be so bad working Sundays if I just had something to show for it. That's what makes me so mad—tired, too."

"I know, Snow. It's a shame, that's what," she sympathized, then told me to see Emily and Buddy to bed.

Shortly after I came back downstairs, Momma rose, yawned, and decided to turn in. As usual, Marie followed close behind, leaving me all alone with Poppa. I would have forfeited the treasured privilege of staying up late and gladly joined the two of them, but I knew my father had something to say to me. One stern glance when I first returned from walking out with Lorna let me know. I pretended to be reading funnies I had already read in the morning. After what, to me, seemed like an hour, he spoke, his voice gruff and strange.

"What's that boy doing pulling on you out there in the street?"

"He wasn't pulling on me," I replied nervously.

His frown deepened. Twisting his mouth, he stared at me as if he were looking at something disgusting.

"You want to go 'way to school, don't you, Miss?" he asked.

"Yessir."

"Then let 'em keep their hands off'n you!" he ordered, speaking as if the words were choking him.

"Yes, Poppa," I murmured, frightened but relieved.

Without another word, he opened the sports section of the paper. He did not say more because he knew there was no need.

Although I was glad it was over, I still felt uneasy. I didn't want Poppa to be angry with me or to worry about me. I wanted to go over and sit on the side of the lounge, as he used to sit on the side of my bed when I was little, and tell him it was all right—that I knew how he felt. But he did not look up from the paper. I straightened up the room, put the chairs back against the wall, and smoothed out the table runner. Yet he never looked at me. Finally, I paused at the hall door, told him I was going to bed, and waited.

"Good night, Honey," he said. "I'll be up soon's I rest a lil while longer." Without a trace of anger in his voice, he looked at me, and he smiled.

Long after I heard him come upstairs, I lay remembering that moment when Billy's cheek touched mine. I wondered again why my parents, especially my father, acted as they did about boys. They knew Billy was a nice boy who never got into any trouble. Of course, he went around with "the crowd," but so did Henry. And I knew there was no need to mention what Henry was allowed to do in contrast to what I wasn't. Henry, they said, was a completely different matter: he was a boy! After extending several invitations, which I could not accept, boys stopped asking me to go out. They knew I couldn't go, and they knew also that I would not try to sneak out as some girls did, even if I could get away with it. I couldn't understand why I had to miss everything others enjoyed. Much of what they did I didn't even want to do, but it didn't seem fair for anyone to have to miss out on everything.

One day, weary of my complaining, Momma dampened a sleeve of the shirt she was ironing, smoothed it out, and fixed a puzzled gaze on me as she asked, "Just what is it you're in such a hurry to do, Child?"

"I want to go out and have fun like everybody else, Momma."

"Hmmm. Then suppose you tell me where's it that's fitting for you to go to. S'pose you talking about that party. Honey, I wish you could go to something nice just much as you. But I keep on telling you that house is no fitting place for you. Got no fault to find with Deborah. Poor child, it's a sin and shame she's got to live in there. I do believe she'd be nice as anything if she didn't have to be in there with them people. But no, I don't fault your father one bit for saying you can't go."

"That's all he ever has said!"

"Wha' cha want him do, Miss, let you run wild like most rest of them girls? Seems to me you ought learn a lesson from them. How you think Ruthie and Louise going to have all that fun when they saddled down with them babies?" Momma asked, getting more upset as she talked.

"But, Momma, this's the first time anybody's invited me any place in I don't know how long. They all say I can't go nowhere. That's why they don't ask me. Now Deborah wants me to come. Can't you get Poppa to lemme go for even a little while, even if I can't stay long—just this once, please?" I begged. "Lorna's going, and Billy, too."

"Now, Ginny, you know good and well your father's not letting you go outen here with Billy."

"But why, Momma? What's wrong with Billy?"

"Didn't say nothing's wrong with him. Just know how your father feels 'bout it, Ginny."

For a long time I sat and thought, knowing nothing I said would cause them to change their minds about letting me go to Deborah's. Nonetheless, I tried again. "You think Poppa's ever going think any boy's all right for me to go out with or even come to see me, Momma?"

"Ginny, your father don't want keep you from enjoying yourself. It's just that he worries about you. He's scared something might happen to you. That's all. Maybe one day you'll thank us."

"*Thank* you?" I cried. "For keeping me penned up here like some prisoner? Bet when you were my age . . ."

"Now, that's enough, Miss!" Momma shouted. "Don't want hear another word. See if you can pick them greens. First, look out and see what the children's doing. It's mighty quiet out there."

Walking slowly to the front porch, I realized that nothing would change for as long as I lived at home and did what my parents considered best. I decided never again to ask permission to go out with other girls and boys or to have dates I could only dream of. It wasn't right. Yet there was nothing I could do about it. I knew one phase of life could not last forever. Still, the knowing didn't help in the least. I took the greens to the sink; for the very first time, I took no pleasure in our new convenience. I washed those greens until Momma protested: "If you wash 'em one more time, won't be a thing left but chaff. Suppose you peel some potatoes. Then go on outen here. Go for a walk or something. Maybe it'll do your disposition some good."

The minute I finished with the potatoes, I headed straight for my grandmother's. It was a relief to find her alone. Seated at the kitchen table, Mom smiled up from a pile of colorful papers that she was rolling into oblong shapes and shellacking. After drying, they would be strung, alternately with assorted beads, into long strands and hung as a portiere in the hall doorway. My greeting probably sounded as glum as I felt.

"Hey there, Sugar! Child, you look like you just lost your best friend. Don't know when Ah seen you lookin' so down-trodden. What's matter?" Mom asked, eyeing me with concern.

"Nothing."

"You mean to tell me you got that great long face for no reason? No ma'am. Ah can see something's matter. Don't you want tell Mom 'bout it, Honey?"

Then it all came out. As I detailed my troubles, I began to cry. Mom waited until the tears stopped.

"Ginny, Honey," she said, "Ah know how you feelin'. Shan't tell you how much time you got for all them things you worryin' about missin' cause that don't help none right now. Maybe Jane and Snow's a lil bit strict on you, but you must never ferget, Child, they only tryin' to do what they know's best for you. You see, Sugar, they didn't have it as good as you, and they want make sure 'taint nothin' around here goin' ruin things for you all. You understand what Ah'm sayin'?"

"Yes'm, Mom, but sometime it makes me feel so bad. I can't do one thing like other girls. Nothing!"

"Ginny," Mom said, turning a solemn gaze on me, "remember way Ah use to tell you about how 'twas with me when Ah was young? Well, maybe Ah oughten told you some them things."

"Why, Mom? I like to hear about how you did and all!"

"Maybe that's the trouble. Just might be Ah made it all sound like somethin' you thinks about like romance. Could be Ah made it sound like a lotta fun. Maybe 'twas sometimes. But, Honey, Ah was wild like that 'cause Ah didn't have nobody to think for me, not way you got. All Ah told you might sound like them *True Story* tales—me gettin' married and just barely in my teens—but it's whole lots more to it than what you reads in stories. It's more'n a notion way me and Clarence done just tryin' to get by. Poor as Job's turkey we was. And it ain't nothin' good about havin' babies one on top the other, when you ain't hardly much more'n one yourself. That's reason you got to be thankful for your folks, even when it seem like somethin's not right. They doing nothin' but trying do what's best for your own good, Sugar. Now, you stop poutin'. It ain't becomin' to you. Won't be long 'fore you be goin' off to school. Then you'll have plenty chance to be around lots a nice young folks. You hear?"

"Yes'm."

"Sugar, Ah made a big pot of soup," Mom said, changing the subject. "Feel like eatin' some?"

"Yes ma'am!" I exclaimed, jumping up to clear one end of the table.

When we finished eating soup, Mom cut thick slices of pound cake, velvet-textured, lemony, and delicious. We talked as we ate, and I told her about Cousin Bill and the Easter bunny that had been a gift to a child whose family Miss Anne, our neighbor, washed for. When the child's mother grew tired of the rapidly growing rabbit, she told Cousin Bill to return her laundry when the child, Beth, wouldn't be home, which he did. And Miss Anne made rabbit stew for supper. Meanwhile, Beth's parents told her the rabbit had run away. But somehow she learned that Cousin Bill and Miss Anne ate it. After that, whenever Beth heard Cousin Bill's wheelbarrow creaking across their yard, she'd run upstairs. One day he wheeled up behind her without making any noise with a new wheelbarrow. As Cousin Bill fussed over Beth, he tried to make amends by offering her a ride in the wheelbarrow. It took a lot of coaxing before she decided to accept the ride; still she would not respond to his questions regarding her opinion of the shiny new wheelbarrow or of the smooth ride—so very different from rides in the creaky old one. Finally, Beth turned large gray eyes up to Cousin Bill and said, "Bill, you needn't try to be all nice to me. I know you and Anne ate my rabbit!" That said, she jumped from the wheelbarrow and flounced into the house. All Cousin Bill could do was scratch his bald head in bewilderment and stammer as she left.

Mom, laughing until tears ran down her cheeks, exclaimed, "Ain't that the very limit! Wonder how she knowed about 'em eatin' it, Ginny?"

That I didn't know, but we sure had fun laughing about it. Realizing it was past time for me to go home, I told Mom how glad I was that I'd come down; and to this day, I can feel the caring in her voice as she said, "Me, too, Sugar. Now you be sweet and don't be worryin'. Things bound to change. You just have to be patient. That's all." Even then, Mom's very special wisdom often amazed me. She, who had very little formal education, was smarter and wiser than many people who boasted several degrees. And I knew, as I hurried down the dusty road, that I always could learn from my grandmother.

✦

As surely as season follows season, time passes, even the year-long months in the lives of frustrated teenagers, and once again I was busy preparing for the opening of a new school year. Henry, having worked on campus all summer, was already in Hampton. My job as a dishwasher in the new restaurant downtown enabled me to save a bit more than I could have by working for the Mudds. Marie was working as a mother's helper at Dr. Hull's. Emily and Buddy earned a little change by running errands and doing odd jobs for neighbors. Every penny was needed, for if all went well, there would be bills corning in from two colleges instead of one, along with all the expenses at home.

Until late summer, my chances of entering college that year were dim. All year our parents had struggled to pay the balance due on Henry's work-study plan. There was no way for them to handle more. Although they knew how miserable I'd been out of school, they probably still felt that, at sixteen, I could wait. Things took a different turn, however, with the arrival of an anxiously awaited response from a college official in Pennsylvania, who wrote that I had been granted financial assistance—a job, a loan, and a scholarship—that would cover practically all expenses. Happiness reigned in our home. But that happiness was short-lived. Upon arrival on the Cheney College campus, we were directed to the office of an official who regretfully informed us that funds for the promised aid had been cut off. So we, disappointed beyond the telling, made the long journey back to the Shore.

In the days following that experience, my parents agonized with me. My father, having seen a long year's hopes shattered in seconds, swore he would find a way to get me into college before the semester was too far gone. Reverend Waller suggested that his friend in Baltimore might be able to help get me enrolled in Morgan College. That friend turned out to be none other than the son of Grandpop's old buddy, Harold Wills. Within a few days, we were on our way to Westover to meet Mr. Wills.

The Willses lived in a big house with a screened porch. My heart pounded as we turned onto the road to one side of the spacious lawn. Mr. Wills came outside to meet us. He was a handsome, dignified-looking old gentleman who reminded me of Grandpop. His chestnut-hued skin was accentuated by silvery hair that swirled in waves and curls as Grandpop's used to.

For what seemed like a long time, they talked about the hard times our people continued to encounter, especially on the Shore, in our struggles for what is rightfully ours, including an education. Then Mr. Wills entertained us with tales about him and Grandpop—tales of their "sowing wild oats," as he put it. In the middle of one tale, he stopped abruptly.

"Snow," he said, "it just now struck me I might have the perfect solution to your problem!"

"What's that, Mr. Wills?"

"What would you say if my son and his wife offered to take Ginny to live with them? They got a big house, and I'm reasonably sure they'd be glad to have her stay there just like one of the family. She could help out with chores same as she does at home. That way, you'd be saving room and board. Just last week he mentioned needing a girl to help out a little. Suppose you let me get in touch with him, and I'll let you know in a day or two. All right?"

"Yessir! Here, lemme give you the garage phone number so you can reach me. Just can't tell you what this means to us, Mr. Wills. Maybe some day . . ."

"Don't mention it, Son," Mr. Wills cut in. "Does me good to be able to do something for Caleb Holden's boy." He walked us to the car, shook Poppa's hand, and wished me well. I could hardly believe it was happening at last!

Before the end of the week, everything was arranged. Mr. Wills had assured Poppa that his son would welcome me as part of his family. And having met Mr. Wills, we assumed that all would be well. So three weeks into the fall semester I left for Baltimore with Reverend and Mrs. Waller, who had volunteered to see me through registration at Morgan.

When Reverend Waller first mentioned the possibility of my attending Morgan College, I had been so discouraged that I would have been ready to go to the far ends of the earth just to be in college, no matter where. But after the Cheney College disaster, my parents knew better than to take anything for granted, especially assurances written on fine stationery with college emblems.

I was almost afraid to hope, but even though I couldn't visualize any part of the overall experience, the prospect of my attending Morgan College was almost too exciting to bear. At that time, all I knew about Morgan was what our high school principal had told us in relating his experiences there. To that, I added information from the registrar's office and whatever Reverend and Mrs. Waller could tell me about that outstanding institution in faraway Baltimore. Thoughts of the big city and Morgan College intimidated me.

Morgan's roots, I learned, stretched far back to the 1860s, when it was founded as the Centenary Biblical Institute by the Baltimore Conference of the Methodist Episcopal Church. In the 1868–69 academic year, total enrollment was just twenty students. Its name was changed to Morgan College in 1890 in honor of the Reverend Lyttleton Morgan, the first chairman of its Board of Trustees. Almost twenty years later its present site in the northern part of the city was purchased. (Area residents fought to have the sale revoked because Negroes, they thought, should not be

The Alumni Memorial Gate at Morgan College, Baltimore, late 1930s

permitted to establish a school in a white community, nor within five miles of Towson Normal School—now Towson University.)

Reverend Waller told me not to expect Morgan to be a rich, fancy college—that just as it had begun as a poor Christian institution, it still was a poor college. Morgan was dedicated to the training and education of our people, he said, noting his belief that Morgan was destined to become one of the most outstanding Negro colleges in the country. Every bit of information piqued my eagerness to become a Morgan student. Nothing I learned, however, could prepare me for the events of the ensuing academic year.

Haltingly but surely, my college experience began. Bewildered by more than the fact that, in Spanish I, students already were speaking Spanish, I wondered if catching up was possible considering the late start, especially in classes with many "citified" students who were products of big city schools.

It was not until that school year—that year of painful experiences—was over and we children were back home that our parents learned the full story of my first year in college. Momma said she suspected something was wrong soon after they entered the Willses' house when they came to take me home. But she had not the faintest idea of what her child had endured during those eight months of live-in service there. She recalled having had the distinct impression the minute she laid eyes on Mrs. Wills that her child should not have been in the care of "that woman" for a week, to say nothing of a full school year. Mrs. Wills's response to my mother's observation that I did not look well was, "The main thing wrong with Ginny is that she's spoiled." At that point, I wanted nothing more than to leave that house for good.

Back home, Dr. Hull took one look at me and said, "Ginny, I was just about to ask how you enjoyed college, but from the looks of things, I won't ask. What in the world happened to you? Was it that bad?"

Tears welled as I shook my head and tried to smile. Momma told him how hard she had been trying to get some answers from me.

"Ginny, you sit right there," ordered Dr. Hull, "and tell us exactly what happened while you were away."

Swallowing tears, I detailed my laborious existence as live-in maid and cook—an ordeal that bore no resemblance to the "member of the family" role envisioned by Grandpop's genial old buddy. In that dismal house, I found, in lieu of a surrogate mother, a cold, self-pitying woman who occupied her time by giving orders and seemingly making bad situations worse, most especially for the vulnerable live-in help I had become.

From the outset, I was given a clear understanding of my role in the household. Daily, I prepared breakfast, cleaned up afterward, and packed lunches—there were children—before leaving for early morning classes. When I returned, a list of chores was waiting. On weekends, instead of having ample study time, I was beset by household chores that kept me working until well after preparing Sunday dinner. By that time, I was too tired to cope with class assignments and, as a result, suffered through the worst academic year of my life.

Having survived the first month in the Willses' house, I focused on holding on until Christmas. Visions of holiday happiness at home helped me through the darkest times. When I received train fare from home, I was overjoyed. However, I said nothing about it because Mrs. Wills already had stated her opinion about anyone's making so much fuss about a holiday. Even so, I had no idea that she opposed my going home for Christmas until I attempted to clarify the date of my departure. A barrage of objections drove me upstairs before she could witness my tears. I could not understand how any mother could be so heartless, but she was determined to deprive me of Christmas with my family. Bewildered, I didn't know where to turn.

It took the unexpected intervention of Mr. Wills's sister, who stopped over on her way to the Shore to spend Christmas with her parents, to get Mrs. Wills's decision overturned by appealing to her brother. Next morning, Mr. Wills drove two Shore-bound passengers to the train station. And I'll never forget the compassion bestowed on a timid homesick girl by that lovely lady. Having escaped the threat of the unhappiest Christmas imaginable, I refused to think about what would await my return to that house. Nothing could overshadow the joyous promise of Christmas with my family. And nothing could have prepared me for what lay ahead.

Pressed to continue, I related trial after trial confronted during the remainder of the year—special punishments for the sin of going home for the holidays. Heavy spring cleaning chores—herculean for a girl weighing little more than ninety pounds—caused serious injuries and permanent scars. Another kind of punishment was inflicted when Mrs. Wills ordered me to eat dinner alone in the kitchen one evening because she didn't want her table crowded, in spite of objections from the two visiting relatives, who pointed to the extra space at the big table. So I was forced to have dinner (that I had prepared) alone, beset by a feeling I had not known before.

Sitting at a counter in that hateful kitchen, I witnessed another kind of prejudice in their table talk. They referred to fair-complected blacks as mulattos; all others as Negroes. As they talked about some kind of mischievous prank involving the light-complected Wills boy and two of his buddies, who were a little darker, I heard the boy's brown-skinned grandfather pretending to be reading a newspaper account of the incident: "Two little Negro boys and one mulatto were apprehended . . ." They also got a kick out of bragging about their fair-complected friends who, after employing the services of white beauticians in white salons, regularly lunched in the downtown stores' spacious for-whites-only lunchrooms. Oddly enough, the guest who repeatedly made a point of the "mulatto distinction" was a brown-skinned man. It was as if he must have felt the need to pay homage to the lighter hued. To me, however, it was an illustration of the ambivalence inherent in my people's intraracial prejudices. On one hand, some of us grew up hearing "black is honest"; "blacker the berry, sweeter the juice"; and other such sayings. On the other hand, we ourselves have been known to give special status to our fair-complected brothers, while harboring uncomplimentary opinions about them and their genealogy.

Another demeaning and equally unforgettable experience that I related to Dr. Hull occurred during one of Mrs. Wills's frequent "recuperations," when she—furious at her husband for going out against her wishes—ordered me not to retire until he returned, but to stay downstairs and be ready to come running if she needed anything. After midnight, I crept upstairs and stopped at her door to see whether she needed anything. No response. But the moment I fell into bed, shrieks and bangings alarmed the place until she paused to demand the bedpan. For no reason, she subjected me to bedpan duty when the bathroom was a few steps down the hall.

Dr. Hull was silent and frowning throughout my account of life with the Willses. Even though he knew my reasons for not telling my parents about the abuse during Christmas—they would have prevented my returning, and I was determined to complete the freshman year—he scolded me. Directing me to the examining room, he muttered, "Want to see how much more harm than good you did by sticking it out there. Sounds to me you stayed with a real Simon Legree."

One part of the doctor's diagnosis was frightening. I already knew that, as he put it, I was "worn down to a frazzle," but he said my appendix had to come out. First, he said, I needed to build myself back up. The thought of surgery terrified me. I had never been inside a hospital, and in my imagination I pictured every gruesome possibility. Even so, I had no idea that aftereffects of one traumatic year could cast shadows through several decades of my life. Nor did I suspect that what should have been my sophomore year at Morgan College would be spent preparing for and recuperating from surgery.

13 · *A Fresh Start*

"Look here, boy!"
Shore whites said,
"Don't expect
no such changes
around here. you hear?
We don't care
what they do—
or claim they doing
away from here."

My return to Morgan in 1937—this time to live on campus—was marked by a mixture of relief and frustration. The relief to be back in school after a year's absence was boundless. It was not easy, though, to adjust to the fact that my former classmates now were juniors and I a lowly sophomore. Nevertheless, the new school year promised to be far better than the first in every conceivable way.

From the outset, I was happy just to be a student again—a sophomore with a grant, a scholarship, a loan, and a job to help defray expenses. However, upon reporting for a job assignment, I was informed that I was not qualified for either the clerical job or the job in the bookstore. Both jobs required some typing, and typing was not part of the curriculum in my little Shore school. The only unfilled jobs were ones in housekeeping that included cleaning bathrooms in dorms. It wasn't what I had hoped for, but it was something I could do, and it would help pay my expenses. After that horrendous first year, life on campus seemed like a daily miracle to me. When disgruntled students complained about the dull routine or the food or the restrictions, they sometimes caught me smiling in the midst of complaints. It was hard for me to see how they could fuss so much when life was so good.

Only one thing troubled me: I had returned to the campus still ashamed of grades I'd made during the freshman year. But even that cloud disappeared when I qualified for the Dean's List. From then on things seemed better than ever. Of course, there were problems, but what mattered most was that the months were filled with hard work and studies, friends and social activities, learning and living. And after the last exam was over, there was the bittersweet business of packing up and returning home for another summer and trying to work in the cannery to save as much as possible until September came again.

Every spring, on the journey home for the summer, I sensed an ambivalence in my feelings toward the Shore. One moment I gazed again at rippling green fields, enchanting woodlands, rivers reflecting swamps, clustered farm buildings—all so ideally beautiful and peaceful. I felt a deep, special love for the home scenes. The next moment I remembered things like the lynchings that happened in Salisbury and Princess Anne. Those horrible memories haunted my thoughts of the Shore. (Even Morgan students from the Deep South declared that, in general, Shore blacks were treated worse than those "back home.")

After a few days' rest, I began looking for work. In Pocomoke, work for me meant cleaning, picking crops, or laboring in the tomato factory. Whenever I think of that tomato factory down by the Pocomoke River, I relive my early work experiences there. Everybody called it the "Can House," that drab, shedlike factory where tomatoes were processed during the hottest weeks of summer when tomato season peaked on the Shore. Poor people, especially blacks, counted on the little they could make working long, tedious hours in the cannery. Although the pay was low, it was all most of them could hope to make. So they counted on the nickels and pennies earned during the weeks that the Can House whistle summoned them very early in the morning. When the crop was heavy, the whistle blew again for a night shift and workers toiled steadily late into the night.

Soon after I was old enough to look after the younger children, my mother went to work in the cannery. When Henry reached hiring age, he got a job there operating a machine that dropped a ball of salt into each can of tomatoes. The endless tales one heard about people and happenings there made me curious about the place where Momma and Henry worked during tomato season. Momma left home early mornings, hurried back for lunch, and dragged herself back exhausted in the evening. Daily she flopped into the rocking chair, handed me her "can-house things" to take outside, and shook the day's coins into her lap from a smelly little drawstring sack, soaked to a rust color with tomato juice.

From the outset, I disliked having to open and handle the bag containing her can-house things. Everything in that bag reeked of soured tomatoes. The old dress, the homemade apron of worn oilcloth, the shabby, smelly shoes, damp galoshes and head cover, even the pointed spoon-shaped, razor-sharp peeling knife—everything was spotted with round yellow seeds and drenched with tomato juice. Each item had to be separated and spread out to air and dry on the side porch. And one had but to go near the porch to know those things were there.

As I grew older, in spite of having been told what the Can House was like, I begged Momma to let me go to work with her and help out by peeling into her bucket, as many girls worked along with their mothers until they were old enough to sign up as regulars. But Momma said she didn't want me exposed to the things I'd hear or see at the factory.

"You stop worrying about going down there," she added. "Do what you can do home here for now. Finicky as you are, how you think you'd make out in all that mess? Try to have a fit if you got to hang up my can-house things. Don't even want to touch 'em! Besides, I don't think much of having you around some them peelers, foul-mouthed as they are. And you womanish enough a' ready without listening to their common talk."

I stayed home, minded the younger children, cleaned, and cooked. But for the next two summers, I started out early worrying Momma about going to the factory with her. She knew I wanted to help out, and there was no denying that I needed the change, which they could not give me. Although she was reluctant to have me around the raw talk at the factory, she gave up when I continued to pester her and said, "I'm going leave it up to your father. See how much you worry him to death!"

The day finally came when I, equipped with oilcloth apron and all the other can-house gear, waited to go back to work with Momma after lunch. By noon it was blazing hot. For weeks we had been hoping for rain, but the weather stayed the same—humid and hot, without a breeze anywhere. I tried to ignore the heat as we hurried down Linden Avenue.

"Walk up, Ginny! You been raring to get down there, so hurr'up. The whistle'll blow 'fore we get half straight if I fool with you. Want make me late your very first day?" Momma fumed, being still apprehensive about my going.

"'Deed I don't, Momma. I'd rather break my neck hurrying than . . ."

"Nobody saying nothing about breaking no neck," she retorted. "Just walk up. And remember what I say about watching me so's you know how to do. And keep your mind on peeling, not on what them women's saying. That knife can slip and cut your hand wide open."

The dreary scene as we neared the Can House grounds was nothing like I had imagined. And there was that indescribably nasty odor—a heavy, sour stench that seemed to press toward us, surrounding us as we walked. It saturated the hot air until one breathed it and tasted it. The factory resembled a long gray tin-roofed shed, with its sides open so that one could see through to the other side. At the shady end of the building, baskets of shiny ripe tomatoes, row upon row, covered an enormous square of ground. Several trucks in varied conditions and sizes and horse-drawn wagons were being unloaded by men whose faces glistened with sweat that trickled down to soak dingy undershirts. Some wore wide straw hats, shading them from the unmerciful sun. The hats also served as fans to stir up the hot air or as swatters against flies and mosquitoes. Several younger men wore bandanna-type red handkerchiefs, greasy and sweat-stained, tied around their foreheads. In shades ranging from ebony to ivory, muscular arms rippled as basket after basket of tomatoes was heaved from wagons and trucks and placed in long rows on the ground. From there, other workers transported the produce to the scalding machine. No one seemed mindful of the mess underfoot, where flies swarmed over the squashed tomatoes and horse manure. Soon, all would be trampled back into the earth.

Scattered about the grounds in small groups, the peelers sat on boxes and stools, enjoying the last minutes of lunch hour. While they rested, they talked—some in quiet groups, others boisterously. A few drank sodas; however, most drank ice water from tomato cans or whatever they had brought in Mason jars from home. Almost immediately I spotted several familiar faces.

"Hey there, Jane! Bless ma soul if she ain't done brought little Ginny down heah. How you, Sugar?" Sara Mae, a neighbor, called out. "Now don't come down heah apeeling so fast cain' nobody keep up with you."

"I won't," I assured her, letting the comical old lady have fun. In a few minutes, Sara Mae had everybody laughing about the perils of new peelers. Everyone said Sara Mae should be in a show—that she was a show all by herself.

When the steam started up, Momma led me inside so she could help me get ready for peeling. We crossed the concrete floor of the packing area, where several men were lounging among big cardboard cartons, making the most of the few free minutes. Momma nodded as we passed, "Good afternoon, Gentlemen."

"Aft'noon, Miss Jane," they said. Then Bob Moore, wiping sweat with a dirty rag, added, "Hot enough for you?"

"'Deed 'tis, just awful."

We reached the peelers' area and climbed a few steps to a small platform, from which one could view peelers on all sides and observe other operations as well. Then we descended to the area where "inside peelers" worked. After we'd put on old working dresses, Momma showed me how to pin a thick layer of newspapers to the bodice for added protection before securing the oilcloth apron in place. When we were all ready, she carefully pointed out every item she had tried to describe for me many times before.

The overall area reminded me of Henry's old train track. Its oblong curved counter was split lengthwise by a metal track, which soon would be squeaking and rattling noisily as it conveyed basins of scalded tomatoes to peelers. Big, heavy buckets, each bearing a stenciled number, lined both sides of the counter, marking peelers' stations. At some places there were tall stools. Knowing Momma's station was on the inside, I imagined the outside stations might not be so hot or, at least, might not smell so bad since peelers there were closer to occasional breezes from the Pocomoke River, a stone's throw away.

The whistle shrilled its signal. Immediately, the clanging of machinery stopped conversations. As one, the workers rose to their feet. Steam clouded the air. Peelers moved to their stations. Within minutes, the first pan, a big, heavy basin of steaming tomatoes, was shoved onto the jerking conveyor. Peelers, in an assortment of protective garb, stood at attention watching the tomatoes roll by until the last gap on the track was filled. Then Harold, the operations manager, shouted for them to begin. Each peeler grabbed a pan from the conveyor, pulled it close to her bucket, and began peeling as if her very life depended on the job at hand.

Every now and then two peelers grabbed the same pan because it was filled with extra-large, perfect-looking tomatoes. Then there were harsh words, threats, and sometimes clashes requiring a referee. Usually, though, they peeled steadily for four or five hours at a stretch, standing on wooden planks raised above smelly juice which ran on the floor, breathing steam and sweating until they were soaking wet. All the while the manager moved stealthily behind them, often getting closer than necessary depending on how a peeler looked to him, trying to find some fault with the work. Obsessed with his power, he was known to blow off his own hateful steam as the mood struck him.

Peeling tomatoes was tedious, unpleasant, backbreaking work. The number of basins of tomatoes needed to fill a bucket depended on how the tomatoes were running. Solid tomatoes, large or average-sized ones, were a peeler's delight. But soft tomatoes took twice as long for the same pay. Upon filling a bucket, the peeler rounded it off and pushed it onto the conveyor to be transported to the other side of the platform, where a man emptied it into a bin. A white woman seated on a stool would drop either change or a token into the empty bucket as it moved down the track back to the peeler, who, meanwhile, was filling an empty pan to get started on the next bucket. At times, in the midst of heavy peeling, the workers got a respite when machinery broke down. Then they sat around cooling off and resting. Even so, they were conscious of the number of times a bucket would have returned with whatever pittance passed for pay at the time, if the machine had not broken down.

Afterward, no matter how hard I tried, I could not remember exactly how things happened that first day. Whether it was before or after Momma and I had filled the first bucket, I wasn't sure. What I did remember was a sudden sense of losing the battle against that powerful stench. It swirled around my head, filled my nostrils, seeped down my throat, stirred up my stomach, and generated such sickness that I could fight it no longer. Tomato juice gushed toward me. The cement floor waved and shimmered. Through a steamy haze, hands moved me from the counter. From far off somewhere, voices reverberated through tin-can clangor:

"Jane, let's get her over heah."

"Bessie, sit her down on that box."

"Rest her head on this."

"What happen, Jane?"

"'Deed I don't know, Miss Mary. She scared me half to death. Didn't say one word. Just leant against me, and I saw she was sick," Momma replied nervously. She held a wet cloth to my forehead while someone tried to pull off my apron.

"Poor child. She ain't use to all this mess."

"She be all right. It's the stink in here. That's what 'tis."

"Here, let her smell this," an authoritative voice cut across the others. It was the white woman who worked in the office. The sting of ammonia jolted my head. I took a deep breath, and felt the nausea begin to lose its hold on me. And before long, feeling shaky but better, I asked Momma to let me peel again. I had to prove I could do it. But she wouldn't hear of it. The whole thing had made her nervous, and as soon as she was satisfied that I would be all right, she began looking for a way to send me home.

The women helped her get me over the counter to the outside, and the battle was lost, at least for that summer.

Another summer, though, I went back to the factory, fought every day to overcome the nausea, learned to stand for hours before steaming pans of tomatoes—pulling, peeling, and pushing heavy pans and heavier buckets. I put my sore, blistered feet down on the pavement gently walking home from work. Aching through every bone in my body, I felt too tired to move. Hot baths and rubbing alcohol helped, but when I started out the next morning, tiredness went with me. Then Fate brought an unexpected change. One of the women who inspected the peelers' work became ill; an immediate replacement had to be found. Henry heard about the vacancy first because his job was located near the inspector's platform. After he came home with the news, Poppa saw a man who arranged an interview for me. The possibility of getting work as an inspector and being paid by the hour made all the hateful things about the Can House seem inconsequential. Even that low hourly wage was more than I'd ever make peeling. I'd be able to buy more things needed for school and eliminate one more problem for my parents. For the first time in weeks, my steps were light as I hurried toward the plant office for my interview. Taking a deep breath, I rapped on the screen door.

Inside, the room was nearly dark. I stood in the doorway trying to adjust my eyes to the gloom. A pleasant-looking white woman, dressed in a neat cotton print, sat behind a big dark cluttered desk. To one side of the desk sat a large, ruddy-faced old man gripping a sturdy white cane. I sensed that even if the dark glasses were removed from his eyes, the cold, scornful expression on his face would be no different. In his crisp short-sleeved shirt and gray striped seersucker trousers, he appeared to be cool despite the record-breaking heat. He was the factory owner. Workers dubbed him Old Man Ludden. Turning to the woman, I said, "Good morning. My name is Ginny Holden. I've come to see about getting the inspector's job."

With a half-smile, the woman spoke, "Yes, Ginny." Then she turned to Mr. Ludden. "Mr. Ludden, this is Snow's girl, the one Harold said might work out up there with Serena."

"Humph," he grunted, turning toward me. "You know what the duties of the job are?"

"Yes, I know. And I'm sure . . ."

"Just answer my questions! How old are you anyway?" he asked gruffly.

"Eighteen."

"What makes you think you ought to get the job? Half of 'em been up there wasn't worth a hill of beans."

"I'm a careful worker. I'll do my best to see that no bad tomatoes or cores or skins get by me."

"You understand, you have to work nights when we're loaded?"

"Yes."

"Yes *what?*" he thundered, catching me by surprise.

"I said 'yes,'" I replied, voice quavering. I wondered what had happened, but I didn't have to wonder long.

The old man exploded. Banging his cane on the floor, he shouted, "Say 'Sir' when you speaking to me! Damn it! What the hell do you think this is? I know your pappy. Knew his pappy, too. Ever' last one of you! 'Yes' to me, humph! Don't start thinking going away to school makes you one bit different than the rest of 'em. Not in this town it don't—not long's I'm around here. Coming back here with a whole lotta them city airs! You going to show proper respect when you're in my presence. And don't you forget it for one minute. You . . .!"

I groped for the door. The sound of his ranting and cursing followed me down the steps. In the blinding sunlight, I no longer had to fight the tears. And, as I ran up Linden Avenue, I recalled another day—a day many years ago, when a tiny third-grade pupil ran home in tears because the white superintendent had yelled at her teacher just because she asked him to call her "Miss Blaine" rather than simply by her first name.

That night my father and brother rushed home, anxious to know if I had gotten the job. When I finished telling what had happened, Poppa sat, clenching his fists and shaking his head angrily as he spoke. "That right, huh? So that's how he treated you. Well, we going see how much you got to do like he says. You children just keep your mind on staying in school, and you not going have to bow and scrape to that old buzzard or none the rest of 'em—not if I have to work my fingers to the bone. No sir!" He banged his fist on the table. Sitting there watching my father, I knew I would never forget the look of pain, anger, and fierce determination on his face.

The next morning Momma said the woman in the plant office was waiting at the door when she passed, and she appeared to be embarrassed as she said, "Jane, I'm sorry about the way Mr. Ludden talked to your girl. He had no cause to act like he did. The child didn't do a thing for him to carry on that way. He's just contrary, and he hasn't been feeling so good. So don't pay no attention to it. If Ginny wants the job, she can start work tomorrow."

"All right, Miss Rose," Momma replied, "but I'll have to see what Snow says about it. Mr. Ludden upset Ginny real bad, yelling and cursing at her."

"I know, Jane. Course, he curses all the time. Don't pay it no mind. He won't bother her again. She won't even have to see him before she starts work," Rose assured her.

The two inspectors worked on a high platform, well behind the conveyor and near the relatively dry, clean packing area. There, elevated to a height slightly above the waist of the inspector, a long trough-like bin held peeled tomatoes to be examined. As buckets were emptied, the inspector's duty was, after noting each bucket's number, to go through its contents for cores, specks, or skin. If defects were found, the manager was to be notified. He, in turn, strode up to the identified peeler and proceeded to berate her before fellow workers.

How well do I remember seeing Harold Johnson in action on my first day as a regular peeler. At that time, Lola Brittingham, second peeler on my left, was hard at work with shoulders hunched forward, head lowered over her bucket, and hands flying in a rapid grasp it–core it–skin it motion. Lola seldom joined in conversations while working. From the time she pulled off the first pan until lunch or quitting time, it was Lola, the tomatoes, and the tinkling of tokens in the dripping cotton sack pinned high on her apron. That day, Harold stood behind Lola for at least five minutes, watching her race against time; she had no idea he was there. The lull in conversation should have alerted her, but she paid no attention, just worked faster and faster. Meanwhile, Harold moved closer. He stood there, arms folded and a hateful sneer on his round red face, waiting to pounce on his prey. When Lola had filled the bucket, she gripped it and shoved it on the conveyor. Instantaneously, Harold grabbed her arm, startling her.

"Pull that bucket back off!" he ordered.

Lola eyed him quickly, glancing at the peelers across the counter as she pulled the bucket off, asking, "Why you want me pull it off?"

"Just do like I say!" he yelled, grabbing an empty pan. "Now take them tomatoes outta there and put 'em in here."

Using both hands, Lola began putting the tomatoes into the pan. After a few moments he shouted, "That's enough." He tilted the pan so others would see as he felt among the tomatoes for defects and found two faulty ones. But that wasn't enough for him. Then he found an uncored tomato, which he held close to her face.

"Here's the kind of work you been turning out," he said. "Look here and here. Now I'm telling you this once, and I'm not gonna tell you again. Damn it! You peel them tomatoes right or you through! Hear me? It's plenty people waiting for this job. I see one more bad bucket from you and you're fired. Now dump that bucket in with them skins, and if you wanna keep on working here, you better remember ever' word I said!"

Looking around at the other peelers, who pretended not to hear, he shouted louder, "Damn it to hell, I'm gonna stop letting you all get by with so much, ever' last one of you!"

Feeling satisfied that he had the attention of everyone within earshot, he strode from the area. And the peelers, trying to console Lola, who had kept her head down throughout the incident, voiced their feelings.

"Wish he come over heah and talk to me like that. Bet I'd tell him where to go. Shittin-assed bastard!" snarled Mattie.

Sue Bruce took it up. "What you expect outen poor white trash like him? He ain't no good."

"Can't stand that sneaky cracker. Know what I'd like to do to him? Treat him just like I'm doing this here tomato. This little knife'd move right good in that fat face of hissun," said Sadie, ges-turing menacingly.

"Lola, don't worry yourself about him. He come back heah bothering you some more, he's going to have us to deal with. We going get in it, too. We good'n tired of taking stuff off'n him. Heah he ain't got nothing to do but come 'round here sneaking up on us. That's ever' last thing he do, except setting on his fat, stinking behind." Mable Reed paused to spit on the ground to show her contempt for Harold before adding, "Never been no better'n a common dog!"

For the first time since Harold left, Lola raised her eyes. Al-though she tried not to show it, we could see the hurt in her tired, old face.

"That's all right, girls," she said quietly. "I thanks you for botherin', but 'mongst you don't be getting in no trouble with that Harold and losing your job on 'count of me. We all needs this little money, such as it be. Guess 'taint much of nothing we can do 'bout it. Nothing atall."

Work on the inspector's stand was not easy. Once inspected, piles of tomatoes had to be pushed with wooden paddles from the bin into a chute, which carried them to the processing area. To-mato juice soaked the inspector's stand, but at least it was located a distance from the steam. Even when juice dripped from my el-bows, ran down my apron, and soaked my feet—even when the ache in my back and feet became almost unbearable—I still pre-ferred working at the bin to the peeler's bucket. There were many days, though, when the plant grounds were a sea of tomatoes. No matter how fast the two of us worked, at times it was impossible to keep the mounds of tomatoes down sufficiently for us to see each other from opposite sides of the bin. And there were days when, after having worked from seven in the morning until six in the afternoon, we had to put in extra hours at night—all in a time and place when our earnings were counted on the basis of a few cents an hour.

Although Momma agreed that I was better off working on the stand than peeling, she never liked the idea of my being around Serena, the other inspector. She didn't know Serena, but she knew *about* her, just as everyone in town did. She was what they called a "high yellar woman." She came to work every day dressed up for Sunday. She wore too much rouge and lipstick and a store-bought, waterproof apron over pretty cotton prints. Folks said she ran with white men! That, among folks down home, was about the lowest thing any black woman could do. Yet, I was fascinated by Serena, whose face wasn't pretty but whose figure and slow, hip-swinging walk, men said, "could make a blind man stare." Serena, in turn, amused by my youth and naivete, enjoyed telling me about her experiences and the lovely things in her home, which she offered to show me if I would visit her. She entertained me with exciting details of trips to New York, Chicago, Atlantic City, and other faraway places that I had seen only in movies, magazines, and daydreams.

It took only one painful incident to make me see Serena for what she was. It happened on a sticky afternoon when the air was heavy with steam and thunder rumbled through the din of clanging machinery. Serena was describing her "good time" of the past weekend, and I, clinging to every word, was being transported to another world. For a few moments, factory noises were muffled amid visions of floating chiffon, soft music, a handsome man's arm circling my waist, a whisper . . .

"Hey you!" a shout suddenly rang out. "Shut your mouth and pay attention to them tomatoes. See this here tomato? It just now come down, specks and all, from that bin. I better not have to tell you about it again. You understand me?"

Harold, a snarl twisting his big red face, stood below my side of the platform glaring, emphasizing his words by pointing the faulty tomato at me. Swallowing hard, I wanted more than anything else in the world to spit down on that white spot between his ugly beady eyes and into his stringy hair. But I nodded that I understood. I knew I probably had said less than a dozen words in the past half hour. Serena had been doing all the talking, but I had been listening. Before I looked away from Harold, I saw him wink and grin at Serena, who caught her bottom lip between perfect teeth and suppressed a smile. In a flash I saw it all: what people said about Serena and that cracker was true! So now she was the one and probably would be until he tired of her. Then, to him she'd be just another "nigger," a slut he'd look past whenever they met on the street.

Why, I wondered, did she let him talk to me like that? She could've told him she was the one talking, not me. He'd never fuss at her. And that tomato—couldn't it as easily have been Serena who let it slip by? Yet when he stood there berating me, she acted like she had nothing to do with me or the work. Why didn't she say something?

In that moment the "Serena fascination" drained from the bin with specks and cores and other waste. I saw Serena clearly for the first time. I understood then why people said the things they did about her kind. "Never again," I vowed, "will I ever be so dumb!"

✦

The sultry days of summer were almost over. Tree leaves sagged, limp and parched, from the long, hot, dry spell. Weeds wilted on ditch banks, in fields, and along crusted cracked road banks. August heat burned the powdery earth on which no rain had fallen since the week of the hurricane when the river overflowed. Then, storms came again with even greater force than before. On Market Street, water rose above automobile wheels. Men in hip boots waded to work downtown. Women and children stayed indoors. The driving force of wind and rain made all outdoors hazardous. Property that was not tightly fastened down, and much that was, sailed past rattling windows and over rooftops, inflicting injuries and damaging anything in its path. Poor families, living in low-built shabby houses, lost their meager belongings to flood waters. Day after day, the violence of nature pounded everything relentlessly as if the Shore itself had angered the gods. Then as suddenly as it had come, the storm was over. Light rain gradually diminished, the wind lost its roar, and an unnatural calm settled over the area. The next day the sun came out, bright and blinding, baring the devastation dealt to the Shore.

No strangers to adversity, Shore men worked together, restoring that which could be restored, repairing damages, and cleaning up. Sodden furniture and other possessions dried outdoors in the sun. And warm, dry sand once again replaced clammy mud. Although the awful storm was over, reminders left in its wake would haunt Shore men for some time.

The Can House whistle had been silenced by the hurricane. Many fields of tomatoes and fall crops were ruined as they lay beneath rivers of floodwater. When, after an uneasy time of waiting, we heard the factory would be running in a few days, we breathed prayers of thanks. The old whistle sounded one day about mid-morning. It gave a hoarse screech, as if it, too, had been ruined by the storm. Within a few minutes it started up again, caught on a harsh note, and blasted out its summons. Male workers, faced with the task of getting the creaking, rusty machinery going again, had been on the job for days. Gradually women from outlying areas filed in and sat around the conveyor resting from long hikes to town. Town peelers put aside everything else, grabbed equipment bags, and covered ground from all directions. But the revival was short-lived. Instead of the daily back-aching pace to which they were accustomed, workers were employed one day and off the next. Even when the factory was running, the most solid-looking tomatoes, often deceptively waterlogged, were apt to burst at the touch of a peeling knife. So the Can House shut down early, and its workers were unemployed before the usual end to the season. They did whatever work they could find and were thankful for the little earned before the onset of winter, when jobs would be even more scarce.

Although it was almost time to get ready to return to school, I worked as relief dishwasher in a restaurant until the week before registration. Then underwear, blouses, and dresses had to be mended, laundered, and packed. A few carefully selected purchases, still downstairs in bags and boxes, were arranged on the sofa.

Remembering my unhappiness when Henry first left for Hampton and I had to stay home, I tried to control my excitement about returning to Morgan whenever Marie and I were together. Having graduated from high school in the spring, Marie would have to stay home for a year and save what she could from her job at Dr. Hull's. So it was understandable that when I showed her my single new outfit and asked how she liked it, she barely glanced at it and mumbled, "It's all right." Without another word, she went downstairs. That night as we lay in bed, I tried to think of something to say that would make my sister feel better about having to stay home after Henry and I returned to school.

"Marie," I said, "the year'll fly by before you know it. This time next year we both'll be getting ready to go."

"Um hum, good night," she said before turning over to end the conversation. She was at work the next day when I left for Baltimore.

14 · *College Reflections*

So many trials
to overcome
while chained, but steeled . . .
by loving . . .

During the long train ride to Baltimore, I reminisced about times shared with friends I soon would be seeing—except for Esther, my former roommate, who wasn't returning. It was hard to imagine being back on campus without her. Ours really was an ideal college-roomie relationship: from the first day, we seemed to get along as if we had been together forever. We shared each other's problems and happiness, and supported one another in all kinds of ways. We knew and respected times to talk and times to be silent in the close quarters of our room.

Thoughts of Esther reminded me of our freshman year and of the unforgettable purchase a mutual friend helped me select. That purchase turned out to be one of the worst mistakes I've ever made. Ashamed of my worn winter coat, I had written home for permission to sell my only piece of real jewelry, the gold diamond-set ring I had found several years ago. Not wanting me to lose the treasured ring, my parents somehow scraped together enough money for me to buy a decent, warm coat.

I remember getting up extra early on that Saturday morning in order to finish working in time to go shopping for the coat. It was late afternoon before my friend Celeste and I began the long walk downtown. Hours later, we returned lugging several packages. With the money, sufficient for an inexpensive, but good coat, I had bought a pretty green coat with a flared skirt, a cute brown hat trimmed with a pom-pom and a pheasant feather, and a pretty orange crepe dress with pleats down the front and flowers

June Week at Morgan State College, 1940

embroidered on the collar. Any time Momma mentioned what had happened to the money they sacrificed for my coat, she fussed. Before winter was over, that coat had changed from pretty green to the color of withered cabbage. One thing was certain: I had selected it, and I had to wear it that winter, the next winter (the year spent away from Morgan), and for part of the following winter, my first on campus.

Embarrassed by the sad-looking coat, I stayed indoors when the weather grew cold and there were special weekend activities on campus. I made up various excuses for not going out. Then, as soon as everyone left the dorm, I watched other students, dressed in their Sunday best, stroll off to the evening's affair. Although I never complained about the coat, my mother sensed my suffering. Still fussing about my folly, she saved up her wash money until there was enough for another coat. But that time she made the selection herself and mailed it to Baltimore.

One Sunday evening, before the arrival of the new coat, Esther returned from a banquet in Spencer Hall with a red rose. Migraine, not the shabby coat, was the excuse Esther concocted for my absence. So Phil, a classmate, sent me a perfect rose pilfered from a table decoration. I wasn't sure what to think of either the gesture or Phil, a rather sophisticated Baltimorean. In spite of his attention, I wondered whether he was attracted to me or simply amused by the little small-town girl he got a kick out of teasing about almost anything, even my name. "Leave off the IA, " he said grinning "and it fits you perfectly—Virginia." Unsuspecting, I put the accent on the wrong syllable before catching on.

Phil never failed to rib me about my Eastern Shore accent and countless other things—common knowledge to city folks but things I knew nothing about. Yet, he often waited for me after class. And I enjoyed talking and studying with him, just as I did with a few other classmates who, for the most part, treated me in the same protective manner as older classmates had done back home.

Then, during the summer, I received notice of a letter being held at the post office for "postage due." I couldn't imagine what it could be. The envelope was long and fat, and Phil's return address was scrawled across the flap. In several pages he described his activities of the summer and his plans for the coming academic year. He closed by saying he thought of me often and would like to hear from me. Phil's letter surprised me; we'd never spoken of writing. And I, knowing the type of girls he went around with, had not thought about it. Still it was a nice letter. In a few days, I answered. The correspondence continued, and I began to wonder how I would feel about him once we were back in school.

"Oh well, I'll see what happens," I thought, suddenly realizing that I had spent most of the long train ride remembering first- and second-year college experiences.

"Baltimore! Baltimore!" the conductor shouted. The train rounded the last bend and pulled into Penn Station.

Junior year proved to be as filled with wonders and problems as I could imagine. Some events were destined to be memories of a lifetime, others, for the moment. Having been granted sufficient self-help to make ends meet, I concentrated on my studies. Nothing, to me, was as important as being able to justify the extreme sacrifices my parents were making to keep all of us in school.

Seizing every opportunity to help out financially, I entered a national essay contest, which was publicized on bulletin boards around campus. For weeks, I worked researching, organizing, writing, and rewriting. Finally, when the paper was finished, I wondered whether I had wasted too much time—time that should have been spent on my courses—working on a paper that, more than likely, would amount to nothing. Surely, many top students from leading colleges had submitted papers. Even Gerald Chapman, "the brain" on campus, was competing. A month passed without word from the contest sponsors. Then one gray

November day a call came from the dean. After a timid knock, I entered the office. Gerald was already there. Dean George's eyes twinkled the way they did whenever he was pleased about something. He wasted no time in sharing a letter from the essay contest sponsors: prize-winning essays had been written by two Morganites! Gerald won first prize and I, second. Hardly believing it actually had happened, I asked if second prize would help with my tuition, which was paid by my job, scholarship, and church loan—leaving a small sum to be paid by my father. But even a small amount was too much, considering all his other bills. Dean George looked over some figures before answering.

"It surely will help a great deal, Ginny. With the prize money applied to your bill, you won't owe one penny from now through the end of the second semester!"

Naturally, I was thrilled about winning, but I was overjoyed to know that my parents would have nothing to pay on my bill for the remainder of the academic year. Dean George praised us for bringing honor to Morgan; then he told us to go spread the good news. If in this life, each person is allowed three perfect days, I'd willingly count that day as one.

Upon receiving word of my winning, my mother said she could hardly wait until lunchtime to tell Poppa. She later related his reactions. For a few minutes after reading the letter, he said nothing. Only the half-smile creeping through his pensive expression signified his pleasure. Finally, he told Momma that, although he knew I did not want them to spend one unnecessary penny on me, maybe—just maybe—they could manage to send "enough so she can join that sorority her friends been wanting her to join," something I had never once hinted for.

A few days later, I received a special delivery from home containing a money order and a note that read, in part, "Your father and me are real proud of you for winning the contest. He said since he won't have no more bills for you this year, he's sending this money so you can join that club you been talking about."

For the next few weeks so many things were right that I wondered how long it could last. One day a photographer arrived on campus to take pictures of the essay contest winners. About a

The Ivy Leaf Club at Morgan College
(Adele, club president, is standing in top row, second from right)

week later, a student burst into the dorm waving the *Afro-American* newspaper and shouting, "Extra!" All of us crowded around to see pictures of the winners. Although Morgan students were accustomed to local press coverage, mainly it was about winning streaks of the football and basketball teams. So the essay winners created quite a stir. Gerald enjoyed a special celebrity status because, in addition to being a scholar, he was captain of the football team. Everyone around campus seemed to be excited about the winnings and publicity.

Thanksgiving came, and Lorraine, my new roommate, invited me to spend the holiday weekend with her family in Baltimore. On Saturday night we were invited to a party. Lorraine's date was Berkley Gray; mine, for a special evening, was Phil. But some students determined to have a ball drank too much. One vomited on the stairs and made such a stinking mess that I felt nauseous for the rest of the night. All I wanted was to get out of there, away from the noise and the odor of whiskey, away from the stench of vomit that assailed my nostrils and sickened my every breath, away from the partygoers and their "good time." Even as I danced with some of the more nearly sober fellows, all I could do was wonder if that was what having a good time meant, whether that could have been all I was missing when I had fussed about not being able to go anywhere or do anything. Even worse, Phil had disappeared, and no one seemed to know where he was. A half hour had passed since Berkley told me Phil would be right in as soon as he returned from an errand. We were packed in Berkley's car, ready to pull off when Phil finally appeared, looking flushed and sheepish. By that time Lorraine already had told me, as gently as she could, that Phil had gotten sick.

"You mean he got drunk, don't you, Lorraine?" I asked, feeling disgusted and ashamed that I had come to the party with the one who had ruined it for me.

Glimpsing Phil from the car window, I turned away, hating the sight of his flushed face. But there he stood, motioning for me to let him into the already crowded car. Worse yet, I had to sit on his lap! Lorraine tried to convince me that I was making too much of the incident when I told her I really did not want to see Phil again. With considerable reluctance, I kept our Sunday night date. The evening was pleasant, as Lorraine had predicted, but nothing erased that unpleasant memory. However, because I kept that date, I gained a lasting friendship when Phil took me to meet a friend, Margret Williams, who was visiting her relatives for the holidays. And ever since that long ago evening, Margret and I have shared the blessings of being best friends.

✦

After Thanksgiving, everyone was caught up in plans for Christmas and going home. I felt sorry for the few who would remain on campus for various reasons throughout the holidays. Some pretended they didn't mind, even bragged about the ball they would have in the minimally supervised dorms. But almost all who stayed knew the campus would be lonely and secretly wished they, too, were homeward bound for the holidays.

I hardly could wait to get to Pocomoke, to see everyone again, and especially to hear about Marie's freshman experiences at Hampton Institute. When the train pulled into the station, my father was waiting. Happily, we embraced. Jumping into the garage truck, we headed down Fourth Street. The gray bare trees and ice-patched, frozen ground made me shiver.

"What's matter? Cold?" Poppa asked.

"Not too much. It just looks so cold, the trees and everything. So much ice all over the ground. Look at the things on Miss Brown's clothesline, Poppa! Don't the long drawers look funny, frozen so the arms and legs're all sticking out?"

"Yeah," he chuckled. "We havin' a real cold snap, Honey. Don't know when it's been this cold. Them clothes probably froze up soon's they put 'em out there. Put you out in near-zero weather, you'd freeze up, too. Well, they say it's no place like home, Girlie. Here you are."

Momma had been listening for us. Before the motor cut off with a jolt, she had flung open the kitchen door, and I ran to her. We embraced, and my world was filled with the happiness of being home again and feeling the love of my parents: smelling sweet potatoes oozing syrup in the oven, warming my hands over the hot wood-burning stove, being a short walk from Mom's and anticipating the magic of Christmas at home—everything good!

"You lookin' well, thank the Lord," Momma said.

"You all sure look good, too. I can't tell you how good it feels to be home."

"We just glad as you, Honey," Poppa assured me. "Well, it's time I'm gettin' back to work. No need to tell you two to enjoy yourself. See you tonight."

"Bye, Poppa. I got a whole lot to tell you," I called as he closed the door against the frigid air.

We talked until we'd exhausted every possible topic. While Momma ironed, I sat resting my head against the high back of the old rocking chair.

"Guess you wantin' to go down Mom's, huh?" she suggested, knowing that I was anxious to go but not wanting to appear to be in a hurry to end our own time together. "Go on, Ginny. I won't think hard. You want to see Mom, and I don't blame you one bit. We going have plenty time to talk all we want. "

"Guess I'll go on then, since you don't mind, but I won't stay too long," I promised, getting my coat and tam from the dining room and holding the coat close to the stove to warm the chill from the lining.

As I neared my grandmother's, I decided to go past the front porch and through the side yard, instead of cutting across the old school yard to the back, where she would be sure to see me pass the kitchen window. Although she knew I was coming home, I still wanted to surprise her. After picking my way across the frozen, rutted yard, I reached the door and knocked once.

"Com'on in!" Mom called.

Pretending to fumble with the doorknob, I slowly opened the door. The sharp glance Mom directed toward the door disappeared in an instant. Laying down her iron, she hugged me to the warmth of her bosom.

"Bless my soul if 'tain't my child! Sugar, when you get home?"

"Just this afternoon. My, but I'm glad to see you."

Smiling, Mom said, "Sugar, Ah declare, Ah'm so glad you home Ah don't know what to do. Been well since you been away?"

"Yes ma'am, except for the same old monthly trouble. That's bad as ever."

"That'll get better, Sugar. Ah use to be same way. You'll grow outen it 'fore long. Just try'n be patient," she advised. "Wish Ah had somethin' good to offer you. Ain't made nary a thing sweet; but don't worry, Mom's going make plum pudding whilst you home. Going bake a coconut layer cake, choc'lit, too!"

"And I'll be ready for 'em, too. Meals at school's all right, but I miss yours and Momma's cooking."

"Well, you sure going get your fill whilst you home," she promised. "Now, Sugar, tell me all about ever'thing."

It was almost supper time when I realized how long we had been talking. Time passed so quickly when we were together. After asking about each relative and friend, I bundled up to brave the cold again.

When Henry and Marie arrived from Hampton next day, the seven of us were together again. It hardly seemed as if we had been apart. Henry took Buddy into the woods and they gathered holly, pine, and cedar to make wreaths for the windows and front door. Soon the woodsy green scent drifted through the rooms, and the house smelled all Christmasy.

On Sunday mornings our household moved at a restful pace. When he did not have to work, Poppa was the last to come downstairs. Then following "good mornings," he always turned to Momma: "Ready, Hon?"

"Whenever you are, Snow," she replied.

"All right, Children," he called, "let's have prayers."

Immediately, each one knelt before a chair and bowed his head, as Poppa prayed:

"Dear Heav'nly Father, we come to Thee this morning with thankful hearts that Thou has spared us to see another Sunday. We thank Thee, Lord, for blessing us to have all our little family together once again under this roof Thou blest us to call our home. We thank Thee, Lord, for bringing our loved ones home safe and sound. Though they been far away, we know they're ever in Thy watchful care and Thou would ever give them counsel. We thank Thee, Father, for watching over us here at home, for giving us courage and hope when the way gets dark and discouraging, for giving us health and strength when many's suffering and dying. We thank Thee for the good wife and mother Thou has blest us with and ask Thee to keep her ever in Thy loving care. Help us to show gratitude for our many blessings. And when our work on earth is done, we ask Thee to take us home in Heaven with Thee. These and all blessings, we ask in the name of Jesus Christ. Amen."

After prayers and breakfast, we dressed for church. And as Marie and I rushed about in our cold bedroom, I thought how good it was just to be home again. There was something about kneeling with the family and listening to Poppa pray—the same as we had done ever since we were small—that made me realize how fortunate I was to have such a mother and father and family and home. Even without a bathtub and basin, even without warm rooms upstairs, to me, that home was dearer than any other in the whole world. And, with the windows all dressed in freshly ironed lace

Good friend Betty Brown and Adele home for Christmas

curtains framing fragrant wreaths and the Christmas tree trans-
forming the front room into a sparkling fairyland, our little house,
in its own way, was as beautiful at Christmas as the finest house
on Market Street.

✦

Back on campus in Baltimore, sitting in economics class as the professor droned on, I wondered how anything I'd waited for so long
and enjoyed so much could come and go as quickly as Christmas. It
seemed almost as though I'd never left the campus. But memories
of those happy times with relatives and friends helped dispel the
loneliness. It helped a bit to remember that, even though it had
been snowing steadily since early morning, before long spring
would come. Still, many things would change and change again before forsythia brightened the taupe-hued countryside. At that time,
the whole world seemed to be a gloomier shade of gray.

There are times when only the onset of more serious problems
can make us realize the relative insignificance of earlier concerns.
Such was the case when in the midst of post-holiday doldrums, a
wave of flu hit the campus, causing a number of students to lose
time from classes. Weeks later, many of us, still not fully recovered
from flu's enervating aftereffects, struggled to catch up, keep up,
and make up missed work.

One day, however, things began to change. The persistent ringing of the hall phone disturbed my concentration. Pushing aside my assignment, I ran down the corridor certain the party would hang up before I could answer. But I made it, and the call was for me—the dean's office! Wondering what could be the reason for the summons, I hurried down the walk. The secretary told me to go right in—Dean George was waiting. The mystery deepened when, after signing some letters, he started talking about world affairs. Then he said, "I hear you've been having quite a time of it. That flu can knock you out, all right. But I believe I have just what it'll take to make you feel better."

He pushed the buzzer. When Mrs. Hughes came to the door, the dean nodded and she left. As soon as she closed one door, the other door to the office opened. I could not believe my eyes!

"Do you know this gentleman?" asked Dean George with mock seriousness.

Standing in the doorway, looking tired but happy, was my father. I ran across the room and hid my tears in the sweater he wore under his old blue serge suit coat. The dean, pleased with his role in the little plot, explained that he had to keep an appointment off campus. Before leaving, he invited us to visit in his office for as long as we liked. He added that my father should feel proud of my record—also that he expected me to save him a piece of the cake, which was certain to be one item in the rope-tied, cardboard box packed by my mother.

Hours after the visit was over, Lorraine and I were still talking about the surprise as we feasted on huge slices of delicious chocolate layer cake. I described every detail of the visit, made possible when my father learned that his old friend Ben was driving to Baltimore to make a delivery. Because my parents were concerned, especially since the bout with flu, they decided it would be good for all of us if he made the trip with Ben. How right they were! Never have I been happier to see anyone than I was to see my father that day.

With the trials of probation and initiation into Alpha Delta chapter of Alpha Kappa Alpha sorority, as well as midterm exams behind me, I felt as if weights had dropped from my shoulders.

Then came time for social activities on campus, along with the new experience of being part of the sorority sisterhood.

During those early days of my being part of that special world, I never imagined anything could cast a shadow over the prideful, sisterly camaraderie I felt. However, an unforgettable experience was lurking in the wings, even then, awaiting the next semester's activities.

Morgan's Homecoming Game was the grand event of the football season, and the selection of Homecoming Queen was an essential preliminary activity. Of course, the queen and her court were an attractive addition to the halftime parade. The queen's ladies-in-waiting were chosen from the different sororities, along with her own. I was delighted to be chosen to represent mine, but that elation was short-lived. It vanished on a bright fall day when I was studying in my dorm room, and an entourage of my sorority sisters paid me a visit—a most unusual occurrence at noon, when most students were at lunch or studying. But I soon learned their mission. They had come to examine what I planned to wear for the homecoming parade.

True, my parents and I could not afford expensive clothes for me, but I always managed to buy one or two attractive outfits, and I always took pride in my appearance. Otherwise, I would have refused the invitation. The lovely black-wool pleated skirt and fine tweed jacket, precious rose angora sweater, and black accessories made a perfect outfit for the occasion. Or so I thought. The facial expressions and murmurings of my "sisters" did not agree. Something flashy was preferred.

I assured them that they should not concern themselves about my participating; they could select a replacement. I did not want to listen to their stammerings; I just wanted them to leave. Their visit was a humiliation. Far worse, at the time, the actions of a few immature students belied everything I believed to be representative of the sorority.

At the big game, I reluctantly sat with my sorority sisters—wearing the tiny, mum corsage that they had selected for each of us—when Phil came and placed the most beautiful beribboned, fluffy chrysanthemum corsage on my lap. "To go with that sharp outfit," he said so my seatmates could hear. As I pinned on his corsage, I knew I never would forget what that gesture meant to me.

There was something else I haven't forgotten about that day. It involves the appearance of my replacement, who wore a flaming red ensemble trimmed with fluffy gray fox fur from neckline to hem. Generously applied makeup matched her ensemble. I was a bit surprised when one of my "fashion critics" came over and said, "I'm so sorry we changed things; you really would have represented us, Ginny." But those words were too late to make a difference, in more ways than one.

Nevertheless, I refused to let one dreadful experience intrude too much into all the pleasurable activities of campus life, especially in a world awaiting the miracles of springtime. After spring vacation, the rustic scenery of the campus was transformed by leafing trees, lush green lawns, crocus, and forsythia. Lovers, oblivious of everything except each other, strolled the grounds. Students from town wandered off in pairs whenever they could manage. Resident students did the same, although we were free to stroll weekdays during the magic hours between dinner and nightfall, as well as during long, wonderful weekends.

Gradually, I began to feel twinges of disappointment whenever Martin, another classmate, was not waiting to walk with me after dinner. At first I denied it even to myself, but Martin made me feel secure and special. He was different somehow—intelligent and attractive, yet unassuming. I liked him, just as I knew he liked me. But he and Phil were friends; in spite of the fact that there was no real commitment between Phil and me, Martin knew there was a relationship of some kind. Even I wasn't sure of what that might amount to. Actually, I liked them both, but I wasn't sure of my feelings for either. All I really knew was the wonder of springtime, especially when one is young and happy. Too soon, however, finals were over. And once again we students were returning home for the summer.

15 · Commencement

So many turns
carved by black men
to make life worth the living . . .

Every summer, many blacks from Pocomoke worked in Ocean
City, Maryland, during the resort's busiest season. Ned Rollins, a
painter by trade and Mount Zion's choir leader, was also an excellent cook. He boasted of having cooked in the same Ocean City
hotel for more than twenty seasons. Young people seeking jobs
depended on Ned's help. He advised them of prospects and
helped place them in "his hotel" whenever possible. They worked
as maids, waiters, dishwashers, cooks, kitchen helpers, janitors, or
on any other jobs they could get. Since room and board were provided at the hotels, practically all the workers counted on saving as
much as possible for the lean months ahead.

After a week at home, I went to see Mr. Ned about getting
work in his hotel. He not only got me a job as a waitress but also
promised to save space in his car for me when they left for the season. I was delighted. It would be a long while before tomatoes
were ripe and work began at the cannery. In Ocean City I would
have a job for the entire summer; then my parents would have
very little to pay on my bills. The idea of working at the beach was
exciting; it reminded me of the yearly Sunday school picnics.

Mr. Ned's hotel was not one of the big, fancy buildings on the
boardwalk. However, its operation required a staff of several employees to work steadily from morning until night, with very little
time off. Workers' quarters, located below the kitchen area, were
dark, damp, musty cubicles. Those tiny rooms appeared to have
been an afterthought to fill in the high open area between the
ground and the floor of the building. Around the corner, near the

rear entrance, was a closet containing a toilet and basin—the sole bath facilities for black hotel employees.

The moment I saw "the room" and the lumpy low cot on my side of it, I wanted to go home. Only the kindness of Hazel, the girl I shared the room with, gave me the courage to stay. Hazel was from Pocomoke, too, but back in school I was too young for her crowd. And there was still another barrier: the few from our hometown who did struggle to go to college were, for some unspoken reason, no longer accepted as regular friends but categorized as "different." So at first, I was uneasy, not knowing how Hazel felt about room-sharing. But we were in Ocean City, not Pocomoke, and Hazel—probably remembering the little girl she and others had sheltered—was friendly and kind. Although she did maid's work, she had experience as a waitress, and she taught me how to lift and balance a heavy tray, along with other tricks of the trade. We really enjoyed each other's company, but nothing helped when, after an exhausting day, I slumped on that hated cot. I could feel my skin crawl beneath the damp, dingy sheet that smelled of mold and mildew and the gritty, dark covers that touched the floor, where sand appeared to rise up between the boards faster than we could sweep it outside.

Whether I would have stuck it out for the season under those circumstances I'll never know, for a frightening incident precipitated an abrupt change. On that particular night, we had been unusually busy, dashing between kitchen and dining room, narrowly missing collisions with loaded trays, trying to please disgruntled guests as the dining room filled up each time a table became available. Finally, the last customer left. Too tired to eat, I had just cleared and set up my last table and headed for my room when Bernice, the white woman in charge of waitresses, told me I was wanted in 307.

"For what?" I asked, not moving from the door.

"Mr. Carey and them want some extra glasses and some ice."

"I'm all through for the night. Let Bob take it."

"They asked for you, Ginny. It won't take but a minute, and more'n likely it's a fat tip in it for you. You better take it on up."

"Go ahead, Ginny," Hazel urged. "I'll wait to you get back."

I knocked, holding the tray ready to hand to whoever came to the door. From the sound of their voices, I knew better than to go into that room. It was apparent at dinner that they had been drinking. Although Carey himself seemed to be a decent person, I was glad when they left the dining room. A short blonde man opened the door.

"Here's your order," I said, holding out the tray, which he ignored.

"Hey, Clyde," he shouted, "didn't you say you want to see Ginny?"

Carey, lounging on a bed, replied quickly, "Sure I do. Come in, Ginny. It's all right. I just want to talk to you a minute."

My eyes flashed from Clyde to the others watching from across the room.

"I can't, Mr. Carey," I said. "I'm off duty now. Just brought this up and I'm through."

"Come on in here, Ginny!" the blonde man ordered, taking the tray with one hand and grasping my wrist with the other. He jerked me inside, set the tray on the bureau, and backed against the door. My heart was pounding, but I dared not let them know.

"Would you please move so I can get out?" I asked the blonde man.

"Wantcha to have a lil drink with us. Tha's all," he said, slurring the words.

I told him I did not drink—that even if I did, I would not drink with them. Then Carey got up. The others watched but said nothing. He motioned for the blonde man to leave the door.

"We just want to be friendly, Ginny," he said. "We're leaving for New York tomorrow, and you've been such a good waitress that we wanted to do something for you."

I reminded him that they could "do something" for me at breakfast. The man sprawling in a chair nearby cleared his throat impatiently, shifted his position, and eyed me from head to feet.

"Do you like New York, Ginny?" Clyde asked.

"I've never been there."

"You haven't!" he exclaimed. "Would you like to go there? You could go back with us."

"With you!" I could hardly believe I'd heard what he said.

"Now don't misunderstand me," he hastened to explain. "Bernice told me you're a college student. I can get you work that will pay you more in one day than you make an entire week here and . . ."

"And you think she's cute, and you've been wanting to get hold of her ever since we got here," interjected the red-haired man, who until then had not spoken, " 'specially since you saw her on the beach in that red bathing suit."

"Okay, Brad, cut it!" snapped Clyde. He turned back to me, as I edged closer to the door, and said, "Don't mind Brad. He's drunk."

"Like hell I am!" shouted Brad. "I'm no drunker'n I was when you sent for her so we could . . ."

"Brad!" Clyde shouted.

At that moment I bolted from the room. But I could not out-run the words that trailed me down the hall:

"You damn fool! Had her right in here and let her go!"

"But we said if she'd take a few drinks. Besides, now you see she's not that kind of girl."

"What the hell are you talking about? A nigger's a nigger! You ever heard of one who wouldn't . . . Oh , forget it!"

"Ye-e-es," a drunken voice sang out, "we have no black bottom . . . we have no black bottom to-oo-da-a-ay . . ."

Although Hazel tried to convince me that everything would be all right after Clyde's party left in the morning, I quit that night. It was clear that Bernice was involved in the plot in 307 when she told me to give them room service. I wanted nothing more to do with her. Hazel asked me to stay with her until I found another job. Having no place else to go, I stayed, but only long enough to find a job that lasted until it was time to return to Morgan for the fall semester.

◆

In 1939, the State of Maryland purchased Morgan College in re-sponse to a commission's findings that the state should provide more opportunities for black Marylanders. There would be an extra air of excitement and pride on the Morgan State College campus, but for a while my chances of returning to college that fall were slim. Money from a few poor-paying odd jobs would not cover what I needed to make to pay tuition and bills. But word came that the church loan could be increased a few dollars. So Poppa, remembering the year that contest winnings had helped pay my bills, promised they would figure out some way to make up the rest. It worried me that my parents would have this unexpected burden added to an already heavy load. The only consolation lay in the fact that, if only we could make it through the year, Henry and I would be graduated. Then I could help with the others.

Senior year seemed to pass with the speed of an express train, pausing to make designated stops but losing no time for those who floundered along the way. In September, May seemed too far away for one to be concerned about all the impossible things to be done before honeysuckle once again bloomed along the campus walls. But September passed to October, and too soon after the first football games, cheers heard in the stadium became applause for feats on the basketball floor. Yet a few students found time to enter the first short-story contest to be held on campus. Participants guarded their creative efforts with utmost secrecy. Whenever the contest was brought up, even in intimate groups, no contestant would talk about his "tour de force."

On a beautiful Sunday afternoon in mid-December, an air of mystery pervaded the spacious lounge in Soper Library.

Students, faculty, and visitors chatted in small groups and enjoyed refreshments until Professor Fisher stood behind the lectern. Then there was total quiet. Without introductory remarks or announcements of the contest winner, she opened a folder and began to read: "In a quiet, little town on the Eastern Shore of Maryland . . ." Martin squeezed my hand as I blinked back a tear. Professor Fisher was reading "The Miracle of Christmas"—my story, the winner!

Professors steered us seniors through weighty term papers, into practice teaching, and endless other requirements for graduation. Deadlines came and went with dizzying speed. We complained that time, racing by so fast, was depriving us too soon of our long-awaited senior status.

When I was invited to spend Christmas vacation in the city with Celeste and her family, I was glad. The train fare for a trip home could be applied to my bill, and I could walk from her house to Enoch Pratt Library to work on term papers and study for exams. Also, the prospect of Christmas in the city was exciting, as were our plans for an upcoming fraternity formal. I even had a gown—black velvet, slim and sophisticated—bought on sale for under ten dollars. Phil invited me, and Celeste was going with her fiancé. "It should be fun," I thought, "to be doing things I'd dreamed about all those years." But I realized that nothing, not even the finest ball with the most dazzling Prince Charming, could equal what I would miss on my first Christmas away from my family and home.

After the formal, Celeste and I talked until dawn about happenings of the evening.

"I saw Martin watching you when you were dancing with Phil," she teased.

"How about when I danced with him?"

"Oh, I saw him then, too, but that's different. Ginny, are you sure about Phil?"

"Sure about him? I don't know what you mean."

"You know exactly what I mean! Phil's about as dependable as my broken watch. He'd even be trying to make time with me, knowing we're best friends, if I'd let him. Now Martin's crazy about you. I just can't figure you out. Martin's sharp and he's got class. From where I stand, he's worth a dozen Phils any old day."

"Martin's got a girl back in his hometown," I interjected.

"And Phil's got a few right here," quipped Celeste. "Girl, you'd better stop being so blind."

"Maybe I'm not as blind as you think."

"Ginny, I'll say this, then I'll shut up," Celeste warned. "If you get seriously involved with Phil—and I sure Lord hope you don't—he'd never treat you the way Martin would. Bet anything, if you and Phil'd get married and were going to have a baby, when it was time to get you to the hospital, Martin would be the one ready to take you. Phil'd be out somewhere with the boys, or worse!"

"You sure don't give him much credit, do you?"

"Just as much as he deserves," retorted Celeste. "Go to sleep, Ginny. It's almost day."

During a hectic last semester, we weathered an extremely cold winter, all the nightmares of practice teaching, an outbreak of flu, numerous crises involving finals, makeup projects, and other incidents both social and academic. However, most of us in the Morgan State College Class of 1940 survived.

✦

An air of expectancy enveloped the campus on June 6, Graduation Day. Outside, hundreds of folding chairs lined the spacious green football field. The speakers' platform was all ready for dignitaries. Cars continuously crunched over the graveled drive past the girls' dorms. Inside the dorms, worn lounges had been spruced up for the arrival of visitors. Amid the clutter of books, boxes, and luggage—packed or partly packed—excited graduates rushed about unmindful of the disorder.

Earlier, while walking back from breakfast, Martin had been unusually quiet. Instead of leaving me at the dorm entrance, he came inside. Clasping my hands, he held me with a strangely unwavering gaze.

"Ginny," he said, "I want you to remember that you mean more to me than anybody ever has or ever will. Do you hear me?"

Puzzled, I answered, "You sound like you're going to China or something."

"It's hard for me to say," he began in a strained voice, "but I want you to know how I feel. Couldn't sleep much for thinking about you last night. But damn it, Ginny! I'm going to get married soon's I go home!"

"You what?" I gasped, not believing what I'd heard.

"Ginny, I've got to! Don't you understand? I hate telling you this. You know . . ."

"I know I had no business believing you. You're just bad as—oh, what difference does it make anyway?"

"Listen to me, Ginny, please," Martin begged, turning me to face him. "Do you think if I had known—but you know me better than that. I had no idea anything was wrong. Not until last night when I got a call from home."

So that was that. Nothing more to talk about. Martin would do what the folks back home expected, the "honorable" thing. From my bedroom I watched him descend the sloping green, cross Cold Spring Lane, and climb the winding quarry stone steps up the hill to Baldwin Hall. Long after he had disappeared behind the shrubbery, I stood staring outside, thinking of Martin and of the years of expectations—nothing to do with Martin—that had preceded commencement day. And I wondered why, when finally that long-anticipated day had come, there was little joy within me.

Outside, excitement reigned. While some students dashed in and out of dorms, others strolled the familiar grounds for the last time before graduation. Alone in my room, I contemplated the irony of it all as tears dampened the lace-edged jabot of my best blouse.

With my parents' arrival, unhappiness was forgotten. And the tears were tears of joy. We were so happy and excited in those moments of talking together, tripping over each other's words.

"Yeah, Henry and Marie's home—you know he graduated last week, thank the Lord. It's a good feeling with you and Henry, all through college. Mom sends her love. Said she can't hardly wait to see you, and she's praying you going get along all right. Won't be too long now 'fore Marie's graduating, too. We know you want to help, Honey. No, I'm afraid Henry won't be able to help—your brother's married, Honey. No need of telling you, Ginny, then you'd been worrying about that, too."

"Ginny," Poppa asked, "they got somewheres we can freshen up and get dressed?"

When he returned from the men's dorm, rested and handsome in his good gray suit, he complimented Momma on the way her hair was styled—courtesy of one of my friends. Then he turned to me as I waited, all capped and gowned.

"Well, Honey," he said, "you made it, spite of ever'thing. Thank the Lord."

Adele's yearbook photo,
Morgan State College, 1940

"Looks like it, Poppa, and all I can say is how much I thank you and Momma. But one day I'm going to do things for you. I won't ever forget all you've done so we could finish college. Don't worry. I'm going to help you with Emily and Buddy. And I mean to make you proud of me."

"We're already proud of you, Honey, graduating with honors and all," he said.

" 'Deed it's the truth," Momma agreed.

"I'll walk over with you so I'll know where to find you when everything's over," I told them. "It's almost time for us to line up."

We found seats for them at the end of a row where they could see everything from processional to recessional. In a matter of minutes there would be standing room only. The band tuned up. Crowds steadily filled long rows of seats. Wondering whether to pinch myself to make sure it wasn't a dream, I took my place in line. On signal, the long column of black academic robes began winding up the hill from the chapel and the music of the band urged the procession forward as we marched between blocks of spectators to our seats.

I felt as if I were in a dream world. The minister's invocation echoed above the audience. Dean George's words drifted through the chirping of birds, and the sound took me back to birdsongs in trees in my grandmother's yard. Memories paddled through my mind, pushing the campus gathering and its sounds farther and farther away until I heard a stream of faraway voices:

In a quiet, little town on the Eastern Shore of Maryland . . . Down by the riverside—land where my fathers died . . . I call you Mr. Bluff; call me Miss Blaine . . . They lynched a man last night! . . . Silent night, holy night . . . Learn one thing if you don't learn nothing else, Child:

you got to think for yourself . . . There is so little learning in the wisest of us . . . We'll do the best we can, and the Lord'll help us find a way . . . world wouldn't come to an end if they'd let our children go to tenth grade out on Market Street . . . She treated me like a slave . . . like a slave . . . Whole town'd be a damn sight better off if we had more citizens like you—white and colored . . . Just hopes you keeps right on like you doing, Sugar . . . Graduating with honors and all—graduating . . . your graduation . . . graduation . . .

" . . . on the memorable occasion of this, your graduation." The dean's words shattered my wanderings, jolting me back from the days of my youth on the Shore to the ceremonies in Baltimore where rows of graduates prepared to receive diplomas. Rising as if in a trance, I moved to the center aisle and marched up to the platform. I saw the student ahead of me accept her diploma. Then the words resounded about me:

"Adele Virginia Holden."

Invisible hands guided me forward. I shook the speaker's hand, grasped my diploma, and with a dizzying sensation of drifting over the floor, I moved across the platform to the steps. And I walked past the sea of faces toward the uncertainties of the much-awaited "after-graduation" world, a world no longer cloaked in dreams.

Epilogue

Long decades past that never-to-be-forgotten graduation day on Morgan's beloved campus, I reflect on a treasure of memories. Memories of my remarkable parents; of the publication in 1961 of *Figurine and Other Poems* and of the full-window display given my book by the Enoch Pratt Free Library; of the recording of the book by the Maryland State Library for the Blind and Physically Handicapped and of its availability to users across the country; of the graduate fellowship award by Johns Hopkins University and of the perfect graduation ceremony on the Hopkins quadrangle; of being named "Dunbar's Poet" at a special assembly at Dunbar High School; and of being inducted into Iota Phi Lambda's "Society of Living Makers of Negro History."

So many precious moments have passed; so many memories remain—memories of a teaching career that began on Maryland's Eastern Shore in the 1940s and ended with my retirement from the Community College of Baltimore (now Baltimore City Community College) in the 1980s. Throughout those years, there were the usual pluses and minuses, but pluses far outnumbered minuses. Each time I managed to take a boldly printed grammar rule from a book and imprint both meaning and clarified use into a student's mind was, for me, a definite plus. It was equally rewarding to inspire a love of literature in a student, who, on being introduced to Shakespeare, muttered, "Why do I have to read Shakespeare anyway? I'd rather take out the trash than read that stuff!" And there were students' comments that eventually circulated back to the teacher: "She's tough, but you learn in her class"; "I learned more about grammar and writing in one semester in Professor Holden's class than I learned in my whole life"; "She must think we don't have nobody giving us homework but her!" Amid the pluses and minuses, there often were humorous mo-

Student Council President and future Chief Judge, Court of Appeals of Maryland, Robert M. Bell congratulates Adele upon her being named "Dunbar's Poet"

ments. I never shall forget the time, shortly after *Figurine* was published, that a group of seventh-graders surrounded me outside my classroom and looked me up and down. Finally, one of them said, "Our teacher told us to come up here and look at you so we can see what a real, live poet looks like!"

I recall days when I wondered whether my students learned nearly as much from me as I learned from teaching them.

Whenever I look back over the trials of my journey, from the little gray house on Pocomoke City's unpaved Bank Street to the station in life my parents envisioned for me, I always marvel. As if poverty were not enough of a curse, their

Adele and sister Dorothy Emily at Adele's retirement party, 1982

Snow, sister Elizabeth Marie, brother Elroy ("Buddy"), and Adele celebrate Christmas
in Wilmington, Delaware, early 1960s

struggles from the early to mid-decades of the twentieth century
were worsened by the fiercely guarded, rigidly enforced "laws of
the land" that dictated a world of deprivation, discrimination, and
segregation for blacks on the Shore. A world in which theirs and
their children's lives were scarred by atrocities, even nearby lynchings, a world wherein questionable laws remained unchallenged
and most blacks held little or no hope for bettering their conditions. Only those who experienced life in that time and place—or
in similar times and places—can truly relate to the circumscribed
world in which we lived.

When my parents moved to Wilmington, Delaware, during
World War II, they noted differences between Wilmington and
Pocomoke; however, they were equally aware of subtle similari-
ties in the matter of race relations. They talked with new friends
about the great expectations our people had when "our boys" returned home after fighting for our country during World War I.
Those hopes soon faded with the lack of change. A world war
later, my own generation tried to believe things would be different after World War II ended. Basically, things remained too

Iota Phi Lambda Sorority, Kappa Chapter, banquet honoring the society of "Living Makers of Negro History," 1963 (from left: Wiley Daniels, program director, WEBB Radio; Dr. William Henry, President, Maryland State Teachers College, Bowie, Maryland; Adele Holden; Dr. Martin Jenkins, President, Morgan State College; Dr. Parlett Moore, President, Coppin State Teachers College; Lillie Patterson, Specialist in Library Services, Baltimore Public Schools

much the same as before. And that lamentable fact hounded blacks throughout the United States of America, not merely on Maryland's Eastern Shore.

Through the years, my brothers and sisters and I have all tried to make our deeds reflect appreciation for our parents' immeasurable gifts to us. As soon as we could manage, the older three siblings held a mortgage-burning, making the Wilmington property completely our parents' own home. They appreciated each thoughtful gesture—too many for individual listings, if remembered. Among my most treasured memories is the joy that shone on my father's face when I gave him the diamond ring he had craved all his life but never could afford; that joy was matched only by my mother's smile when she received her first, and only, personal bank account. Both were special Christmas gifts to them. But no gift from me evoked the prideful glow that beamed from their faces as they admired the full-window display for *Figurine* at the Enoch Pratt Free Library. Perhaps I should have said no gift other

Window at the Enoch Pratt Free Library in downtown Baltimore honoring Adele's book of poetry, *Figurine and Other Poems*

than the dedication in that book: "To my dear parents, Laura Jane and Snow Holden . . . who have given so much to their children."

Just as I always tried to express my love and appreciation to my parents, I never forgot to remember my precious grandmother with visits, gifts, and newsy letters. To me, Adell Dickerson was and always had been a best friend, as well as a wonderful grandmother. As far back as I can remember, it was Mom who used to take Mame and me for long walks in the country. It was she who had calmed my fears as she explained the naturalness of the changes taking place within my prepubescent body. I never forgot the gentle assurance in my grandmother's parting words that afternoon:

"Now, Sugar," she said, "don't be aworrying about nothing. Time come for you to commence and you going be just fine. Hear me? And if's anything atall you wants talk about—don't make no never-mind what 'tis—just c'mon down Mom's."

That's the way it was with Mom and me. We shared secrets, freely talking about anything. Over the years she occasionally warned me to keep our conversations to myself: "Jane'd get mad if she finds out we talk about certain things. No need upsettin' her." And that very special relationship never changed. Although we saw each other less often after my family moved to Wilmington in order for Poppa to make a living wage, we never lost touch.

Mom never revealed her exact age throughout her eighty-some years. She enjoyed a healthy, fulfilling life. But when aging's infirmities struck with a vengeance, she had to be admitted to Peninsula General Hospital in Salisbury. Although doctors assured the family that she should have several reasonably good years left, Mom wanted no part of living life any less than to its fullest. So my dear grandmother died in 1960, while I, convalescing from surgery, was not able to comfort her. Heartsick and struggling to bridle a lifetime's worth of tears, all I could do was send a corsage of the tea roses she loved—a token from me to be forever close to her, as close as her presence has often been to me since the day I returned to Pocomoke twelve years after Mom's death. I would not have returned even then if not to visit my critically ill cousin Mame, who so long ago walked out to Hall's Hill with Mom and me.

After spending most of the day reminiscing with Mame, I took the long-delayed walk up Bank Street to the house where Mom always had welcomed me home. Just for a moment it seemed as if she should come around front, drying her hands on the hem of a bib-topped gingham apron. Torn between dread and desire, I turned into Mom's yard and went into the house where my Aunt Weezie now lived alone.

Inside, the house was at once different, yet the same. Although Weezie stirred up the ashen coals in the old kitchen stove, a kind of quiet chill permeated all downstairs. Furniture, replaced or rearranged, seemed strangely impersonal and unrelated to the warmth of the past.

Standing at the door to Mom's bedroom, I caught a whiff of a long-forgotten odor. It stung my nostrils—carbolic acid! Mom used to paint it on the bedsteads and springs to keep chinches away. The instant I smelled the carbolic acid, I experienced the sensation of being transported somehow so that I stared not into a cold, darkened room but into a familiar one, warm and bright, where shades no longer were drawn at windows rattled by winter winds.

A summer breeze rippled white organdy, alternately sucking curtains against window screens then ballooning them inward to strain against tiebacks. White woodwork accented wallpaper columned in pink and blue morning glories. In varied browns, the heavy unmatched furniture, which had been bought, piece by piece, by Mom from the women she used to wash for, looked the same as before.

In one corner on a dull tan washstand was a china washbowl-pitcher set in white and shades of cool green, along with a matching smaller pitcher and a covered, loop-handled soap dish. Partly hidden by towels hanging on the side rack, a matching slop jar sat on the floor beside a cracked chamber pot.

The oval mirror attached to the shiny squat bureau tilted forward so that it reflected articles on its hand-embroidered runner: Mom's wood-backed mirror, comb, and brush, exposing long gray hairs tangled in its sparse, uneven bristles, along with some trinkets in a tarnished dish.

Near the side window, a worn leather-cushioned rocker moved slightly with the breeze. On the matting-covered floor were two pieces of Mom's handiwork—a round rug which she had made out of old nylon stockings and an oval rug, multicolored, made of plaited rags.

The big double bed, with its intricately carved headboard almost as high as the ceiling, was covered with a pebbly textured off-white spread. And folded across the foot of Mom's bed was her worn, but treasured, "crazy quilt," that handmade patchwork in which stitches still held together fragments of lives: memories, once sewn together by her dear hands.

From the moment I entered Mom's room, I just stared from one familiar object to another, feeling lonely and alone, touching nothing. Then something moved me to caress her patchwork quilt, and for the very first time since her death, I sensed the warmth of her presence as surely as if she were standing there beside me. Overwhelmed with indescribable feelings, I rushed out of her room, closed the door, and ran downstairs.

Many times since that unforgettable moment, I have felt the certainty of my grandmother's nearness, no longer frightening, but kind and assuring, as she always was to me.

✦

"Three things," my parents used to say, "we always hoped we'd see happen in our lifetime—and we're still waiting to see the third." Through hard work, determination, and much sacrifice they managed to "see" the first two: a nice home of their own and the college education of their children. Although they expected no miracles, they never gave up hope for the third: equal rights as guaranteed by the Constitution of the United States of America. They had witnessed denials of too many of those rights—rights still being denied their children, just as they had been denied generations of their ancestors.

The seeds of yearning for their rights had been planted in the deprived, segregated world in which each generation had struggled, even fought, for the enforcement of constitutional rights—rights for which they never should have had to fight. Yet, many brave men, including my father, fought for those rights long before the term "racial equality" was breathed aloud on the Shore. In those years, few blacks could imagine a way out of that world in which their every dream was cursed by poverty and segregation.

Many years passed before heavy rumblings of black discontent were heard and felt in various parts of the country. During that time my father retired from his job as an automobile mechanic; soon afterward, he accepted a job as an automobile mechanics instructor in a Wilmington vocational school. However, just when the breaks he deserved finally came his way, his health began to fail. Long years of overwork and stress soon took an irreparable toll, and he had to give up the job he took such pleasure in doing. Too soon, while still in his sixties, he seemed to be far older than his years.

Having worked since he was a child, going to work was, for my father, as natural as getting out of bed mornings. The abrupt shift from his daily routine to totally unscheduled days was too difficult for him even to pretend to appreciate. Too much was missing from his life; he did not know how not to "be on the job." It seems that even the lifetime enjoyment of his favorite sports, baseball and boxing, wasn't the same for him. One thing, however, did capture his attention: he found kinship in the civil rights movement.

My father became a "you-are-there" supporter of "the movement" and followed every event with a passion. Whenever I spent a weekend with my parents, he briefed me on whatever I had been too busy to follow in detail. Yet, even as I listened, I often wondered what might have been the future for one motherless, bright, little boy had he been given a small fraction of the opportunities he had made possible for his children. And I recalled his regret—apart from the fact that he never had the chance to go beyond elementary school—that he never had the opportunity to take violin lessons, a regret that he repeated whenever we heard the melodious strains from a violin.

Poppa made sure that I should not miss anything significant. He likened a much-publicized lynching to one we had suffered back home; he praised Thurgood Marshall's expertise during the University of Mississippi case; he agonized over not having been there to keep a seat beside Rosa Parks; he prayed for the Little Rock nine; he expressed varying opinions of leaders in the Student Non-violent Coordinating Committee; he applauded the brave Greensboro students at those hate-filled lunch-counter sit-ins; he pored over the first Civil Rights Act since Reconstruction, The Kerner Commission Report, and the '63 Voting Rights Act; he worried about riots that were erupting across the country and wondered what, in the end, it all would mean for blacks, as he grieved for four little black girls who were killed in a church bombing.

My father kept up with every media-covered move of Martin Luther King, from King's church in Alabama to that fateful day in Memphis, Tennessee. When an assassin's bullet stopped Dr. King on April 4, 1968, it jarred hopes, both long-deferred and newborn, throughout black America. With the silencing of the century's voice of equality and justice, we—not only the black race, but all the people of the United States of America—suffered an inestimable loss.

Troublesome times following the assassination of Dr. King exacted a heavy toll on us as a country, as a people, as a race, and as individuals. There is no doubt that the unrest affected my father's already serious condition. Nevertheless, he resisted my urgings that he see a specialist in Baltimore by insisting that his own doctor was taking good care of him. During my September 1968, weekend visit, I persuaded my parents to plan to visit me within the next two weeks. Meanwhile, I made plans to get him to a cardiologist during the proposed visit. They took me to the station; we waved as the train pulled off. Exactly one week later, my beloved father died in his sleep.

He was the bravest, most dedicated man I have known. Without fanfare or applause, he literally fought for our rights—alone. But he died without realizing most of the changes for which he had hoped, prayed, and fought. The sudden death of the pillar of our family left a void that cannot be filled.

There have been numerous times, however, when I have been thankful that my father did not live to see much that has happened since he died. Because he was ill, I did not tell him about the "just wait" note signed "KKK" that I found under the door of my apartment in a brand-new high-rise building. That happened in the mid-'60s shortly before the law "allowed" blacks to live where they chose in Baltimore. I still have the note.

Another incident occurred well over a decade after my father passed. I had just moved into my new residence when I happened to be on the elevator with a very old man. After a cursory glance in my direction, he asked, "What floor?" I stated my floor, adding a "thank you." Then he looked straight at me and asked, "Who you work for?" When I told him I work for myself, he gave me a long, puzzled stare before exclaiming, "You *live* here?" As I confirmed his suspicions and we reached my floor, he shouted my apartment number. The alarm had been sounded; even the very old and decrepit knew the exact location of the "alien" who had invaded what always had been "their territory," a place where blacks were supposed to work, not live.

My mother survived my father by nearly three decades. She often spoke about the things they had hoped to see happen during their lifetime. Although she never relegated the chances for a race-relations miracle to the class of things that might happen "when turtles trot and canaries crow," she said she knew better than to try holding her breath until it happened. Nevertheless, she held fast to the hope that change was bound to come, if not in her lifetime, then during the lifetimes of her children and grandchildren.

She was in her midnineties when she suffered a broken hip and, for the first time in her life, was hospitalized. After being discharged from the hospital, she was confined to a nursing home in Wilmington, where she learned to enjoy the companionship of

Margret Williams Land, Bill Faison, Leon Henry, Adele, Claudia (Elroy's wife), and
Laura Jane Holden at her one hundredth birthday celebration

new friends and looked forward to the visits of her devoted children and a few faithful friends.

For my mother's one-hundredth birthday, I hosted a well-deserved celebration, and she enjoyed everything: the rosebud corsage on her new gown; the American Beauty roses from Elroy ("Buddy") that accented the beautifully decorated table; the special program, greetings, and gifts from family and friends; the repast; and most especially blowing out the single candle with a single puff—one candle, symbolic of a century of life and living.

I often recall the conversation my mother and I had while I was putting up the tree in her room for what proved to be her last Christmas. We reminisced about the magical Christmases that we once enjoyed so very much, those Depression-poor, beautiful-beyond-words Christmases. She sighed a longing sigh; then she surprised me, when, in the midst of our sharing happy memories, she began to talk about lifelong hopes that things really would get

Jane and youngest son Elroy ("Buddy")

better down home. I remember her rueful tone of voice as she spoke:

"From all I hear, it's not much different right now than it's been anyway. And if truth be told, it's not much better nowhere else neither—not from what you see on TV. I know you must remember how Mom use to say that if people don't start doing right by each other, it's going be suffering in this world like never before. I can hear her right now, plain as day. Wonder what in the world she'd say if she was living now? I can just about tell how she'd say, 'One of these days, Children, God's going move, and it's going be a whole lots more'n gnashing of teeth around here. Mark my words!'"

My beloved mother died on January 24, 1998, less than three weeks after the sudden death of my older brother (the two persons I wanted most to have this memoir). The Holdens, who once were a loving family of seven, now are but three. Of the former seven, three died suddenly: my father, in 1968; my sister and best friend, Dorothy Emily, in 1984; and my brother, Leon Henry, in 1998. If there are words to spell out the depth of such loss and grief, I do not know them; however, I must try:

> Your sudden death ripped moorings from my world—
> I felt my chilled brow in your shrouded form.
> I smoothed the velvet quilt; they closed the lid.
> Words only edge pain of good-byes unsaid.

✦

For my people, it has been a long and burdensome journey from the Pocomokes in our world to this place and time. As Jacob wrestled through the night at Peniel, we have wrestled through centuries of long-imposed darkness. But we have refused to let hope be wrestled from our grasp. We, who have suffered the vilest atrocities and who still are beset with their hate-filled remnants, have survived through everlasting faith in God and the hope He has given.

If, by some means, all people can will themselves to relate to one another as individuals—each one sheltered under the umbrella of humanity—there yet is hope.

Looking back . . .
I don't wonder
how we have come
this far.
I know.

Looking there . . .
I still ponder
the long, long way
we have
to go . . .

About the Author

Born shortly after the end of World War I, Adele Virginia Holden grew up in the segregated world known simply as "the Shore," an isolated patchwork of counties wedged between the Chesapeake Bay and the Atlantic Ocean.

She graduated from the Snow Hill Colored School after her father made it possible for black children to continue their high school education through the tenth grade in their hometown of Pocomoke City, located between Salisbury, Maryland, and the Virginia line.

Adele then journeyed to Baltimore where she graduated from Morgan State College (now Morgan State University) in 1940. During her distinguished career, she taught English at Dunbar High School, where she was honored as "Dunbar's Poet," and was Professor of English at the Community College of Baltimore, from which she retired in 1982.

Adele started taking classes at Johns Hopkins University and soon amassed enough poems to publish her first book, *Figurine and Other Poems,* in 1961. She received letters of praise from Langston Hughes, Sterling Brown, Josephine Jacobsen, and Gordon Parks among others. Based on the strength of the work in *Figurine,* Adele was awarded a full fellowship by Hopkins for study in the university's prestigious Writing Seminars, from which she graduated in 1965.

In 1963, Adele was inducted into Iota Phi Lambda Sorority's Society of "Living Makers of Negro History." Her writing has appeared in several publications and has been presented on educational radio and television programs.

Set primarily on Maryland's Eastern Shore during the 1930s, *Down on the Shore* portrays the truth about a people, a place, and a time. It reveals the reality of a lifestyle meted out and

7/6/20

rigidly enforced by Shore whites—a way of life both humane and cruel.

Down on the Shore depicts the trials and achievements of determined parents in their struggles to offer their five children a better quality of life. It recalls the children's own battles to fulfill goals instilled by parents who saw education as their only chance in a segregated world wracked with barriers. This story, then, is a portion of America's story.

Adele reading from her first published book, a collection of poetry titled *Figurine and Other Poems* (Adele also designed the book's jacket)

Adele wrote the book with the conviction that the sharing of underlying truths can produce positive changes in the human condition and improve humanity's chances for peaceful coexistence.